BLACK COMMUNITY IN
THE 20th CENTURY

HANSIB PUBLICATIONS

BLACK IDENTITY IN THE 20th CENTURY

Expressions of the US and UK African Diaspora

Mark Christian
Editor

HANSIB

First published in Great Britain in 2002
by Hansib Publications Limited
London: PO Box 34621, London E17 4GL
Hertfordshire: Orchard Road, Royston, Hertfordshire SG8 5HA

www.hansib-books.com

ISBN 1 870518 87 X

Cover design by Graphic Resolutions, Hertfordshire, England

Production by Books of Colour, Hertfordshire, England

Printed and bound by Interprint Limited, Malta

*In memory of
Ian, Denys and Roger Christian.
They died too young.*

CONTENTS

ACKNOWLEDGEMENTS

I would like to thank the Fulbright Scholarship board and Miami University, Ohio, for their support. Chapter Three is based on a paper I presented for the Lemnitzer Lecture at Kent State University's Center for NATO and European Studies, February 25, 1998. Chapter five is based on a paper I presented at The Ohio State University, May 23, 1998, via the African American and African Studies Department's conference: The Black Intellectual in Africa and the Diaspora. This conference was also in honour of the African American writer Harold Cruse.

Thanks also to my colleagues, and to those who have contributed in their criticisms of earlier drafts of chapters, collectively they made my task as an editor arduous but certainly rewarding. Lastly, many thanks to the students I have taught on both sides of the Atlantic based at The Ohio State University, Department of African American and African Studies; Kent State University, Department of Pan-African Studies; Charles Wootton College in Liverpool, Liverpool Hope University College and University of Liverpool; and presently at Miami University in Ohio. Without their interest in Black history and culture prompting my mind on a daily basis it would have been difficult to complete this project. I thank you all.

CONTRIBUTORS

WILLIAM ACKAH

William Ackah is Black British and a lecturer in community & race relations studies at Edge Hill University College. He is currently completing his PhD at the University of Manchester. His latest book is *Pan-Africanism: Exploring the Contradictions* (Aldershot, England: Ashgate, 1999).

HAKIM ADI, PhD

Hakim Adi is Black British and a senior lecturer in African & Black British history at Middlesex University. Among his numerous publications relating to Africa and the African Diaspora is *West Africans in Britain: 1900-1960: Nationalism, Pan-Africanism and Communism* (London: Lawrence & Wishart, 1998).

MOLEFI K. ASANTE, PhD

Molefi K. Asante is an African American and a professor in the Department of Africology at Temple University. A pioneer in Afrocentric philosophy, and a prolific writer, he is arguably the major contemporary theorist in African centred discourse. Among his latest works is *The Painful Demise of Eurocentrism: An Afrocentic Response to Critics* (Trenton, NJ: Africa World Press, 1999).

DIEDRE L. BADEJO, PhD

Diedre L. Badejo is an African American and Chair of the Department of Pan-African Studies at Kent State University. Along with her knowledge of African world literatures, she has spent many years in Nigeria studying among the Yoruba people. Among her publications is *OSUN SEEGESI: The Elegant Deity of Wealth, Power and Femininity* (Trenton, NJ: Africa World Press, 1996).

MARK CHRISTIAN, PhD

Mark Christian is Black British and a professor in Black World Studies and Sociology at Miami University in Ohio. A senior Fulbright recipient, his primary research and publication focus is on the African Diaspora experience in relation to the UK, US and Caribbean regions. Among his recent work is *Multiracial Identity: An International Perspective* (London: Macmillan, 2000).

MEKADA GRAHAM, PhD

Mekada Graham is Black British and a lecturer in Social Policy and Social Work at the University of Hertfordshire, where she is also completing her doctoral studies. She is a leading exponent of African centred theory and practice in social work studies in the UK. Among her latest publications is *Social Work and African Centred Worldviews* (Birmingham, UK, BASW: Venture Press, 2001).

WILLIAM E. NELSON, JR., PhD

William E. Nelson, Jr. is an African American, a leading political scientist and pioneer in the field of Black Studies based at The Ohio State University. His latest book, *Black Atlantic Politics: The Dilemmas of Political Empowerment in Boston and Liverpool* (New York: SUNY, 2000), is a ground breaking comparative analysis involving two African Diasporic communities.

STEPHEN SMALL, PhD

Stephen Small is Black British and a professor in the Department of African American Studies, University of California at Berkeley. He is a key theorist in 'race' and ethnicity studies. Among his publications is *Racialised Barriers: The Black Experience in the United States and England in the 1980s* (London: Routledge, 1994).

SHIRLEY TATE, PhD

Shirley Tate is of African Caribbean descent and has lived in Britain most of her adult life. She is a lecturer in Cultural Studies at Lancaster University. Her research involves an ethnographic approach in comprehending the complexity of Black identities.

INTRODUCTION

TO WRITE a book that encapsulates 'Black Identity in the 20th Century' is an almost impossible task. Therefore some caveats are appropriate before the reader delves into the thematic chapters presented. This stated, a major aim of this book is to provide a number of key 'markers' that had a significant influence on Black identity in the twentieth century, specifically from the perspectives of Black British and African American experiences.

Second, the term 'Black' is defined here as: persons/groups who can claim African heritage throughout the world. No doubt such a definition of the term 'Black' will cause consternation to the many Black cultural theorists, particularly in the UK, whose contemporary vision of 'Blackness' often explodes into such minutiae that it has become an almost futile concept in a theoretical sense.

Accordingly, it is important to state here that 'Black' means something tangible, that it relates to a myriad of social groups and experiences that share, in all their complexity, African heritage. The fact that many millions of people of African heritage have been displaced from the motherland of the African continent for centuries and have resided in African Diaspora locations throughout the world is merely part of the social complexity, but this does not negate the reality of one's African heritage. Indeed, to paraphrase an African proverb, one can put a log deep in a river for hundreds of years and it will change colour, shape and texture, but fundamentally it still remains a log.

Does this mean that I am an essentialist? This depends on how one defines the term essentialist in relation to the subject matter. Let me be both bold and brief. If it is to suggest that there is something in 'essence' about being of African descent in this postmodern world, and that this can be traced back to various social histories that have profoundly influenced the twentieth century Black experience (as the theme of this book indicates), then I submit: I am an essentialist.

However, this does not mean that I fail to see the diversity of Black people's lives and experiences. It means simply that, regardless of the nuances in the Black world, there is an open acknowledgement regarding a commonality of experience that Black peoples have had. Particularly, in regard to the collective struggle against the social forces of white racism and racialised discrimination. Arguably this has been the major factor in the social struggle of Black people collectively during the twentieth century.

Moreover, the fact that a book written by a group of Black scholars concerning 'Black Identity,' largely from the UK and US, is a rather unique phenomena per se. On one level, it gives credence to the proposition that Black people continue to be a marginalised social group in Western intellectual circles, but on another it denies the notion that Black people have no collective thoughts outside of white-led intellectual circles. Due to this latter point alone, one should take heed of the relevance of such a much-needed volume at the dawn of a new century.

It is also important to note that while the contributors to this book share a commonality of African heritage, each provides his/her own way in expressing what Black Identity has meant through a particular theme. In other words, the writers each approach their topics from a specific perspective. The authors speak for themselves and yet each chapter resonates with the common themes of resistance and struggle. In this sense, the reader is able to profit from these diverse and unique expressions of Black or rather African centred thought.

OUTLINE OF THE BOOK

The multidisciplinary and interdisciplinary chapters have been put into three sections. *Part I* gives an account of both historical and political aspects of Black identity. In chapter one, William Ackah examines the role of Pan Africanist thought and practice and outlines some of the major themes to have emerged, along with a look at some of the key thinkers. Chapter two by Hakim Adi focuses on the political identity of West Africans in Britain from 1900-1960. Dr Adi gives an in-depth analysis of the early expressions of African organisation in Britain. Chapter three gives an insight into the historical roots of British racism via a discussion of the 1997 European Year Against Racism. And finally, in chapter four, William E. Nelson, Jr. examines the development of Black political consciousness in the US.

Part II considers the social and cultural markers that form key aspects of Black identity. Chapter five, by Molefi K. Asante, offers a strong challenge to Western intellectual hegemony. While chapter six discusses the tradition of Black intellectual activism. Finally, Mekada Graham in chapter seven proposes an African centred social work paradigm for the UK.

Part III is fundamentally concerned with the inner workings of Black communities and how identity is most often both complex and contradictory. Chapter eight looks at the issue of Black people who can claim a 'mixed racial heritage'. Stephen Small shows, via careful assessment, that 'Black' is indeed a contentious and profoundly socially constructed label. The need to move to a more inclusive 'African Identity' is apparent. Shirley Tate, in chapter nine, also gives an account of the complexity of Blackness and how it can cause unnecessary division within Black communities already beset with a myriad of problems. Lastly, in chapter ten, Diedre L. Badejo discusses the themes of race, class and gender via the literary talents of Zora Neale Hurston and Toni Morrison. In doing so, she provides us with a folklorist view of Black identity and it is in this chapter that we capture the vitality and humanness of Black folk.

Overall, this collection of essays provides students, scholars and teachers with an array of source material. It is openly eclectic, yet framed within an African centred discourse. The book has been created to meet the needs of readers interested in comprehending the breadth and diversity of Black identity in regard to the US and UK African Diaspora, and how it manifested in the twentieth century. However, it does not claim to be the last word on the complexity of African Diaspora history and culture. But we confidently predict that the themes and perspectives herein will continue to impact well into the twenty-first century.

Mark Christian
Miami University, Ohio
July 2002

PART I

Historical and Political Markers

Chapter One

PAN-AFRICAN CONSCIOUSNESS AND IDENTITY: REFLECTIONS ON THE TWENTIETH CENTURY

William Ackah

PAN-AFRICANISM as the collective endeavours, experiences, dreams and aspirations of people of African descent across the globe has no precise date for its birth. In attempting to chart and define Pan-Africanism, historians and other academics are faced with a number of questions that are beyond the realms of simple research. In analysing Pan-Africanism, the issue arises as to when did the people called Black or African in the twentieth century, first perceive of themselves in such terms? When did these same people, whether in Africa, the Caribbean, Asia, or the Americas, first think that there was a connection that somehow united them on the basis of originating in Africa?

Perhaps the genesis of these ideas emerged in the fifteenth century, when the Portuguese began to transport Africans to the old, old world made new by the iniquity of enslavement and conquest.[1] Maybe the notion of a connection came earlier in the eighth and ninth centuries, when Arab and African Muslims traversed parts of Asia, Africa and Europe spreading the message of Islam and creating new empires.[2]

Whether the idea of a Black existence, an Ethiopian ideal, or an African personality stems from the dawn of time, or emerges on to the world stage as a result of more recent tragedies, (slavery and colonialism) is beyond the scope of this particular work,[3] but what is evident is that the twentieth century has witnessed some of the most important manifestations of a sense of African consciousness or Black global connection which are features of Pan-Africanism.

It was in 1900 in London, at the dawn of the twentieth century, that Pan-Africanism comes into formal usage and begins to assume a formal political dimension.[4] The event that ushered in this new era in Black political life was the first Pan-African Congress, organised by the Trinidadian Lawyer, Henry Sylvester Williams.[5] That significant event at the commencement of the century was matched in the last decade of the century when the final great Pan-African struggle against the imposition of the white man on the continent was won: that being the ending of apartheid in South Africa. Looking back at these two events and others of significance in the twentieth century it is evident that the era under discussion has been a pivotal one in terms of African-derived, political, economic, social and cultural expression. The overarching manifestation of that expression is collectively housed under the broad umbrella of Pan-Africanism.

It is not the intention of this chapter to provide a comprehensive review of Pan-African inspired events of the twentieth century. The focus of the work is to reflect in general terms on Pan-African successes, clashes and failures in order to provide some pointers to the way in which Pan-Africanism should and can develop in the future. The twentieth century has been crucial in terms of the development of Pan-Africanism, so an essential task of academics, policy makers and activists interested and concerned about Africa and its Diaspora, is to learn lessons from the words and deeds of twentieth century Pan-Africanists and to assess the ramifications of twentieth century Pan-Africanism for Black/African consciousness and identity beyond the century in question.

PAN-AFRICAN SUCCESSES: THE MEETINGS

An easily forgotten aspect that assisted and fostered a sense of Pan-African identity in the twentieth century is the simple fact that throughout the period, people of African descent and origin had meetings. The fact that people met does not by itself suggest much, but in London in 1900, Paris in 1919, London and Brussels in 1921, London and Lisbon in 1927, New York in 1927, Manchester in 1945, Dar-es-Salaam in 1974 and Kampala in 1994, Africans and those interested in the plight of people of African descent globally, met under the auspices of the Pan-African Congresses.[6] These meetings, although not significant numerically, were of major importance, due to the content of the discussions and the variety of people from Africa and the African Diaspora that attended. It was that sense of unity in diversity exemplified by the Congresses that brings an added dimension to the notion of Black identity in the twentieth century and makes them worthwhile exploring.

People from as far afield as the African continent, the West Indies, North and South America and Europe, came together in the belief that they had things in common. They believed that they could work together to realise their common aspirations as essentially brothers and sisters and sons and daughters of Africa. This was indeed a fascinating realisation, given the different cultural, language, religious and other barriers, both pre and post-enslavement, and colonialism that worked against the construction of such common goals and beliefs. A brief survey of some of the themes that stemmed from the meetings this century is illuminating. Early meetings focused and ranged on the need for Africans to self administer parts of the African continent, to the condemnation of the practice of lynching in the United States (Congresses 1900, 1919).

Later Congresses, in particular, 1945, sought to dismantle the colonial system particularly in Africa but also in the West Indies and other parts of the world, as a precursor to African Unity (Congress 1945). More recent congresses have focused on the need to tackle neo-colonialism and embracing the women's movement (1974, 1994). Some of the early meetings were only sparsely attended, sometimes due to poor organisation or to the unwillingness of European colonial powers and the US to have issues concerning the welfare of Africa and the African Diaspora discussed by people who were, by and large, the victims of their actions.

For all this, however, what was significant is in the fact that Africans from the continent met with West Indians, African Americans, Africans in Europe, and non Africans from around the globe. In their meetings they discussed issues and passed resolutions indicating a sense of shared purpose and identity that they hoped would lead to action being taken by some of the most oppressed people in the world, for some of the most oppressed people in the world.[7]

The Congresses are usually cited as important meetings in the history of Pan-Africanism, and rightly so. It is also important to recognise that, in the twentieth century, many people of African descent met and formed associations all over the globe. These organisations were formed to defend African interests where they were and also to harbour and maintain a sense of African identity in the West as well as African self-determination and unity on the continent. Of crucial importance alongside the meetings were the journals and papers that were produced in this century. Papers like the *African Times and Orient Review* of Dusé Muhammad that was read by African students and Black intellectuals of the Diaspora in the early 1900s.[8] Influential magazines like the *Crisis and the Negro World* galvanised Black hearts and minds in the Diaspora and also in Africa, creating a sense of common goals and purposes for people of differing class backgrounds and geographical locations.

These journals made a major contribution to nurturing a sense of a common identity in the diverse surroundings of the global African community.[9] All people of African descent, to some degree, were haunted by the shadow of white supremacy and imperialism in the first half of the century. Hence, these meetings and publications were a critical source of hope and encouragement helping to keep alive a sense of Pan-African consciousness.

It also gave those Black people engaged in Pan-African activities an opportunity of being part of organisations with a sense of focus. It enabled activists to develop ideas and strategies and work with others to see those ideas come to fruition. Early Black publications also enabled Black creative writers to have their work read and critically appreciated by Black audiences and readers. The number of publications and organisations established by people of African descent, both in and out of Africa in the nineteenth and twentieth centuries, is testament to the desire on the part of Black intellectuals and activists to assist the striving mass of Black humanity.

Finally, it is important to recognise that the journals, organisations and meetings that people of African descent and origin had, provided Black intellectuals and activists with a sense of stability in a very precarious world. In a century dominated by colonialism, racism and oppression, where even Black elites often scrambled from region to region and country to country, trying to eke out an existence. It was meetings, journals and organisations that provided the basis which helped to foster, however fleeting, Black aspirations and energies. It also enabled Black intellectuals and activists to remain committed to the cause of liberation and justice for the sons and daughters of Africa at home and abroad. The fact that it is through the recorded histories of Black organisations and Pan-African meetings that the story of Pan-Africanism this century unfolds, is itself an indication of how critical those meetings were and are in fostering a sense of Pan-African identity, then and now.

LIBERATION

Pan-African meetings and the protagonists attending them have for the most part been concerned about, and engaged in, struggles against oppression. Looking back on the twentieth century, it is staggering to think that at its commencement, Africa and the Caribbean were colonised; that the US was an officially segregated and institutionally racist nation; and that Black people across the globe were treated as second class citizens, if they were recognised as human beings at all.

At the end of the century, it is significant that it can be recorded in ink that Africa and the Caribbean are free, politically; that the US is no longer officially segregated on racial grounds; and that even though Black people are still subjected to racism and various forms of exploitation, their prospects and aspirations are different to what they were at the beginning of the century. Pan-African inspired struggles played an important role in bringing about those changes of circumstances for African peoples worldwide.

The twentieth century has been a long struggle for African peoples, but it is true to say that a lot has been achieved from a very weak starting position. In 1900, the delegates at the Pan-African Congress in London resolved to only ask the dominant colonial powers in the Black world, to treat the people under them better, and to see a way in the future, when the Africans were ready and tutored enough in European ways to have some form of self rule.[10] In 1999, by contrast, the first Black president of the last country in Africa to break the political shackles of white supremacy, South Africa, was able to be succeeded by the second Black president, Thabo Mbeki. The personal struggle of Nelson Mandela and the struggle of Black South Africans to end apartheid, with support from around the Black world, exemplifies the spirit and the tenacity of the liberation struggle that has taken so much of Pan-African energy in the century under consideration.[11]

Total liberation, in the sense of Africa being free economically, and the Diaspora in white majority nations being liberated from the scourge of racism, has still to have been achieved, but this century has seen giant strides taken in that direction. Liberation provided a platform for new ideas, personalities and ultimately identities to emerge out of the wreckage of enslavement and colonialism and hopefully pave the way for a new African personality to be born.

MESSAGE

A major element of twentieth century Pan-Africanism has been the messages that have been conveyed under that broad umbrella. It has already been alluded to that the formation of associations, the writing of journals and the meetings of Black intellects were crucial to the development of Pan-Africanism, but what was it that the intellects and activists of the twentieth century were trying to say? And how have their messages contributed to an understanding of Pan-African identity in the century under analysis?

In order to have a better grasp of the predominant Pan-African inspired messages of the century, it is essential to understand the context out of which they emerged, and for this, a foray into the nineteenth century is required. A combination of missionary education in Africa and the opening up of educational opportunities for Black people in the Diaspora meant that a small but privileged Black elite emerges in both Africa and the Diaspora in the nineteenth century. These elites were, for the most part, products of a Western-orientated education system. They had all been subjected to the racism of that system, yet paradoxically relative to their uneducated Black brothers and sisters, they occupied privileged positions in very oppressive times. Being in such a position for these people, mostly men, was not an easy one, and they were confronted with many questions concerning their own positions in a world that had helped to educate them, yet, at the same time, still sought to deny them, and people like them, rights and opportunities afforded to white people.[12]

Men such as E.W. Blyden, the West Indian who arose to prominence in Liberia,[13] J. Horton, the Edinburgh educated doctor, who also spent long periods in West Africa,[14] and M. Delaney, the African American soldier and intellect with notions of a return to Africa,[15] were all forced to consider the role and place of the African in the World. This was before revolutionary notions of dependency, imperialism and overthrowing the shackles of European colonialism had come into vogue in the twentieth century. Hence, when faced with questions concerning their identities and standing in the world, men like those mentioned above had only their religious-inspired education, and their own perceptions of themselves and insights into their histories, with which to guide them. These were set against a context of Western domination of the world economically, politically and culturally, which undoubtedly was an imposing background to confront.

In light of the intellectual, economic and political obstacles that seemed to be in front of them, it is no wonder that these Western-educated Africans asked questions and made enquiries into whether Africans were really a 'lesser race'. Were African cultures, because of their pagan origins, somehow deficient and unable to progress? Were Africans really the cursed descendants of Noah, destined to roam the

earth and be the servants and slaves of other races?[16] It was the desire
of Black intellectuals to answer these questions, and to make sense of
their place in a Western world, that had, on the one hand, educated
them and yet, on the other, had often despised and rejected them, that
provides insight into the thinking behind some of the key Pan-African
inspired messages of the twentieth century. The key components of
the twentieth century message can be broken down into three major
ideals, these being pride, unity and progress.

PRIDE

In the twentieth century, with more resources at their disposal than
ever before, a key task of Black scholars and activists has been to
refute strongly the idea that Black people were inferior peoples, and
that their cultures and histories were somehow deficient when
compared to Europe. Powerful voices and philosophies vigorously
argued that Africans were the creators of great civilisations, that they
were the equals of any of the races of the world and that they, therefore,
deserved to be given due respect. A variety of messengers have preached
the message of Black pride, from Marcus Garvey, to Negritude, to
Malcolm X, to the Black Power Movement in the US and the Black
Consciousness Movement in South Africa. What echoes throughout
the various protagonists and their messages was that Black people are
a people with a history, dignity and accomplishments, which they need
to take pride in and utilise as a means of restoring African dignity,
pride and greatness across the globe.[17]

UNITY

Closely associated to Black/African pride, was the notion of unity. It
was perceived that enslavement and colonialism had broken, but not
destroyed, the essential aspects of African-derived life and culture. If
African people were to be strong again, and their dignity and place in
the world respected, then they had to be united. This unity needed to
take place on the continent first with it leading the way in terms of
becoming a political and economic power block in the world, and
then the Diaspora would follow. This was part of the vision outlined
by Kwame Nkrumah.[18] Also the notion of unity in the twentieth century
was seen in a broader sense of third world peoples and working class
peoples joining together to fight for justice and equality, preaching a

message of the brotherhood and sisterhood of humanity in opposition to Western imperialism and capitalism.

This wider unity found expression at the 1945 Pan-African Congress, which welcomed a broad array of non-African interests to the Congress.[19] Expressions of unity also came in the form of the short-lived Afro-Asian Solidarity Movement of the 1950s[20] and the Non-Aligned Movement, which brought together diverse nations from Africa, Eastern Europe and Asia.[21] At the cultural level, twentieth century religious faith, notably Rastafarianism, emphasised the idea of the unity of all peoples of African descent across the globe and unity as a process of healing and strength for the scattered children of Africa lost in the wilderness of Western Babylon.[22]

PROGRESS

This theme has resonated strongly throughout the Pan-African inspired messages of the century. From Booker T. Washington to Garvey to the Nation of Islam, elements of the African Diaspora have preached that Black people need to help themselves to catch up and even surpass the achievements of the West. In Africa, too, Pan-Africanists have seen unity as a precursor to progress. The need for the continent to develop and make economic and technological progress has been a constant theme at OAU and other continental African forums in the latter half of the century, including the 1994 Pan-African Congress.[23] However, a tension has existed within Pan-African thinking as to whether progress meant abandoning traditional African culture and adopting Western values or rejecting the West and reclaiming traditional African virtues. The activities of regional groupings in Africa, to date, suggests progress in practice and has owed a lot to Western ideals and plans, not withstanding the dynamic of the other two Pan-African inspired themes of pride and unity. Grand ideas tend to dominate the regional agenda, ideas that need Western input, technical know-how and capital in order for them to materialise into reality. It is argued that a Western-orientated notion of progress has undermined the effectiveness of Pan-African regional groupings to break the shackles of neo-colonialism, dependency and poverty.[24]

The messages of pride, unity and progress were necessary for the era under discussion as it enabled Africans and people of African descent across the globe to position themselves in relation to a changing world that, at the beginning of the twentieth century, continued to deny them basic rights and freedoms. Even at the end of the twentieth century, Africa and the African Diaspora were still preoccupied with questions such as who are we? Where are we going? So it is evident that it was necessary for Black thinkers and activists to pursue goals and messages that would empower people with a sense of purpose and destiny to accompany their struggles. Whether that is still the message that is necessary in the Pan-African world in the future, is something that will be considered at the end of the chapter.

PAN-AFRICAN CLASHES

The twentieth century has seen some amazing successes in terms of meeting Pan-African aspirations. Inevitably, it has also been witness to clashes and disputes between some of its leading individuals and nations. These clashes have impacted on the development of Pan-Africanism as a movement/ideology and they have contributed to the fluctuating and fragmentary nature of Black identity at the end of the twentieth century, as Black people search for role models and philosophies to which they can align themselves. This reason alone makes these clashes an interesting focus for analysis.

In attempting to traverse continents, nations, language, class, racial and gender barriers, clashes within and about Pan-Africanism were bound to emerge. Of all the clashes that have taken place, this work will focus on two of particular significance. The first is a clash of individuals, Marcus Garvey and W.E.B. Du Bois, two immense figures in the history of Pan-Africanism. The second is that between nations, the Monrovia and Casablanca groups of African nations, both with different conceptions of African unity in the late 1950s and 1960s. Clashes between individuals and nations reveal the kinds of tensions and anxieties at the micro and macro levels that hinder the development of unified identities in Africa and the African Diaspora, making them relevant areas of study.

MARCUS GARVEY AND W. E. B. DU BOIS

The apparent dislike between the two early twentieth century giants of Pan-Africanism has been well documented.[25] A combination of two powerful egos vying for pre-eminence in the African Diaspora, coupled with class and racialised distinctions, conspired to keep the great mobiliser /orator, Garvey, apart from the intellectual genius of Du Bois. Interestingly, in terms of political philosophies, the two men were of similar mind. Du Bois was a rather eclectic figure but his desire to see Africa strong and independent, for Blacks to be economically self sufficient in the Diaspora and for Black culture to be promoted through art and literature to elevate the 'race', also resonates throughout the work of Garvey.[26] Marcus Garvey's journal the *Negro World* and the activities of the Universal Negro Improvement Association, were dedicated to advancing the cause of Black men and women all over the world, something with which Du Bois certainly had empathy. For all the two men's protestations and sincere work concerning Black progress and the development of Pan-African consciousness, it is evident that it was their own historical backgrounds that played an important role in preventing them transcending race/class barriers and forging the ultimate Pan-African 'dream team'.

For Garvey, it was growing up under the tripartite racialised system of Jamaica, exemplified by the ditty "if you're white, you're alright, if you're brown, stick around, if you're black, get back," that lies at the root of his dislike for Du Bois. He was snubbed by the mainly light skinned middle classes of Jamaica when he wanted support for his programmes in the early 1900s, and it was this, it can be argued, that fuelled his misguided obsession with notions of racial purity and his mistrust of light skinned middle class Black leaders.

It is a little harder to read into Du Bois's motivations for not getting along with Garvey. Maybe it was the fact that Garvey did not fit his ideal of a 'talented tenth' leader, yet he was so successful that it meant that Du Bois, out of rivalry, was predisposed to dislike his rival, while admiring aspects of his programme.

Du Bois's clash with Garvey is significant because it has echoes in the lives of many people of African origin and descent around the world, particularly in the twentieth century. The idea that light skinned and dark skinned Black people are different and act with antagonism towards each other still resonated in the US and in parts of the Caribbean, even at the end of the century. Divisions in Europe between Africans and Caribbeans, both migrants to major cities like London and Paris, were also still very much in evidence. Ethnic tensions and violence marred the lives of many people in the African continent, yet, as with Du Bois and Garvey, actual differences in terms of wants and desires have been minimal, but historical baggage, racial and class distinctions still emerge to resurrect divisions between people of African descent and origin. This work is not arguing that there are total similarities between ethnic tension in Rwanda, and differences in skin tone leading to tension in Kingston, Jamaica. Each case is routed in its own historical specificalities that are constantly being examined and re-examined.

However, one common theme that links antagonisms between people of African heritage, or indeed, exacerbates them, has been the hand of white supremacy. Whether it has been in the form of enslavement and colonialism, with its concomitant miscegenation, and divide and rule tactics between groups, or whether it has been with more modern forms of racist discourse focusing on notions of beauty and desirability, white supremacist thought and action has widened the cracks in the notion of a unified Pan-African identity. Du Bois and Garvey, at a micro level, provide a succinct reminder that for all the wise words concerning the need for unity and the desire of Africans everywhere to come together, what divides has been as potent, as what has united, and that is why Pan-African identity still remained unresolved, by and large, in the twentieth century.

CASABLANCA AND MONROVIA
The second clash that is under consideration here stems from the debates and divisions that emerged concerning Africa's future direction in the late 1950s and early 1960s among its leading nations. In 1958, an historic meeting took place in Ghana, the first meeting of independent African states on African soil. This meeting, with delegations from Ethiopia, Liberia, Morocco, Sudan, Tunisia, the United Arab Republic and the hosts, Ghana, was remarkable in that it traversed religious, racial and geographical boundaries and held out hope of a new, post-colonial, vibrant Africa.[27] A continent that would work together, take responsibility for African affairs and make the dream of Pan-African unity a reality.

Although, in 1958, not many African states had gained independence, the fact that these new African nations were prepared to meet with bright leaders like Nkrumah of Ghana and Nasser of Egypt, appearing committed to the idea of African unity, augured well for the rest of the continent as it pursued freedom and independence from European colonialism.

As more former colonies became independent, particularly those that had been formerly French colonial entities, such as Ivory Coast and Cameroon, it became evident that there were differences in the community of African states as to what direction the continent should take and what Pan-Africanism should mean in practice. For the former French colonies and, later, nations such as Nigeria, independence and nationhood had to be stabilised before continental unity was to be considered. Whereas leaders like Nkrumah, and Sekou Toure of Guinea (a former French colony out of step with the majority) wanted Africa to come together politically and economically to ultimately form a United States of Africa, for the other nations this seemed too drastic a step too soon.

Most leaders wanted a gradual approach to unity to be adopted, so that they could consolidate the independence they had just achieved.[28] These differences in approach and belief concerning Africa's future, manifested itself openly in the crisis over the Congo, whereby African countries took different positions on the conflict that erupted in that country soon after it became independent in 1960. The Congo crisis of 1960, that ultimately led to the death of the legendary Patrice Lumumba, was a complex affair that is beyond the remit of this particular piece. But suffice to say, as far as African unity was concerned, the fact that African countries adopted different positions and basically split into two groups – the Casablanca group led by Ghana and most of the original states to gain independence (named after a meeting they had in May 1961), and the Monrovia group, with Nigeria prominent alongside the former French colonies (named after a meeting in Monrovia in January 1961) – did not bode well for future African unity.[29]

The two groups were able to come together later to form the ultimate in African solidarity, the Organisation of African Unity (OAU), in Ethiopia in 1963. This new organisation was something of a compromise between the positions of the Monrovia and Casablanca groups, but the organisation, even with its Pan-African pretensions, could not prevent the divisions that would emerge between nation states all over Africa.[30] Tension, mistrust and a strong tendency to put national interests over general African interests have plagued the continent since the original disagreements between the Monrovia and Casablanca groups.

It is sadly ironic that even at the end of the twentieth century it is again in the Congo that conflict has erupted which again has caused splits between countries in East and Southern Africa as they adopt different positions and actively support the different factions that are engaged in a bitter civil conflict.

As with the earlier clash around 'race' that pre-occupied Du Bois and Garvey, the clash between the Monrovia and Casablanca groups, that led to subsequent tensions within the OAU, have been matters of degree rather than substance. All African leaders since the Second World War, have spoken about the need for unity and closer co-operation, so most differences have been about the pace of change, rather than the need for change. Also, as in the earlier case, personal egos have played a large role in undermining prospects for genuine African unity. In the early 1960s, African leaders were suspicious of Nkrumah, believing that he had designs on taking over the continent. In recent times, African leaders all over the continent have preached unity but, at the same time, they have pursued policies in their own locales designed to maintain power and control at all costs. This has had the effect of slowly killing off Pan-African dreams of unity in reality, while aspiring, or even conspiring, to keep the dream alive through conferences and rhetoric.

The consequences of the clash between nations at the highest level of African continental affairs have had drastic consequences for hope of a strong Pan-African sense of consciousness and identity. Perceptions of Africanity, African Personality and Pan-African identity have been undermined by a failure to match rhetoric with deeds. The ordinary African, whether in Cairo or Cape Town, Mauritania or Malawi, has been so consumed by internal struggles and everyday battles for survival, that there has been little time to muse on identity, beyond the family and the locality. Such has been the draining nature of the clashes in Africa between states and with the wider international community, that opportunities to conceive, believe and really live as sons and daughters of the continent, have been fleeting, to say the least.

PAN-AFRICAN FAILURES
An initiative as big as the Pan-African project, that has developed over the centuries, and with no rigid set of doctrines or ideology, is bound to have some fault lines. These lines, from time to time, open

up and cause ripples, vibrations and even quakes in the notion of genuine Pan-African identity. In the twentieth century, three such fault lines can be identified in Pan-Africanism that can account, in part, for its failure to really imprint itself on the consciousness of the majority of people of African descent, whether on the continent or in the Diaspora. The three fault lines identified here are, one, the fact that Pan-Africanism was mostly elite driven; two, it was male-orientated; and three, it has been very fragmentary.

ELITE DRIVEN

Pan-Africanism in the twentieth century has been an elite driven project that, for the most part, has not really engaged the hearts and minds of the vast majority of people in Africa and the Diaspora. At the beginning of the century, it was the educated elites of the Black world that met in Europe and the US to contemplate the future of the 'race'. They believed that they were acting in the interests of all African people, yet they did not really include them in their deliberations. Like the Du Bois conception of a 'talented tenth', these elites saw themselves as having been destined to lead the masses to some kind of African redemption. Aside from Garveyism, and the mass appeal of some magazines, journals and Black cultural icons, the trend in twentieth century Pan-Africanism has been to lead rather than listen to the masses. While the goal has been to unite the disparate parts of the African experience, the practical experience, to date, has seemingly worked against the fulfilment of this objective, in part, because it has not been widely transmitted.

At the end of the twentieth century, Pan-Africanism was largely talked about by academics and postured on by African leaders, but no trans-national organisation of people of African descent can boast of having a membership of more than a fraction of all the people of Africa and the Diaspora. The only organisations that command any allegiance of Black people in large numbers across countries and continents are religious groups, with their goal of unity being heavenly, as opposed to African unity now. The failure of Pan-Africanism to really move beyond the privileged circles of a few people to the wider realms is hard to fathom.

In the twentieth century, expressions of Blackness and Africanity have become very popular at the consumer/mass level. The legendary

Pan-African singer/songwriter, Bob Marley shone like a beacon for many who were directly and indirectly acquainted with the message of African unity. Yet, for all his expression, and that of others in the music and entertainment industries, such messages rarely translated into anything concrete. Hence, while Black sports personalities, writers, singers and artists from Africa and the Diaspora convey a sense of Africanity through their offerings, this has not been matched consistently in the political arenas, where the elites of Africa and the Diaspora have operated. The leaders of many nation states in Africa and the Diaspora have not readily accepted the idea that they are servants of the people. They still regard them as they did at the beginning of the century, as the uneducated masses that need to be guided by the 'talented tenth'. Unfortunately, under the direction of the elites, the vibrancy, diversity and dynamism of Pan-African identity has ossified and become a museum ideal, that academics at conferences come together to discuss, but which has lost its contemporary relevance for the people of African descent that still sorely need it.

WOMEN
The elite nature of Pan-African organisation and development in the twentieth century can also account for the fact that women are seemingly omitted from the historical and contemporary accounts of the movement. Du Bois, Garvey, Malcolm X and Kwame Nkrumah, are names that leap off the page when discussing significant figures and their impact on African and Diasporan experience in recent times. But few women leap off the page in the same manner. Yet, Amy Ashwood Garvey and Amy Jacques Garvey were crucial to the development and memory of Garveyism as a key marker in the history of Pan-Africanism.[31] Jessie Faucet, too, was another unsung personality who worked with Du Bois on the Pan-African Congresses of the 1920s.[32] Angela Davis, the legendary Black Power/communist activist, engaged not only Africans but also a host of 'Third World' peoples who were inspired to struggle against imperialism and injustice as a result of her experiences in the US.[33] Women have been at the forefront of many Pan-African activities in the twentieth century, but they, for the large part, have not been recognised or given the significance that they deserve.[34]

It can only be surmised what difference to the direction of Pan-

Africanism a more Black womanist-orientated agenda would have made. Perhaps it would have been less blighted by the destructive capacity of divisiveness to get in the way of unity. Perhaps if the influence of Black women's thought on the movement had been more keenly appreciated and explored, then Pan-Africanism might have been less ego-led and more spirit-led. It might have had more concern for the masses, and less regard for proving, pride and progress. Perhaps issues of equality and fairness would have come to the top of the agenda of Africans sooner rather than later. It can be seen as significant that on the African continent in the twentieth century, no woman has exercised power as a head of state, and few as significant elites with power to determine policy at either national or Pan-African level. Again, it is speculation as to the significance of this kind of omission, but what is evident is that the failure of Pan-Africanism to really appreciate the dynamic that Black women's experience could have brought to bear on the movement/ideal this century, has been to Africa's and the Diaspora's loss, rather than gain.

FRAGMENTATION

The final failing within Pan-Africanism in the twentieth century, which is of significance, is the fact that it has not been able to prevent increasing fragmentation between African-derived communities across the globe.

This chapter is not arguing that multiple identities are bad or that all Black people, regardless of where they come from, should expressly identify with Africa. It is apparent, however, that particularly at the end of the twentieth century, people of African origin and descent were increasingly ready to embrace a whole host of different identities, aside from African-orientated or derived ones. Hence, the connections between people of African descent on the continent, in the Caribbean, South and North America, Europe and Asia, are not what they were. The broad sense of togetherness of peoples of the Developing World that marked events like the Bandung Conference of 1955 and the Afro-Asian Solidarity Movement,[35] seem like pre-wedding romantic days, in hindsight, with the parties now very much divorced wondering what brought them together in the first place.

In the great capital cities of places like London and New York, people of different cultures and identities come together and support each other politically and culturally, but it is evident that there are no guarantees on the conditionality of that support. Like Africans, West Indians and African Americans may join together to complain about police brutality, as in the Diallo shooting in New York in 1999. However, if a different issue emerges, something like the Salman Rushdie affair, or support for the state of Israel, then the same groups that showed solidarity over the policing issue, may fracture and be on opposing sides on the basis of religious, racial or ethnic loyalties. Hence, there is a strong sense in the twentieth century, particularly at its latter stages, that identities are less internationalist, less Pan-African, and increasingly African American, Caribbean, Black British, Jamaican, South African, Zulu, the fragmentation goes on and on. It is further evident that these identities, at the end of the century, were more contingent on locale and circumstance than they were on principled beliefs and values, calling in to question their durability.

The dream of Pan-Africanism was that it would override any sense of localism and fragmented identity and be an umbrella under which the different varieties of African in the world could find a shelter from the vagaries of racism, neo-colonialism and balkanisation, that, as a separated people, had done so much to undermine their experience in the world. In unity there was meant to be strength, but in the twentieth century, a sense of permanent unity was not to be realised, and most people of African descent are still found relatively weak in comparison to other groups in the world.

For the most part, political and economic developments, out of which a Pan-African identity might arise, have thus far proved disappointing. So, for example, whereas West Indian cricket, from the late 1960s to the latter part of the twentieth century, provided a sense of focus and identity for disparate Caribbean islands and peoples, attempts at developing a West Indian Federation, and its modern incarnation the Caribbean Community and Common Market (CARICOM), have been noticeably disappointing in creating the conditions for collective endeavour and a sense of Caribbean unity at the political level.

The Caribbean is not alone in being at fault for not genuinely fostering and nurturing a sense of Pan-African identity. The pattern was repeated across the Diaspora and the continent. This is perhaps Pan-Africanism's greatest past and present weakness. The looseness, in terms of organisation and identity, has meant that, ultimately, no-one and everyone in Africa and the Diaspora is responsible for it. It has many mission statements, as opposed to one. Many beacons and sources of identity, as opposed to an overarching one. With no-one directly responsible and with no singular core set of beliefs and principled values, goals and objectives, it is not difficult to see why, even at the end of the twentieth century, Pan-Africanism has not been able to cement together the fragmented elements of the global African experience.[36]

TWENTIETH CENTURY LESSONS
The last century of the millennium was an immense period in the history of Pan-Africanism. It was full of brilliant characters, intense struggles, amazing victories and some inglorious failures that one chapter in a general text could not possibly convey. However, if Pan-Africanism is not to be regarded just as an interesting historical adventure or interlude in the experience of African peoples, then it is important that some lessons are learnt from what has undoubtedly been a very dramatic Pan-African century.

DEVELOPING THE ORGANISATIONAL BASE
Throughout the history of Pan-Africanism, and particularly in the twentieth century, there has been a steady proliferation of organisations established to cater for the political, social, economic, educational and spiritual interests of African peoples around the world. In this chapter, aspects of the work of specifically Pan-African associations have been touched upon, but it is true to say that Pan-African groupings account for a tiny proportion of all the Black-led organisations that exist throughout the globe. In most parts of the world where people of African origin and descent live, there are schools, colleges, community organisations, churches, mosques, political organisations and even economic regional organisations with an implicit or explicit African or Black-orientated focus. Many of these organisations struggled to establish themselves and many still struggle to survive today. If a Pan-African sense of identity is to emerge beyond what was already evident in the twentieth century, then it is apparent that these institutions need to grow and become stronger.

Black or African-led organisations, whether on the continent or in the Diaspora, need to attract more members. They also need to come together with like-minded organisations and associations at national and international level, so that there are more exchanges of people, information and ideas across Africa and the Diaspora. This needs to take place not solely at the elite level, but at the level of the vast majority of people of African descent. In the future, a lot more political interactions between people of African descent need to take place in order to give Pan-Africanism a sense of direction and to give Pan-African identity concrete expression. These interactions need to take place at every level of society. Mass-based political, economic, cultural, and social interactions will mean that Pan-Africanism will not be dependent on a few famous egos to take it forward, but that new ideas with mass appeal and support on the future of Pan-Africanism will emerge.

A confederation of Black organisations, stretching from one end of the globe to the other, has the potential to be a major pressure group, able to mobilise millions on issues such as Third World debt and fair trade for poorer nations. It also has the ability to be a major self-help force for African peoples everywhere, pooling resources, sharing initiatives and offering practical support to communities in different parts of the world, that are often isolated and existing with no sense of hope or tangible prospects for the future. Such notions may appear to be fanciful and unrealistic, but it is only through concrete partnerships that one can see whether Pan-African aspirations have any chance of mushrooming into a vibrant and successful African unity. This chapter is, itself, an example on a small scale of the kinds of Pan-African initiatives that need to take place.

In the twentieth century, it was assumed, and still is in many quarters, that Black people, on the basis of their race and ancestry, would have that desire to come together, that it was somehow their God-given destiny. Yet, the twentieth century has proven that Africans, because they are Africans, are not predestined to love each other, work together and live happily ever after. The century teaches us that new connections between the Diaspora and Africa, and within the two spheres, need to be established connections based on mutual benefit. It is only once connections are established and projects developed and initiated, can it then be maintained that the historical ties that perhaps once bound all these multiple African identities, can be revived as a living, breathing expression of African identity beyond the twentieth century.

STRONG MESSAGE

The twentieth century witnessed the words and actions of some very powerful Pan-African messengers from Africa and the Diaspora, preaching the message of pride, unity and progress. In the latter part of the century, however, when post-modern cynicism and disbelief pervade the intellectual horizon, those earlier messages lost their potency, somewhat. At the end of the century, the modern messengers of the Diaspora speak either the language of despair and self-destruction,[37] or they look back into the past for positive reinforcement and inspiration.[38] From this analysis of the messages of the twentieth century, it is felt that the basic messages of the early Pan-Africanists are still needed to inspire new generations interested in the future of Africa and the Diaspora. The self-help messages of Garvey, Washington, and in more recent times Nkrumah and the Nation of Islam, still need to be preached.

The global economy, as we are constantly being reminded, is interdependent and no one can survive on their own. That is true to a certain extent, but that does not prevent African peoples working together to build a better environment and infrastructure for its people. It is painful to write that, since independence, efforts to integrate transport, telecommunications, education and other sectors of potential continental collaboration, has been woeful. Africa is poor, admittedly, but that does not mean that practical steps cannot be taken to restructure and rebuild. Because many nations are too small or too poor on their own to engage in infrastructural enterprises, then it makes sense to work together to foster a sense of self-help coupled with mutual dependence. Which is the same, simple, Pan-African message of pride, dignity and unity leading to progress.

The pride rhetoric of the past has to be reinvigorated to enable modern Africans and their partners in the Diaspora to reconnect and find ways of supporting each other. Great achievements five hundred years ago, and two thousand years ago, are fine in themselves, but as people that need to progress, Africans and those of African descent need to be inspired to think about future achievements. They need to be able to envisage what a Pan-African-inspired continent and Diaspora would like, what it could achieve for its people, and the standing that it would have in the world. This is the kind of message that is required, a message that will inspire people to action. Garveyism's message was very simple, but it inspired people to action. At the end of the twentieth century, however, it is very difficult to assess what the dominant message for African people is and who should carry it forward.

It is evident that a key lesson to learn from the experience of the twentieth century is that Pan-Africanism does better and inspires more people when the cause is clear, the message is simple, and when those carrying forward the message have a clear vision with attainable targets.

INCLUSIVE PAN-AFRICANISM

Another message that emerges from this assessment of twentieth century Pan-Africanism is that Pan-Africanists cannot afford to get bogged down in arguments over who is, or who is not, an African. Divisions, whether based on racial, ethnic, or religious differences, have been detrimental to the development of the African continent and to the Diaspora in the past, and this analysis should teach all those interested in the welfare of all the disparate Africans around the world that it is time to move on from the "who are we" scenario and consider more thoughtfully what "we ought to be".

The enemy of African unity and progress in the twentieth century was not skin tone, but it was systems that have helped to undermine a sense of African identity and shared purpose. Even some of the greatest Pan-African thinkers lost sight of the bigger picture of African progress because they got bogged down in questions of colour difference. It seems that in the twentieth century the victims of anti-Black racism have been so scarred by the experience, that issues such as shades of blackness, or a racialised Africanity, still consume at the expense of other critical issues such as survival and sustainability. A difficult issue in relation to trying to move forward, in relation to a new Pan-African identity, is what role past oppressors of African peoples should play in the creation of a sense of Pan-Africanism beyond the twentieth century.

The twentieth century, itself, has not provided many clues as to what that role should be, as, unfortunately, the external factors that continue to undermine and negate African experiences across the globe still stem from white supremacist-dominated systems. Whether it has been the World Bank or the International Monetary Fund, Afrikaner farmers, or the police and prison systems in many Western capitalist democracies, it is plain to see that white racism still continues to undermine African identities and life chances. Thus, although Pan-

Africanism needs to be inclusive and not exclude on the basis of race, its membership needs to include only those who are committed to the development of Africa as a continent and to improving the life experience of those people of African descent that live in the Diaspora. That commitment can only be determined by deeds and actions which, up to now, have been sadly lacking in certain quarters, due to the racist practices and activities outlined. However, the test of Pan-African consciousness and identity is not racial, but primarily mental and physical. Meaning that membership is determined by ideological and personal commitment to the development of Africa and the African Diaspora.

The first meeting of independent African states in 1958 provides a benchmark for the kind of inclusive Pan-African identity that is possible. That grouping was racially and ethnically inclusive, it comprised nations that had different religious convictions and it traversed the so-called 'Sahara divide' that was to separate so-called 'Black Africa' from so-called 'Arab Africa'. These diverse nations were able to come together because they had shared the experience of colonialism and now they wanted their new found freedom to mean something, and by working together they believed that this could be achieved. The fact that things did not work out, then, does not negate the inclusive nature of the meeting, and the common purpose that existed. It is principle and purpose that Pan-Africanism sorely needs if it is to be successful in creating an identity that will be more relevant to African peoples than the fragmented picture that existed in the latter part of the twentieth century.

ECONOMY, ECONOMY AND ECONOMY

One element of Pan-Africanism and its connection to Black identity in the twentieth century that has not been touched upon, greatly, has been the subject of economics. Ultimately, for all the notions of identity, pride in Africa and organisational competence that have been expounded. It is economic progress, or the lack of it, that has, chiefly, determined the lack of Pan-African progress in the twentieth century, and which will determine its progress in the future. In the twentieth century, the re-emergence of Asia as a continent and major influence on the world scene, has largely been due to the success and development of the continent's economies. Economic success has enabled cultural expression to come alive, has meant more political influence in the international community and has provided prosperity and opportunity for more and more of the ordinary people that live on the continent. That is not to say that Asia has had a perfect ride, and that every nation on the continent has prospered. Asia has shown, however, that economic progress lifts one status in the world and enables a regional identity to emerge and flourish, so that even the US looks as much to the East for its future as it does to the West.

Africa in the twentieth century, by contrast, has not been successful in terms of economics, which has meant that Pan-African aspirations, although much talked about, have always been vulnerable. In both Africa and the Diaspora, it has meant that Black people have been heavily reliant on benefactors, donors, or non-governmental organisations in order to survive. This state of affairs has meant that Africans everywhere, for the most part, live quite precarious lives, making it difficult to plan, hard to develop and strenuous to create the kinds of platforms that future generations can add to and make stronger. With no secure base it is hard for a stable sense of identity to emerge. Hence, the key twentieth century lesson that needs to be learnt, before it is too late, is to develop a sound economic base so that a sound sense of Pan-African identity can develop and flourish.

CONCLUSION: THE NEED FOR SUCCESS

The twentieth century in the history of Pan-Africanism can, with hindsight, be seen as the era when so much was achieved but, in achievement, the feeling still remains that there was, and still is, so much to do, if Pan-Africanism is to be more than just an aspiration of Black identity. There is no disguising that identities in the twentieth century have come under tremendous buffeting. Technological developments have expanded people's horizons and possibilities, whereas religions, governments and nineteenth century ideologies have lost credibility. With the loss of old certainties and the emergence of new perspectives, comes the potential for new searches and discoveries in relation to self and others. With new opportunities for identities to flourish, also come new opportunities for closure and the narrowing of identities. These narrowings have stemmed from wars, from harsh economic climates and for the search for old and new certainties in a world that seems disjointed and fragmented.

Africa and Africans around the world have not been immune to these changes. In fact, their struggles against racism and colonialism, and the distinctive positioning of the Diaspora in the Western hemisphere, has contributed much to the dimensions of opportunity and closure that has accompanied searches for identity this century.[39] As this chapter reflects on the response of Pan-Africanism to this search, the question arises, "why are Africans still searching, if Pan-Africanism was to provide the answer?"

I would argue that Pan-Africanism needs another success to ignite the dormant fires of African identity that linger in the Black experience, and provide answers for seekers after African-derived truths. The Black experience needs something big to believe in again, for it is evident that even with all the turmoil and mesmerising struggle that Black people have been engaged in, the century reached its end with the children of the twentieth century protagonists still empty handed, looking for the lasting achievement, the continuing success story to believe in and identify with. Africans need a Pan-African success on which to hang their aspirations and desires. This may seem fickle but, nevertheless, having analysed and conjectured on this, I believe it to be a very simple truism.

It is apt to give an illustration from sport in order to emphasise the point. Manchester United is Britain's most famous football team. They have more fans outside of Manchester than in it, with people supporting them in places as far away from Britain as China and Australia. The fans have an identity with the club even though it is thousands and thousands of miles away from the majority of their homes. The affection for Manchester United probably stems from the 1958 Munich air disaster, where most of their first team were killed, and then in 1999, when they won three major competitions in a single season, a major achievement. For a single football club in a rather provincial city of Britain, that is probably the best supported team in the world, and one of the most profitable, this is remarkable, and it reveals that identities today can be based on singular events, memories and ultimately success as much as roots, connections and racialised identities.

Pan-Africanism has potentially millions of followers in and outside of its core focus, the continent. Its potential followers have the memories, the distant and recent connections, to readily identify with the continent. If this analysis of Pan-Africanism in the twentieth century has taught anything, it is that Pan-Africanism needs a tangible, lasting, success in order to generate the renewed enthusiasm for it in the new millennium. Importantly, there is a need to reconstruct an inclusive and viable sense of Pan-African identity. Unfortunately, this goal was all too elusive in the twentieth century.

NOTES AND REFERENCES

1. Reynolds, E. *Stand the Storm: A History of the Atlantic Slave Trade* (London: Allison and Busby, 1985).
2. Van Sertima, I.(ed.) *Golden Age of the Moor* (New Brunswick: Transaction, 1982).
3. Segal, R. *The Black Diaspora* (London: Faber and Faber, 1995).
4. There is still some debate among academics as to whether the 1900 meeting actually constituted a Congress. Although the term Pan-Africanism is generally considered to be used for the first time at that event, it is not usually referred to as the first Pan-African Congress.
5. Various terms are used in this chapter such as of African descent, African origin, African Diaspora, Black/African, to emphasis the linkages and also the separations that exist between people that would have traced their historical origins to Africa before the advent of enslavement and colonialism.
6. Geiss, I. *The Pan-African Movement* (London: Methuen, 1974) See also note 4.
7. Abdul-Raheem, T.(ed.) *Pan-Africanism Politics, Economy and Social Change in the Twenty-First Century* (London: Pluto, 1996).
8. Fryer, P. *Staying Power: The History of Black People in Britain* (London: Pluto, 1984) pp. 287-290.
9. Martin, T. (ed.) *African Fundamentalism: A Literary and Cultural Anthology of Garvey's Harlem Renaissance* (Dover: Majority press, 1991).
10. Fryer, P. *Staying Power...* pp. 281-287.
11. Meer, F. *Higher than Hope: The Authorized Biography of Nelson Mandela* (New York: Harper and Row, 1990).
12. Ackah, W. 'The Complexities of the Black Experience in Theory and Practice' in Torkington, N.P.K. (ed.) *The Social Construction of Knowledge: A Case for Black Studies* (Liverpool: Hope, 1996) pp. 149-160.
13. Lynch, H. *Edward Wilmot Blyden: Pan-Negro Patriot 1832-1912* (London: Oxford University, 1967).
14. Davidson, B. *The Black Man's Burden: Africa and the Curse of the Nation State* (London: James Currey, 1992) pp. 36-43.
15. Delaney, M. *The Condition, Elevation, Emigration and Destiny*

of the Colored People of the United States (Baltimore: Black Classic, 1993; first published 1852).

16.   Drake, S.C. *Black Folk Here and There* (Los Angeles: University of California, 1990).

17.   Ackah, W. *Pan-Africanism: Exploring the Contradictions, Politics, Identity and Development in Africa and the African Diaspora* (Aldershot: Ashgate, 1999).

18.   Nkrumah, K. *Africa Unite* (London: Panaf, 1970).

19.   Adi, H. and Sherwood, M. *The 1945 Manchester Pan-African Congress Revisited* (London: New Beacon, 1995).

20.   Kimche, D. *The Afro-Asian Movement* (New York: Halstead, 1973).

21.   Chazan, N. et al. *Politics and Society in Contemporary Africa* (London: Macmillan, 1992) pp. 412-414.

22.   Campbell, H. *Rasta and Resistance: From Marcus Garvey to Walter Rodney* (London: Hansib Publications, 1985).

23.   Abdul-Raheem, T. *Pan-Africanism Politics, Economy and Social Change...*

24.   Ackah, W. *Pan-Africanism: Exploring the Contradictions...*

25.   Clarke, J.H. (ed.) *Marcus Garvey and the Vision of Africa* (New York: Random House, 1974).

26.   Martin, T. (ed.) *African Fundamentalism...*

27.   Ajala, A. *Pan-Africanism Evolution, Progress and Prospects* (London: Andre Deutch, 1973) pp. 9-65.

28.   Ackah, W. *Pan-Africanism: Exploring the Contradictions...*

29.   Ajala, A. *Pan-Africanism Evolution, Progress and Prospects...*

30.   Sesay, A. *The OAU after Twenty Years* (Boulder: Westview, 1984).

31.   Hine, D.C.(ed.) *Black Women in America: An Historical Encyclopedia, Volume A-L* (New York: Carlson, 1993).

32.   Ibid.

33.   Davis, A. *Angela Davis: An Autobiography* (London: Women's Press, 1990).

34.   Towards the end of the century, women appeared to be having a more prominent role within Pan-Africanism as evidenced by the establishing of a Pan-African women's organisation at the 7th Pan-African Congress.

35.   Kimche, D. *The Afro-Asian Movement...*

36. A permanent Pan-African secretariat was established as a result of the 1994 Congress; see Abdul Raheem (1996, note 7).
37. West, C. *Race Matters* (New York: Vintage, 1994) pp. 15-31.
38. Browder, A. *Nile Valley Contributions to Civilisation* (Washington: Institute of Karmic Guidance, 1992).
39. Gilroy, P. *The Black Atlantic: Modernity and Double Consciousness* (London: Verso, 1993).

Chapter Two

WEST AFRICANS AND POLITICAL IDENTITY IN BRITAIN: 1900-1960

Hakim Adi

THE HISTORY of the African Diaspora in Britain can be traced back to the Roman period, but current documentary evidence suggests that it was only from the sixteenth century onwards that Africans regularly visited or resided in Britain. From this time, western Africa and its peoples in particular became closely linked with Britain through the trans-Atlantic slave trade, and subsequently when large parts of West Africa were conquered and placed under British colonial rule. During the entire period of slavery and colonial rule, West Africans have been compelled or forced, through various circumstances, to leave their homelands and sojourn in Britain. Some, like the famous eighteenth century British residents, Olaudah Equiano and Ottobah Cugoano, had to endure the forced migration brought about by slavery and the slave trade before their eventual liberation and celebrated abolitionist activity in Britain. Others, in more recent times, were compelled to journey to Britain to seek employment or educational opportunities that were not available in their homelands as a consequence of colonial rule.[1]

The aim of this chapter is to outline some aspects of the history of West Africans in Britain during the first sixty years of the twentieth century. In particular, it will explore the political experiences of those African students who came to Britain to further their education. Their political activities and organisations were often influential in Africa and throughout the Diaspora and reflect changing identities, consciousness and historical conditions. They also reflect the particularities of political and social conditions in Britain, conditions which were, in turn, shaped by the African presence itself. During the twentieth century, it has been the political identities that West Africans have adopted in order to counter the twin problems of racism and colonial rule that have been particularly significant. In this context, it has been the ideologies of Pan-Africanism, West African nationalism and Communism that have played the principal role in shaping these changing political identities.[2]

Africans abroad were often those most able to play a pivotal role in the development of the politics of resistance to slavery, colonialism and European imperialism that has developed since the eighteenth century. What is more, as the history of Africans in Britain shows, there has been a very important relationship between the growing political consciousness of those Africans who sojourned abroad, even if only temporarily a part of the Diaspora, and the political consciousness of their compatriots in Africa. It was often while they were in Britain, or because they were in Britain, that their political awareness was sharpened and their political training began. New political identities were forged and important networks were established, linking those overseas in Britain and their organisations and those in Africa with the organisations and politics that existed in the wider Diaspora.

West Africans in Britain, whether we consider them part of the Diaspora or not, have certainly been influenced by their experiences in Britain, and their contact with other Africans and those from the Diaspora. Of course, they have, themselves, been influential, particularly in the development of a wider Pan-African politics, identity and consciousness. It should not be forgotten that they have also made their contributions to the development of radical, working class and anti-imperialist politics in Britain. Indeed, there is a long tradition of these political contributions, ranging from Equiano's membership of the London Corresponding Society in the eighteenth century to Desmond Buckle's lifelong membership of the British Communist Party in the twentieth century.

West Africans' political identities have changed over time and according to specific historical conditions. A Pan-African consciousness, for example, can be seen in the writing and activities of Equiano, Cugoano and other 'Sons of Africa' in the eighteenth century.[3] In the twentieth century, West Africans' political identity has sometimes been subsumed under a general Pan-Africanism, which in the early part of the century often manifested itself as Ethiopianism. But it was also sometimes seen in terms of an identification with a West African 'nation'; or in terms of an affiliation with the polities created by colonialism itself and, of course, with a more narrow ethnic nationalism (often disparagingly called tribalism), depending on the period and the historical conditions.

Many of the West Africans who have sojourned in Britain have been students. Even in the eighteenth century, West African rulers and merchants and their business partners in Britain found it mutually advantageous to educate African children, especially males, in Britain, and each party strove to maximise advantage from this arrangement. British commercial, political and 'humanitarian' interests also hoped that by means of a "good Christian education", West African students, who eventually might become political rulers or leaders, would be influenced to govern according to "plans more or less similar to those inculcated in them in England".[4] Thus began attempts to develop a class of Africans who would be sympathetic to the interests of the British ruling class, attempts to establish neo-colonial links and political identities that would further the interests of British imperialism in Africa. Of course, African students were generally keen to establish their own political identities and, where possible, to further what they considered their own political interests. In this endeavour they were often assisted by their allies in Britain, who had their own reasons for opposing the activities of British imperialism.

West African students from those areas which were ultimately to become the British colonies of Nigeria, the Gold Coast, Gambia and Sierra Leone, continued to come to Britain for schooling and higher education during the nineteenth century. Most, but not all, came from wealthy families and were often those who were destined to be influential future political leaders and thinkers. One of the most prominent was the Sierra Leonean, James Africanus Beale Horton who graduated from Edinburgh University in 1859. The writings of Horton, together with those of Edward Blyden, did much to establish the notion of West African unity and nationalism and their writings proved to be extremely influential among many West African students and intellectuals during the twentieth century. One of the consequences of the slave trade and its abolition in West Africa, was the prominent role subsequently played by the 'recaptives', those freed slaves and their descendants, who constituted a kind of West African diaspora, throughout the region and in particular in the four British colonies. This West African Diaspora, which settled throughout the region, also contributed to the notion that the four British West African colonies had much in common and constituted a West African nation.[5]

African students were often as much educated by the prevailing social conditions they found in Britain, as they were by the formal education they received. Racism and prejudice were constant reminders that Africans, whatever their background, were often considered merely second class citizens in Britain. Such problems were, of course, greatly exacerbated by the rise of imperialism and the partition and conquest of Africa at the close of the nineteenth century. Colonial rule and racial discrimination in its many forms, led Africans to form their own organisations and to unite with others in Britain who saw the need for a common struggle.

PAN-AFRICANISM AND ETHIOPIANISM

Many of the organisations formed in the early part of the twentieth century with a West African membership were also Pan-African in character. At this stage, some Africans did, on occasions, organise themselves separately to campaign over specific grievances. In 1902, for example, concerted action by West African medical students at Edinburgh University, persuaded the Dean of the Faculty of Medicine to write to the Colonial Office in complaint at the openly discriminatory policies of the West African Medical Service, which barred from appointment those of 'non-European parentage'.[6] More usually, however, West Africans allied with all those of African descent who faced similar problems. That is to say, political identity was seen in broad terms, as it was recognised that all those of African descent faced similar problems resulting from colonial conquest and racism, the legacy of slavery and the slave trade.

One of the first of these modern political organisations was the African Association, formed in London in 1897 by the Trinidadian, Henry Sylvester Williams. The aims of the organisation were:

> To encourage a feeling of unity: to facilitate friendly intercourse among Africans in general; to promote and protect the interests of all subjects claiming African descent, wholly or in part, in British colonies and in other places, especially in Africa, by circulating accurate information on all subjects affecting their rights and privileges as subjects of the British empire and by direct appeals to the Imperial and local governments.[7]

The Association included several prominent African members. A Sierra Leonean law student, T.J. Thompson, became its vice-chairman and its assistant secretary was the Nigerian, Moses Da Rocha who, at that time, was a medical student at Edinburgh University. It was the African Association that was responsible for convening the first Pan-African conference which was held in London in 1900.

Ethiopianism was another early form of Pan-Africanism, popular among both African and Caribbean students in Britain. There was an Ethiopian Association in Edinburgh in the early part of the century and an Ethiopian Progressive Association (EPA) was formed in Liverpool in 1904. The EPA was formed:

> to create a bond of union between all other members of the Ethiopian race at home and abroad, and to further the interest and raise the social status of the Ethiopian race at home and abroad; and to try to strengthen the friendly relations of the said race and the other races of mankind.[8]

The EPA does seem to have been relatively short-lived and was probably only in existence for two or three years. However, during that time it did publish at least one edition of a journal, *The Ethiopian Review*. As its aims and its attempts to contact both W.E.B. Du Bois and Booker T. Washington in the United States show, the EPA clearly saw itself as part of a wider Pan-African world.

Political writing by Africans also often concerned itself with aspects of Ethiopianism. The young Nigerian student activist, Bandele Omoniyi wrote *A Defence of the Ethiopian Movement* in support of the struggles of Africans throughout the British empire, and in South Africa in particular, which was published in Edinburgh in 1908. Indeed, most of Omoniyi's student life in Britain was spent attempting to defend the interests of Africans. As a result, like many of the student-politicians who would follow him, he fell foul of the Colonial Office, and official indifference probably contributed to his early death in Brazil at the age of twenty-eight. J.E. Casely Hayford, a future leader of the National Congress of British West Africa, had his autobiographical novel *Ethiopia Unbound* published in 1911. The novel gives us some idea of the political concerns and sense of identity of West Africans in Britain at that time. The influence of the views of Edward Blyden is clearly apparent and one of Casely Hayford's main aims is to extol the glories of Africa's past as the 'cradle of civilisation'. He also looks forward to the emergence of an 'African nationality', 'race emancipation' and the modernisation and regeneration of African societies.[9]

Both individual West Africans and those organisations they joined or formed tended to be Pan-African in their orientation. In their activities and writing, Africans in the early part of the century were most usually concerned, as the EPA expressed it, with "matters of vital importance concerning Africa in particular and the Negro race in general". They wished to raise the status of the African and Africa; to extol the glories of the African past; to combat the colour bar and the virulent racism of the period, and to voice their protests about the imposition of colonial rule. Their stay in Britain often served to heighten their awareness of such political issues, often as a result of the racism they encountered, but their sojourn also provided the opportunity for joint protest action with other Africans and all those of African descent. A vital part in forming the political identities of Africans in this period was played by the emergent Pan-African press both in Britain and throughout the world. The West African press routinely commented on issues affecting its compatriots in Britain, but a strong Pan-African orientation and identity was provided by such London-based publications as the *African Times and Orient Review* founded by Dusé Mohammed Ali in 1912, and *The African Telegraph*.[10]

Political identity, therefore, emerged from the historical conditions and ideas of the time. Even so, it is clear that such identity remained fluid. Omoniyi, for example, was as concerned with events in his country, the colonial state of Nigeria, as he was with Pan-African issues. Attempts to form distinct African student organisations were first made during the First World War. An African Students' Union was formed in 1916, and the same year a West African Christian Union was established in London. Both were short-lived and in the period following the war and throughout the early 1920s it was the Pan-African-oriented African Progress Union and subsequently the Union of Students of African Descent that were the most influential organisations in Britain, although their activities were mainly confined to London.

The African Progress Union (APU) was formed in 1918 as an organisation for "voicing African sentiments" and "furthering African interests". It described itself as "an Association of Africans from various parts of Africa, the West Indies, British Guiana, Honduras and America representing advanced African ideas in liberal education", and emphasised that it was "actuated by love of country and race". The first president of the APU was John Archer, Britain's first Black mayor, and although the Union demanded self-determination for the colonies following their contribution during the First World War, and reparations for 'the Black race', it was also quick to express its loyalty to King and Empire. The APU continued with its activities throughout the early years of the 1920s, and it played a prominent role in the two Pan-African congresses of 1921 and 1923. Professionals and businessmen were the dominant force in most of the APU's activities and by the early 1920s many of the younger African students were openly critical of its leadership.[11]

The Union of Students of African Descent (USAD) grew out of the activities and membership of the London-based West African and West Indian Christian Union which, after attracting some non-Christian members, changed its name and grew in size. It became particularly popular among West African students following the election in 1923 of a new president from the Gold Coast. Although the USAD declared itself to be apolitical, since in its president's view, "a premature participation in politics does not seem likely to serve the best interests of the average student", there is ample evidence that it soon involved itself in many of the major political debates of the day. It was through USAD activities that West African students were able to come to the fore, and to create some of the conditions for the development of their own separate organisations.[12]

Even before the First World War, the attempts by Africans and others of African descent to organise to combat the consequences of colonialism and racism had come to the attention of the British government and other interested parties. For the defenders of empire, Pan-Africanism and anti-colonialism, in whatever form, had to be combated. At the same time, measures to shield Africans from racism had to be taken if Britain's imperial interests were to be maintained. If the dignity of the 'British race' was to be upheld, African men also had to be shielded from the subversive effects of contact with British women. Above all, there was concern that African students might follow in the footsteps of their Indian counterparts who, in 1905, had formed the Indian Home Rule Society and engaged in vigorous campaigning for self-determination for the peoples of India. In 1909, despite police surveillance, one member of this society, Madan Lal Dhingra, assassinated Sir William Curzon Wyllie, an assistant to the Secretary of State for India. From this time on, more concerted efforts were made by government and other defenders of the empire to control and monitor the activities of African students. The politics and political identities of Africans in Britain were, therefore, also shaped by their relationships with government, especially with the Colonial Office, the government department responsible for colonial rule. Initiatives by the Colonial Office, and other defenders of the empire, designed to monitor the students and closet them away from what were seen as 'subversive' influences, were in existence throughout the colonial period.

One of the most interesting of these initiatives was the aim to provide a hostel for the students, which would combat some of the problems associated with overcoming the colour bar and finding accommodation in London. The ubiquitous colour bar was one of the most obvious factors shaping the political identities of the students. It took little or no account of class or national origin and even the London University Graduates' Club announced in 1914 that Africans would be ineligible for membership. Stirred by such indignities, the students and other African residents began to organise themselves to try and establish a hostel, in rivalry with the plans of the Colonial Office and other 'well wishers'. As the *Lagos Standard* explained:

> It is necessary for our advancement as a race that our young men studying for the professions in the United Kingdom should be proficient not only in the professions but imbibe also some of that spirit of independence, freedom, fair play and justice so characteristic of the Britisher in his own home.[13]

Both the APU and the USAD made attempts to establish their own hostels, but these plans came to nought. But the struggle over the hostel was an area of confrontation that would continue until the 1950s. The issue at stake was who would control such a hostel and what would such control mean for the future political welfare, political independence and identity of Africans in Britain? Eventually, during the 1930s, the Colonial Office was able to establish a student hostel called Aggrey House, which had to be partly financed by the Carnegie Foundation and other benefactors, owing to the impecunious state of the Colonial Office. However, Aggrey House could only be established in rivalry with the hostel that had already been opened by Africans themselves. Officials from the Colonial Office even tried to hide their involvement in the scheme. When the machinations of the Colonial

Office were exposed by the students and their supporters, the whole affair turned into a cause célèbre. It served to radicalise the students, not least by encouraging them to seek the support of the very 'subversive' elements so much feared by the Colonial Office. On other occasions, the Colonial Office and the defenders of the empire were more successful in their attempts to influence the activities of African students, especially through financial means. But they often had to do so by recognising some of the political demands that were made on behalf of Africans both in Britain and in the colonies.[14]

WEST AFRICAN NATIONALISM
During the 1920s, West African student activists began to consider forming their own separate organisations. This was partly in response to attempts to control their political activities by the Government and others concerned with the welfare of the empire. But it was also as a consequence of a concern that the Pan-African organisations such as the USAD did not fully represent their interests. At the same time, West Africans in Britain were also responding to a growing political awareness in the West African colonies and the emergence of a peculiarly West African nationalism. It was these developments which had led to the formation of the National Congress of British West Africa (NCBWA) in Accra, the capital of the Gold Coast, in 1920.

It is perhaps, therefore, something of a paradox that the first African organisation to emerge in Britain in these circumstances was not a pan-West African one, but the Nigerian Progress Union (NPU). This was co-founded in 1924 by a Nigerian law student, Ladipo Solanke, and a Jamaican, Amy Ashwood Garvey, the estranged wife of Marcus Garvey.

The NPU was formed "to promote the general welfare of Nigerians from an educational not a political point of view", but it was clearly influenced by the ideologies and policies of the emergent West African nationalist organisations such as the NCBWA. It marked a transition from the extensive Pan-African concerns of the earlier organisations to the initially more limited and narrow focus of the West African Students Union (WASU). However, the NPU also had Pan-African aspirations, regularly contributed to the African American journal *The Spokesman* and, in 1925, published an 'Open Letter to the Negroes of the World'. According to the NPU:

> the time has now come when the Negro at home and the Negro abroad should find their way out to understand each other better with a view to co-operating for the final emancipation of the whole of the Negro race educationally, industrially, politically and commercially.[15]

For the members of the NPU, it was Nigeria that was at the centre of the Pan-African world. It was a country "full of immense possibilities" and "undeveloped sources of wealth", that might one day become a "mighty Negro empire or republic". Although the NPU was only in existence for a year, its Nigeria-centred policies and many of its members, including Solanke, remained prominent in the WASU founded in 1925.

The founding of WASU was directly influenced by the visit to Britain of Dr Herbert Bankole-Bright, one of the leading members of the NCBWA, who urged the students to forge a unity that would mirror that established by the NCBWA in West Africa. The WASU aimed "to afford opportunity exclusively to West African Students in Great Britain and Ireland to discuss matters affecting West Africa educationally, commercially, economically and politically, and to co-operate with the NCBWA."[16]

Interestingly, the decision to found WASU created some dissent among West African students. Ladipo Solanke and his supporters were branded "segregationists" who wished to put West African unity before Pan-African unity. The 'segregationists' replied that they wished to be self-reliant and solve their own problems and that organisations such as the USAD and APU had achieved little. During the next thirty years, the WASU would become the main African organisation in Britain, a training ground for future political leaders and an important anti-colonial force in its own right. It did not completely move away from a Pan-Africanist orientation. It did aim to foster "racial pride amongst its members" and to "present to the world a true picture of African life and philosophy, thereby making a definitely African contribution towards the progress of civilisation". But in its early years, WASU was ideologically attached to the notion of West African nationalism, and the aspiration for a West African nation.[17]

The idea of a West African nationality did not suddenly emerge in the 1920s. Horton and Blyden had both attempted to develop this concept which, above all else, reflected the strivings of the emergent West African bourgeoisie to develop their own polity. Colonial rule, itself, and the beginnings of anti-colonial agitation, had in some ways fostered the idea of a united West Africa. This notion had been further developed by the addition of various elements of cultural nationalism, which initially comprised the main ideological response of the West African merchants and professionals to the onset of colonial rule. As a consequence of WASU's concern with the concept of a West African nation, and the development of the economic, cultural and political unity of this nation, the Union's journal, *WASU*, featured many articles on West African history, culture and languages. An editorial in 1928 explained:

> We members of the WASU believe that the study of our African customs and institutions together with the adoption and reverent preservation of our African idiosyncrasies leads to the formation of a national character which is the cornerstone of nationhood.[18]

The students saw themselves as the vanguard needed to form a West African nation, "as helping to create a healthy national sentiment throughout West Africa". However, they also saw West African unity as important for the whole continent, as the basis of Pan-African unity, an idea that would later find some favour with another WASU member, Kwame Nkrumah. As WASU's president explained:

> You cannot make a nation of Africa, but by securing ...unity in West Africa, and by securing rights in the western portion, you thereby raise the general standard of African welfare and lay down an ideal of life which the African in the east and south will strive to realise. If Africans are to survive, West Africa must become a nation, it must unite under the sentiment of national progress.[19]

The quest for a West African 'nation' was the main subject of two important publications during this period, Solanke's *United West Africa at the Bar of the Family of Nations* (1927) and J.W. de Graft Johnson's *Towards Nationhood in West Africa* (1928). Both writers presented a spirited defence of Africa's past but also looked towards the future, "of a free Africa ... stepping into her rightful place as a unit in the powerful army of the human family".[20] Solanke, in particular, argued that WASU had an important part to play as "a training ground for practical unity and effective co-operation", and was the means to assert "West African individuality" in Britain.[21]

Although the founding of the WASU and its initial political philosophy owed much to political developments in West Africa, it soon began to see itself as playing a leading role in West Africa's political future. During the 1930s, it established over twenty of its own branches throughout the four British colonies in West Africa and even in the Belgian Congo. These subsequently formed the nucleus of the anti-colonial 'youth movements' in both Nigeria and the Gold Coast. In addition, the WASU established itself as a lobbying organisation for a variety of West African political and economic interests and bombarded the British government with its own demands for colonial reform.

In the course of such activity, the WASU, which soon included non-student members, became very much more than a students' union and it became influenced by the range of political philosophies that existed in Britain and further afield. In the late 1920s, it became temporarily connected with Marcus Garvey and accepted some of the tenets of Garveyism. Then, during the 1930s, many students came under the influence of a radical and Marxist-influenced Pan-Africanism, largely as a result of the activities of the Trinidadian former communist, George Padmore, the Sierra Leonean trade union activist, Isaac Wallace Johnson, and organisations such as the International African Service Bureau.

Other organisations, such as the Negro Welfare Association, an affiliate of the League Against Imperialism, also had an influence on some students, and began to train and recruit African communists. Communism gradually became an increasingly influential ideology among African students and some African workers in Britain. During the 1930s, the Pan-Africanist approach of the Profintern's International Trade Union Committee of Negro Workers and its publication *Negro Worker*, was also influential. In the late 1930s, Desmond Buckle, an ex-medical student from the Gold Coast and a leading figure in the Gold Coast Students' Association, became the British Communist Party's first African member.[22]

During the late 1920s and 1930s, African students became increasingly aware of the plight of other African residents in Britain. Significant numbers of African workers, mainly seamen, resided in London, in the major port cities such as Liverpool and Cardiff and elsewhere throughout Britain. Through such organisations as the Negro Welfare Association and the League of Coloured Peoples, African students became more closely linked to the concerns and struggles of African workers and their children and joined with others in the Diaspora to confront the common problems of racism and the colour bar. One of the responses of the African students to these problems was to establish their own hostel in London, and they organised a special fund-raising mission to West Africa for this purpose. Known as Africa House, the hostel pre-dated the Colonial Office's Aggrey House, and became a meeting place, restaurant and centre of anti-colonial activity for all those concerned with Africa and its future. It was one of the first African centres to be established in Britain and for WASU was of major significance as an article in *WASU* explained:

> It is not enough for us to fight in the colonies for freedom that we have. It is of the utmost importance that in the heart of the Empire we own and man a Hostel which will fight for our cause on the spot and give the lie to traducers of the race whenever they say we have not the capacity to manage our own affairs.[23]

Africa House was seen as "a symbol of West African Nationalism . . . a miniature West African Federal State under the management of a miniature West African Federal Authority popularly known as WASU."[24]

THE SEARCH FOR A BLACK UNITED FRONT

However, despite this strong sentiment for West African nationhood and the influence of wider Pan-African concerns during the 1930s, anti-colonial politics in the individual colonies gradually assumed greater importance among Africans in Britain, particularly as a consequence of the emergence of the various youth movements in West Africa. At the same time, differences of interest and orientation regularly surfaced between African students in Britain, particularly those from the Gold Coast and Nigeria, and were never entirely overcome. At times, the WASU found that it was in rivalry with other student organisations throughout the country, and particularly with the London-based Gold Coast Students' Association (GCSA). The GCSA had also been founded in the 1920s to "promote and protect the social, educational and political interests" of the Gold Coast, and to "encourage common understanding, co-operation and unity among the Gold Coast students in Europe".[25]

The GCSA often shared its membership with the WASU but, in spite, or perhaps because, of this fact, there were often disagreements between the two organisations. Political identity was therefore often fluid. Sometimes it was Pan-African concerns that were paramount, at other times West African, while on occasions the interests of the individual colonial states took precedence. Very often it was external political events which could contribute to either temporary or lasting unity. During the late 1930s, events not only in West Africa but also elsewhere in the African continent, helped to bring about increasing unity, not only between the West African organisations, but also to contribute to a wider Pan-African unity that culminated in the Manchester Pan-African Congress in 1945.

One of the most significant events during the 1930s was the Italian invasion of Ethiopia in 1935. Throughout the Pan-African world, Ethiopia was seen as a symbol of African independence. The invasion was, therefore, often viewed by those in Africa and throughout the Diaspora as something of a 'racial war'. At the same time, it served to intensify sentiments of anti-colonialism as well as anti-fascism throughout the colonies. There is no doubt that the invasion of Ethiopian and the activities of various organisations in Britain, including WASU, the LCP and the International African Friends of Abyssinia, did create the basis for greater Pan-African unity.[26] Such sentiments were further strengthened by the fact that due to the demands for colonies from Italy and Germany, the whole colonial system came under the spotlight. This was particularly the case, as it was rumoured that parts of the British colonies in West Africa might be transferred to Germany.

As a consequence, greater unity developed between the West African students, a unity that was further developed during their support for the halting of cocoa production and boycotting of British goods in protest at economic exploitation in West Africa in 1937. By the time of the outbreak of the Second World War, therefore, a stronger sense of West African and also Pan-African unity did exist among Africans and their organisations in Britain. Indeed, shortly after the declaration of war, a deputation from WASU, the LCP, the Negro Welfare Association and other organisations including the League Against Imperialism, met with the Colonial Secretary to question Britain's war aims and to demand political and other reforms in the colonies.

The war was to have a profound impact on the students and all those from the colonies in Britain. The British and other Allied governments found it necessary to call for support from the colonies and therefore emphasised that the war was being fought for freedom, democracy and self-determination, and that at its conclusion, major changes would be made to Britain's colonial empire. The expectations of people in the colonies and Africans in Britain were consequently raised by the declarations made in the Atlantic Charter and elsewhere by leading politicians. At the same time, the student organisations were increasingly seen by the Colonial Office as important barometers of colonial opinion, which should, wherever possible, be appeased and courted. This encouraged such organisations to step up their activities and make ever more militant demands including calling for the independence of the colonies.

During the war, a much greater unity existed between all the African organisations in Britain, and between them and the anti-colonial organisations in West Africa. It was in Britain that the first demands for self-government and complete independence for the West African colonies were made and agitated for. The Pan-African unity that had often seemed somewhat illusory during the 1930s, was also aided by the circumstance of the war and the continuing problems of racism and the colour bar. WASU and the LCP, which had hitherto often viewed each other as rivals, worked more closely together and in 1939 the LCP held a conference on 'African Peoples, Democracy and World Peace' in London which played a significant part in bringing together many of the African organisations in Britain.

PAN-AFRICANISM, NATIONALISM AND COMMUNISM

In 1944, following the initiative of the International African Service Bureau, representatives of various African and Pan-African organisations gathered in Manchester to form 'a Pan-African united front movement', to be known as the Pan-African Federation (PAF).

The PAF did not include the LCP or WASU, but these organisations often allied with it on matters of general concern. This was the first occasion that so many organisations had joined together to forge this kind of Pan-African unity. Perhaps even more significant, was the fact that the PAF included representatives of three African organisations; two from West Africa, the West African Youth League and the Friends of African Freedom Society, and one from East Africa, the Kikuyu Central Association. It was the united activity of these organisations that created the basis for the organisation of the historic Manchester Pan-African Congress in 1945. The war had certainly contributed to this new unity. Africans and their organisations in Britain were now concerned to formulate policies for the post-war world, which could place Africa and the Diaspora at the centre of world affairs, and which would enhance the struggle against racial discrimination and for colonial independence. Although both the WASU and LCP were involved in discussions about the need for a post-war Pan-African congress, it was the PAF, under the political leadership of George Padmore, that finally took the initiative to summon a congress in Manchester in 1945.[27]

Not only did the African and Pan-African organisations unite to convene the Manchester Pan-African Congress, they were also jointly involved in organising two Subject Peoples' conferences in 1945. As always, political identity also included a consciousness of the colonial status that was shared not just with other Africans or those from the Caribbean, but also with those from Asia and other parts of the British Empire. The organising committee of the Subject Peoples' conferences included the Ceylon Students Association, the Burma Association and the Federation of Indian Associations in Britain, who jointly comprised what was referred to as a 'Provisional Committee of United Colonial Peoples' Federation'. Indeed, there was much talk of establishing a 'Colonial International' and agreement among the participants that their struggles were 'fundamentally the same' and that they needed to build unity and work more closely together. As Wallace Johnson, one of the participants, expressed it:

> This unity among the coloured races, the vast majority of whom are workers and peasants, may yet lay the foundation for the wider unity among all workers and exploited and oppressed.[28]

The Subject Peoples' conferences, therefore, gave further impetus not just to the idea of Pan-African unity, but also to African and Asian solidarity and the need for a broad anti-colonial and anti-imperialist front in the struggles for national liberation. All this occurred some ten years before the famous Bandung Conference.

The unity between the African and Pan-African organisations was maintained throughout the preparatory work for the Manchester Pan-African Congress. Most of the organisations supported the *Open Letter* that was sent to the new Labour Prime Minister and approved of a *Manifesto on Africa in the Post-War World* that was sent to the United Nations conference in San Francisco. The African student organisations attended and played a leading role in the Congress itself. Student delegates stressed the need for unity between workers and students and highlighted the problems faced by Black seamen and 'coloured' children in Britain. There were also many demands for an end to the colour bar and racial discrimination in Britain. But, most importantly, the Congress raised the demand for "full and unconditional independence" for the colonies, especially those in Africa. Kwame Nkrumah, one of the leading figures at the Congress claimed that it "provided the outlet for African nationalism and brought about the awakening of political consciousness."[29]

It certainly demonstrated the political militancy and optimism of Africans and their organisations in Britain, and that Pan-African unity was very much based on the ideas and analysis of the movement's Marxist wing. Politically active West Africans in Britain apparently saw themselves as part, not only, of a wider Pan-African world, but also as an integral part of the exploited and oppressed struggling for liberation.

But such apparent unity hid existing divisions and differing orientations. After 1945, many separate organisations reflecting different West African political identities emerged, especially among Nigerians. There were organisations of the various Nigerian nationalities, such as the Ibo Union and Yoruba Egbe Omo Odudwa, and organisations affiliated to particular political organisations in Nigeria, such as branches of the Action Group and National Council of Nigeria and the Cameroons. As in the past, Africans in Britain provided many of the leading members of political organisations in West Africa, and at times were instrumental in developing important aspects of the emerging political ideologies too. New organisations such as the Nigeria Union and Gold Coast Union were also established in the post-war period and, for a time, seemed to diminish the importance of WASU. By the early 1950s, however, WASU had established plans for its re-organisation into a federation that could include the most important of the new organisations, the Nigeria Union and the Gold Coast Union.

Paradoxically, it was also during the post-1945 period that the notion of West African nationalism again assumed some prominence due to the activities of the West African National Secretariat (WANS). The founding of WANS in 1945, following the Manchester Pan-African Congress, demonstrates the complexities and contradictions inherent in the political identities and consciousness of Africans in Britain. Kwame Nkrumah and Wallace Johnson were two of the principal organisers of the Congress. However, as soon as it had concluded, they and others formed the WANS. It continued the tradition of its predecessors and aimed to work, both among organisations within West Africa, "with a view to realising a West African Front for a United West African National Independence", and "among the peoples and working class in particular in the imperialist countries", to educate them about West Africa's problems.[30]

The aims of the WANS make it clear that it saw itself very much in the vanguard of the struggle for "absolute independence for all West Africa", but also in the struggle to unite West Africa as "one country". At a time when internationalism and Pan-Africanism on the one hand, and narrow political nationalism on the other, seemed to be growing more prevalent among West Africans, it may appear strange that the notion of West Africa as one country would again become popular. However, what was new and dynamic about WANS' conception was that West African nationhood was now seen in terms of a West African 'Soviet Union', which would stretch as far as Kenya and the Sudan in the east and included not only British colonies, but French and Belgian as well. Thus, one of the most significant features of WANS' West African nationalism and sense of identity and politics, was its internationalism. It believed in a united West Africa "irrespective of artificial territorial divisions". At the same time, WANS never divorced itself from Africans from other parts of the continent or the Diaspora.[31]

The ideology guiding the WANS and much of the political content of the Pan-African Congress, demonstrates that in the post-1945 period, Marxism and communism played an important role in the political consciousness of many West Africans in Britain. The expectations that had been raised during the war were not met by the actions of the post-war Labour government, which was slow to put into practice any of its wartime promises and which was responsible for the violent suppression of anti-colonial protests in Nigeria and the Gold Coast. These circumstances further radicalised many of the students and propelled them towards more radical critiques of colonialism and racism in Britain. Even during the 1930s, the Marxist-influenced Pan-Africanism of Padmore, Wallace Johnson and others, had developed in Britain and had attracted many West Africans.

The war years also did much to raise the status of both communism and the Soviet Union, and by 1948, the Colonial Office was lamenting what officials called "the addiction of so many of the young West African intelligentsia to form communist associations in the UK".[32] One of the consequences of communist influences was that many of the students developed a new internationalist perspective, and began to see their political identity in much broader terms. WASU, for example, was now affiliated to the International Union of Students (IUS) and had its own representative on the executive of the World Federation of Democratic Youth, which were both viewed by the British government as 'communist-front' organisations.

West Africans also participated in the First International Conference of the Peoples of Europe-Asia-Africa Against Imperialism and in other international gatherings. Many students began to travel to Eastern Europe where they witnessed, "the deep sympathy of the people of these countries for the struggles of the African people for self-determination and human rights".[33] It is evident that, as a consequence of such visits, and in particular the links with the IUS, the perspective of the students was considerably widened. As *WASU News Service* explained:

> As colonials we realise that we cannot and must not isolate ourselves from the struggle of our people for independence. For it is when this is achieved that we can enjoy fully the fruits of education and use it for the building of a better society for our peoples. We realise too that our struggle is part of the universal

one for a better world and as such we must co-operate with all those who are engaged in this battle fully realising that it is a joint struggle that can rid the world of its present day conflicts.[34]

The WASU continued to support the IUS even after the National Union of Students in Britain had left it on the basis that it was "a partisan political organisation which is little more than the student section of the Cominform".[35] During the 1950s, many West African and their organisations used Marxist phraseology in their statements, or were sympathetic towards the Soviet Union. For example, in 1953, the Nigeria Union declared "there is common ground between the colonial peoples and the communist world."[36] By the early 1950s, the British Communist Party even had its own West African branch in London and reported over one hundred and fifty African members.[37]

The attempts by the Colonial Office and others to steer the students away from such 'subversive' influences, therefore, only had limited success. Of course, many students were not sympathetic to the 'proletarian internationalism' which became increasingly popular in the post-war period, but it was not difficult to explain why many were. As one Colonial Office official explained:

> What drives African students into undesirable political fields is what has happened and is happening in Africa . . . African colonial government is not 'democratic', until it is, there will be political feelings and agitation among students of a kind which plays into the hand of Communists and other propagandists.[38]

Internationalism was, of course, also an important part of the Pan-Africanist orientation of West Africans and their organisations throughout the century. There had always been attempts to establish links between those organisations in Britain and their counterparts in the United States and elsewhere. In WASU's early years, for example, the students established links with organisations in the Caribbean, South Africa, the Belgian Congo and Brazil, as well as establishing agents in the United States. As early as 1926, two of the organisation's members had attended the World YMCA Conference in Finland. By the 1950s, many of the African organisations in Britain, including WASU, had more extensive international contacts, including those with their counterparts in France, the Rassemblement Démocratique Africain and the Fédération d'Étudiants d'Afrique Noire en France.

It must not be forgotten that Africans contributed to the political life of Britain as well as being influenced by it. From the beginning of the century, they contributed to the anti-imperialist and anti-racist movements in Britain and acted to put political pressure on the Colonial Office and other government departments and win the support of the British public. In this regard, WASU even had its own parliamentary committee that had a membership of Labour Party MPs. Many other Africans joined the major and some minor political organisations, including the Communist Party, Union of Democratic Control and the National Council for Civil Liberties, and took part in a range of political activities in Britain. They recognised the importance of the written word and wrote articles and published papers and journals accordingly. They were often involved specifically with anti-colonial and anti-imperialist organisations ranging from the League Against Imperialism to the Movement for Colonial Freedom, but also with a host of other organisations as varied as the Young Liberals International and the Women's Co-operative Guild.

There is no doubt that the time the students spent in Britain and the activities they engaged in during their sojourn were of direct importance to political advance in the colonies as well as political life in Britain. The period in Britain was also important in the political development of individual students and in the development of various ideologies of resistance including Pan-Africanism and West African nationalism.[39]

The political identities of both individuals and their organisations changed over time, according to particular historical conditions and influences. It was often remarked that the radicalism of many students vanished when they returned home, and that they were simply 'proletarians in Westminster and bourgeois in Lagos'. There is undoubtedly some truth in this remark, just as it is true that some students, and many other Africans in Britain, took little or no part in the struggles against racism and colonialism. Nevertheless, it is also true that student politics in Britain was significant in its own right and that political and social conditions in Britain were an important influence on many of West Africa's most prominent politicians. In this regard, Kwame Nkrumah, despite the brevity of his stay in Britain, was a notable example.

The political identities and ideologies adopted by Africans clearly changed and varied throughout the century, yet while they were in Britain, most students suffered from very similar problems and all suffered as colonial subjects. It was for this reason that, whatever the language and phraseology used, they generally shared a common political agenda. They were compelled to unite in action against racism and the colour bar, and in opposition to colonial rule. As a consequence, their activities and political thinking made an important contribution to political life throughout the West Africa colonies and, indeed, throughout the Diaspora, as well as in the heart of the British Empire.

NOTES AND REFERENCES

1.   For a general history of Africans in Britain see Killingray, D. *Africans in Britain* (London: Frank Cass, 1994) and Fryer, P. *Staying Power: The History of Black People in Britain* (London: Pluto, 1984).

2.   For further information on these issues see Adi, H. *West Africans in Britain 1900-1960: Nationalism, Pan-Africanism and Communism* (London: Lawrence and Wishart, 1998).

3.   'Sons of Africa' was the name by which Equiano, Cugoano and other African abolitionists collectively referred to themselves.

4.   Shyllon, F.O. *Black People in Britain: 1555-1833* (Oxford: Oxford University Press, 1977) p. 53.

5.   On Horton's ideas see Langley, J.A. *Pan-Africanism and Nationalism in West Africa 1900-1945* (Oxford: Oxford University Press, 1973) p. 111.

6.   Adi, H. 'West African Students in Britain, 1900-60: The Politics of Exile', in Killingray, D. *Africans in Britain* p. 108.

7.   Fryer, P. *Staying Power* p. 280.

8.   Adi, H. *West Africans in Britain...* p. 11.

9.   Ibid. On Casely Hayford, see Jenkins, R. 'Gold Coasters Overseas, 1888-1919: With Specific Reference to their Activities in Britain', *Immigrants and Minorities*, 4/3 (1985) pp. 5-52

10. See Duffield, I. 'Dusé Mohammed Ali, Afro-Asian solidarity and Pan-Africanism in early twentieth-century London', in Duffield, I. and Gundara, J.S. *Essays on the History of Blacks in Britain* (Aldershot: Avebury, 1992) pp. 124-150.

11. Adi, H. *West Africans in Britain...* pp. 17-19.

12. Adi, H. Ibid. pp. 23-27.

13. *Lagos Standard*, 7 June 1914.

14. Adi, H. *West Africans in Britain* pp. 58-62.

15. Ibid. pp. 29-30.

16. Olusanya, G.O. *The West African Students' Union and the Politics of Decolonisation, 1925-1958* (Ibadan: Daystar, 1982) p. 19.

17. *West Africa*, 15 August 1925, p. 1002.

18. *Wasu*, 1/6-7, August 1928, p. 1.

19. *West Africa*' 27 September 1926, p. 49.

20. De Graft Johnson, J.W. *Towards Nationhood in West Africa: Thoughts of Young Africa Addressed to Young Britain* (London: Frank Cass, 1971) p. vi.

21.   Solanke, L. *United West Africa (or Africa) at the Bar of the Family of Nations* (London: African Publications Society, 1969) p. 64.

22.   Adi, H. *Africans in Britain*, especially pp. 76-82.

23.   *Wasu*, 4/3, September 1935, p. 35.

24.   Quoted in Adi, H. *West Africans in Britain* p. 63

25.   Ibid. p. 43.

26.   The International African Friends of Abyssinia was formed by C.L.R. James and others in 1934 with the aim "to assist by all means necessary in their power in the maintenance of the territorial integrity and political independence of Abyssinia".

27.   See Adi, H. and Sherwood, M. *The 1945 Manchester Pan-African Congress Revisited* (London: New Beacon, 1995).

28.   Ibid. p. 25.

29.   Quoted in Langley, J.A. *Nationalism and Pan-Africanism* pp. 355-356.

30.   Adi, H. *West Africans in Britain* p. 129.

31.   Ibid. See also Sherwood, M. *Kwame Nkrumah, the years abroad 1935-47* (Legon: Freedom Publications, 1996) pp. 125-159.

32.   Quoted in Adi, H. 'West African Students in Britain', p. 123.

33.   *Wasu News Service*, 1/8, March 1953, pp. 6-7.

34.   *Wasu News Service*, 1/4, November 1952, p. 12.

35.   *Wasu News Service*, 1/6, January 1953, p. 2.

36.   Obahiagbon, E.E. 'A Preface to Policy' quoted in Adi, H. *West Africans in Britain* p. 205.

37.   See Adi, H. 'West Africans and the Communist Party in the 1950s', in Andrews, G., Fishman, N. and Morgan, K. *Opening the Books – Essays on the Social and Cultural History of the British Communist Party* (London: Pluto, 1995) pp. 176-195.

38.   Quoted in Adi, H. 'West African Students in Britain' p. 124.

39.   West African women played a significant part in many of the organisations mentioned in this chapter. However, they only began to form their own organisations in the 1940s and 1950s. By that time, the vast majority of women students came to Britain to train as nurses, but a minority embarked on a career in medicine, law and in other fields. The first women's organisation was the West African Women's Association, formed in London in 1946.

Chapter Three

REFLECTIONS ON THE 1997 EUROPEAN YEAR AGAINST RACISM: A BLACK BRITISH PERSPECTIVE

Mark Christian

THE MEMBER States of the European Union officially declared 1997 as the 'European Year Against Racism'. In this sense, the European Union openly acknowledges that xenophobia and racism is deeply ingrained within the social body of Europe. As such, during 1997, the political power structure's objective was to resist the rise and spread of racism in the Member States. In view of the European Union's 1997 Year Against Racism, this chapter will give an insight into the Black British experience, taking an historical view and perspective on the racism that has beset Black communities throughout the UK, due to the British Empire and its colonial heritage. The analysis will also adopt an historical frame of reference in order to show how racist ideologies are deep-rooted and have had 'intellectual' durability in Europe since at least the eighteenth century. This apparent longevity of racist thought and practice is something that will be central in the discussion, as it is not addressed by the European Union in the literature that launched the 'year against racism' and xenophobia. Rather, racism is articulated as something only unique to twentieth century social conditions. This perspective, as will be contended, is erroneous. Indeed, racism, in a British sense, is as old and as popular as Shakespeare.

> We call upon all European institutions, public authorities, private organisations and individuals at both European, national and local level, to contribute in everyday life, at school, at the work place, in the media to struggle against racism, xenophobia and anti-Semitism.[1]

The above citation is an extract from a 1997 European Commission newsletter promoting the need to tackle the growing problem of racism within its various national borders. This begs the question: how and why did this contemporary political concern about racism in Europe develop? In point of fact, it was during the 1990s that a key feature of European political debate began to revolve around the growing problem of racism and xenophobia.

The Member States[2] that have had a significant role in the debates surrounding racism, range from Germany, France, Belgium, Austria, Italy and the United Kingdom. The current political interest concerning racism in Europe has occurred largely via the disintegration of the Soviet Union, which brought about a high degree of social unrest in the shape of racist nationalist movements. Some major Eastern European nations, such as Hungary, Poland and the Czech Republic, also had growing far-right nationalist groups emerging during the 1990s. Yet, it is the example of the break-up of Yugoslavia that shocked the Western European powers into doing something about the ugliness of racism or 'ethnic cleansing', which plagued this particular internal conflict. Essentially, this is the backdrop to what developed as the '1997 European Year Against Racism'.

At the outset of 1997, the European Union had fifteen Member States. Each country organised its own events and programme of action to ensure that the message of tolerance, respect and understanding got across to as many people as possible. In his speech that launched the importance of the year against racism, Jacques Santer, the European Commissioner, stated: "Racism is against all that Europe stands for in protecting human dignity and promoting mutual respect and understanding."[3] The same sentiment was echoed by the European Union's Social Affairs Commissioner, Padraig Flynn. He called the event a "very practical vehicle for the EU and member states to take action together and stamp out the evil of racism in our societies."[4]

In terms of the United Kingdom's response to the year against racism and its launch, before his government was ousted from office, the Conservative Prime Minister, John Major, in January 1997, presented British school children with art awards. The children had participated in a national anti-racist art competition whereby they were asked to create a poster employing artwork or photography that represented the cultural diversity of the UK's population.[5] In presenting the awards, John Major stated: "There must be no position, no job, no opportunity, no right from which people are excluded because of their creed, their colour or their race."[6]

In reference to the contemporary concern about the spread of racism throughout Europe, this chapter will essentially examine the experience of Black Britons. In addition, there is also an attempt to put forward an historical analysis of British racism in the Western world. An historical approach in understanding racism is necessary to fully comprehend the nature and scope of it in the present day. Indeed, it would be analytically deleterious to overlook the impact to, and origins of, European racist ideologies and practice. That is, in relation to understanding the Black British experience.

ROOTS OF EUROPEAN RACISM AND RACIST IDEOLOGIES

Racism is the spurious belief that there exists distinct human 'races' which are superior and inferior to each other. Although the social development of 'racism' has been examined in different ways, in terms of the roots of European racism, many writers have located the era of mercantile expansion by Europeans, specifically from the fifteenth to the nineteenth centuries, as the period whereby racist ideologies flourished.[7] In particular, it was with the growth and development of the European 'slave trade' that required the enslaved labour of Africans and Asians, even though white indentured labour was initially used.[8] The labour was necessary in order to produce the staple crops on the plantations in the 'New World'.[9]

Writers, within the Marxist school of thought, such as Eric Williams (1944) and Oliver Cromwell Cox (1948), argued that the rise of racism (Cox, however, preferred to use the term 'race prejudice') was essentially due to the development of industrial capitalism. Moreover, the difference in skin colour and other phenotype characteristics, between the white European and darker nations of the world, was just a useful coincidence for those slave traders/merchants who wanted a demarcated and exploited labour force. It was this dire need for labour that brought about the barbaric European trade in African humanity. Once it developed and the profits of enslavement came flooding in for those who were heavily involved, there grew an 'intellectual' class of Europeans who espoused pseudo-scientific theories claiming the inferiority of Africans and Asians. That is, inferior in comparison to the superiority of the white Anglo Saxon 'race'.

Some writers see this line of reasoning as the way in which white European slave traders/merchants justified the barbarity of human enslavement. As industrial capitalism developed in the eighteenth and nineteenth centuries 'racism' changed to a new set of social circumstances. To put it another way, racist ideology was and never has been static, it has altered to fit the particular time and place where it is a necessary component of the social structure within a given society.

In South Africa, for example, the ruling white minority of both British and Dutch European heritage, established a stratification system based primarily on skin colour. The 'pigment pyramid' saw whites at the top, 'coloureds' in the middle (meaning Africans of mixed origin descent and Asians), while the majority Black/Africans occupied the bottom sphere. Yet in Brazil, racism, in terms of the social stratification in the eighteenth and nineteenth centuries, was not as rigidly structured, compared to that found in South Africa (prior to formal Apartheid). In Brazil, it was still primarily related to skin tone, but there was room for social mobility – racism based on skin colour and other phenotype characteristics was not as harsh.

Another example, is that of the United States of America – any person having 'one drop' of African heritage is deemed to be Black or African American. Crucially, in terms of the roots of European racism and its notions of 'race', it is important to comprehend it as a social construct, which has little to do with actual biological science. Racist ideologues merely endeavoured to justify the enslavement of Africans with often elaborate and fanciful pseudo-scientific theories. Nevertheless, although the racial theories relating to superior/inferior human stocks were scientifically dubious, they still have had a powerful impact in creating the myth of there being distinct 'pure racial types'.

18TH AND 19TH CENTURY BRITISH RACIST IDEOLOGUES

It was the eighteenth and nineteenth centuries that saw a significant increase in literature espousing the notion of white supremacy in terms of humankind. Of those who were the main contributors to racist propaganda in the British context, it was Edward Long and Bryan Edwards in the eighteenth century, with Thomas Carlyle and Anthony Trollope in the nineteenth century, who furthered the cause of white supremacy over the darker peoples of the world. Collectively, their literary works helped shape and cement the popular consciousness of the specific times in which each of them were writing.[10]

EDWARD LONG AND HIS 1774 HISTORY OF JAMAICA

Edward Long (1734-1813) was born and raised in England, and had gone on to live in the British colony of Jamaica for twelve years as a young man. He later wrote a three-volume *History of Jamaica* in 1774. In volume two there is a section on the 'Negro'[11] and it is here that Long outlines his overt antipathy for African humanity. The Long family had a strong financial connection with the island of Jamaica. It reached back as far as when Britain had gained it in 1655 through conquest over Spain. In this regard, Edward Long was a staunch supporter of African enslavement, plantocracy and the colonisation of peoples of

African descent. In his works, Long deplores the idea of Africans gaining any amount of freedom in order to exercise power, either on English soil or in the Caribbean colonies. Certainly, his brand of racist ideas did not fall on deaf ears, according to the noted British historian James Walvin, Long's *History of Jamaica* became a classic planter's text which promoted white supremacy. As Walvin states:

> Long was a much respected author and his opinion on the Negro, enveloped in scholarship and supported by experience and technical expertise in government, made a profound impact. He was among the most extreme in his animosity towards the slaves and, as a propagandist, the most widely read.[12]

It is important to note the degree to which writers such as Edward Long profited financially from racial propaganda in a manner which was insidiously regarded as 'scholarship'. Indeed, to understand the roots of British racism and bigotry in the late twentieth century, it would be senseless to neglect the historical forces that helped shape the consciousness of the British people and Europe as a whole. Edward Long represents a class of intellectuals who were far from objective in their analyses concerning the humanity of Africans. This was primarily due to the fact that they had substantial economic holdings in the enslavement of Africans, and it was in their interest to protect the plantation economy in the British-held Caribbean islands.

BRYAN EDWARDS' 1793 HISTORY OF THE BRITISH COLONIES IN THE WEST INDIES

Bryan Edwards (1743-1800), a friend and associate of Edward Long, was a merchant who had also made his fortune from the enslavement of Africans in the Caribbean. He was also an avid supporter of African enslavement and saw white Anglo Saxons as the superior human 'race'. In 1797, Edwards published his *History, Civil and Commercial, of the British Colonies in the West Indies*. Although its content was not as hostile as Long's *History of Jamaica*, it still peddled vicious stereotypes that denigrated African humanity. Again, it should be noted that Edwards' book also became a 'classic' in the field of British colonial literature. However, both Edwards and Long, as social commentators in the eighteenth century, conveyed in their works one-sided accounts designed to legitimate the continued exploitation of enslaved African labour. Specifically in the Caribbean colonies held by the British and where they each had a vested interest. Accordingly, there was no genuine attempt to view Africans in a positive frame of reference. In this sense, they did great harm, particularly to the abolitionist push for the ending of slavery, by promoting racist theories and stereotypes. This was the apparent intention of both Long and Edwards, along with the many more writers who justified the enslavement of Africans. Unfortunately, their racist ideas continued to gain wide approval and went very much 'alive and kicking' into the nineteenth century.[13]

THOMAS CARLYLE'S 1849 THE 'NIGGER QUESTION'

Thomas Carlyle (1795-1881), a distinguished British historian, was a key nineteenth century figure who also promoted the notion of white supremacy. He felt that it was natural for Africans to serve white Europeans. As did his predecessors, Long and Edwards, Carlyle attacked the ideas of white philanthropists who were working toward social justice for the Africans in the 'New World'. In his essay on the 'Nigger Question' (1849), Carlyle exemplifies his racist beliefs, in the age of ever-expanding British colonialism, as he explains what a person of African descent means to him:

> Do I, then, hate the Negro? No; except when the soul is killed out of him, I decidedly like poor Quashee [name for an African]; and find him a pretty kind of man. With a pennyworth of oil you can make a handsome glossy thing of Quashee, when the soul is not killed in him! A swift, supple fellow; a merry-hearted, grinning, dancing, singing, affectionate kind of creature, with a great deal of melody and amenability in his composition. This certainly is a notable fact: The Black African, alone of wild-men, can live among men civilised. While all manner of Caribs and others pine into annihilation in presence of pale faces, he contrives to continue; does not die of sullen irreconcilable rage, of rum, of brutish laziness and darkness, and fated incompatibility with his new place; but lives and multiplies, and evidently means to abide among us, if we can find the right regulation for him.[14]

As with Long and Edwards in the eighteenth century, Carlyle's racist propaganda was widely circulated and read by the British public.[15] In the extract above Carlyle is explicit in his opinion of the inferiority of both Africans and Asians to that of the white European. What is more disconcerting is the fact that eighteen years on from 1849, Carlyle is of the same opinion regarding white supremacy. In an article written in 1867 and entitled 'Shooting Niagara: and after,' he merely paraphrases his earlier piece, as he states:

> One always rather likes the Nigger; evidently a poor blockhead with good dispositions, with affections, attachments – with a turn for Nigger Melodies, and the like – he is the only Savage of all the coloured races that doesn't die out on sight of the White Man; but can actually live beside him, and work and increase and be merry. The Almighty Maker has appointed him to be a Servant.[16]

Carlyle unashamedly viewed the English as the 'chosen people' whereby they were destined to take up the 'white man's burden' (*pace* Rudyard Kipling) to civilise the world. It was this form of jingoism that informed the era of British colonialism, the Victorian period, and was nurtured by its racist ideologues. What is important to note, again, is that these dubious ideas did not exist in a vacuum. On the contrary, they fed into the growing popular culture that emerged in Victorian Britain. The vast majority of people relied heavily on the insights of writers such as Thomas Carlyle for an understanding of Africans and other peoples beyond Britain.

ANTHONY TROLLOPE'S 1859 *THE WEST INDIES AND THE SPANISH MAIN*

Anthony Trollope (1815-1882), a contemporary of Carlyle's and a famous novelist (interestingly the favourite author of the former British Prime Minister, John Major), also believed in white supremacy and the inferiority of Africans. In his book, *The West Indies and the Spanish Main*, which was the outcome of his travels to the island of Jamaica in 1858, he writes: "God, for his own purposes - purposes which are already becoming more and more intelligible to his creatures - has created men of inferior and superior race."[17] Explaining what he thinks about the character of the African Caribbean in comparison to the white European, he candidly points out:

> They are more passionate than white men, but rarely vindictive, as we are. The smallest injury excites their eager wrath, but no injury produces sustained hatred. In the same way, they are seldom grateful, though often very thankful. They are covetous of notice as is a child or a dog; but they have little idea of earning continual respect. They best love him who is most unlike themselves . . . When they have once recognised a man as their master, they will be faithful to him; but the more they fear that master, the more they will respect him. They have no care for tomorrow, but they delight in being gaudy for today. Their crimes are those of momentary impulse, as are also their virtues. They fear death; but if they can lie in the sun without pain for the hour they will hardly drag themselves to the hospital, though their disease be mortal. They love their offspring, but in their rage will ill use them fearfully. They are proud of them when they are praised, but will sell their daughter's virtue for a dollar. They are greedy for food, but generally indifferent as to its quality. They rejoice in finery, and have in many cases begun to understand the benefit of comparative cleanliness; but they are rarely tidy. A little makes them happy, and nothing makes them permanently wretched. On the whole, they laugh and sing and sleep through life; and if life were all, they would not have so bad a time of it.

Trollope concludes his summation of the African: "These, I think, are the qualities of the negro."[18] He goes on to compare the African to a dog in terms of obedience and loyalty to its master. There is clearly the notion of African inferiority openly espoused by Trollope in his penmanship. What is significant is in the fact that he is one of Britain's most celebrated authors and is widely read even today in British college and university courses. Indeed, his writings are considered among some of the British classics and notable literary works of the nineteenth century. As mentioned earlier, Trollope is also the favourite author of the former British Conservative Prime Minister, John Major. This begs the questions: what influence does the work of an avidly racist writer, which one admires, have on the reader? Moreover, is it ethical to support the work of a person that is ardently racist in his or her views, even though the writing is from another century? These questions may be too complex to answer here, but they should at least be considered for further debate.

THE LEGACY OF EUROPEAN RACISM AND IDEOLOGY

It has been necessary to give the above literary examples of a number of key and prominent British writers who helped shape the common opinion concerning African humanity in the eighteenth and nineteenth centuries. By the mid-twentieth century, and the aftermath of World War II, and specifically the Jewish Holocaust, the modern Western world, in a scientific sense, began an in-depth study into what 'race' in human terms actually means. From the 1950s, up to the late 1970s, the United Nations Educational, Scientific and Cultural Organisation (UNESCO) conducted a number of inquiries into 'race and racism'. The research was carried out by a variety of respected European scientists who came from different disciplines. Although there was an intellectual developmental process in regard to the four major statements on 'race', due to disagreements and the need for further clarity on certain points (i.e. in 1950, 1951, 1964 and 1967), in 1978 the UNESCO General Conference proclaimed its Declaration on Race and Racial Prejudice. After noting the four previous statements, Article I reads:

> All human beings belong to a single species and are descended from a common stock. They are born equal in dignity and rights and all form an integral part of humanity.

> All individuals and groups have the right to be different, to consider themselves as different and to be regarded as such. However, the diversity of lifestyles and the right to be different may not, in any circumstances, serve as a pretext for racial prejudice.[19]

By the late-twentieth century, then, the political climate in Western Europe had apparently morally outlawed racism in both ideology and practice. Moreover, humanity is now considered deriving from a 'common stock' that is born 'equal in dignity and rights'. As shown above, regarding the evolution of the human family, this political position is a far cry from what was considered by the white European power structures in the eighteenth and nineteenth centuries. Indeed, in relation to how people of African descent are viewed, there has occurred a major shift in the way humanity is regarded politically by Western Europe. This may be partly due to the influence of the many post-World War II African and African Caribbean nations who secured a degree of independence from their erstwhile colonial rulers. Along with the independence struggles, there was the development of the Civil Rights Movement in the 1960s in the US, and this had a tremendous impact in promoting the notion of Black pride and consciousness across the globe. However, regardless of these tremendous social forces, racism across Western Europe still remains a social fact at the dawn of the twenty-first century, no matter what political rhetoric is put forward to reduce its prevalence. In short, the history/legacy of racist ideologies continues to blight human relations throughout Western Europe, and the rest of the world, for that matter, hence the '1997 Year Against Racism in Europe.'

BLACK PRESENCE IN BRITAIN

The European Union has over ten million immigrants and people who are considered 'ethnic minorities'. In terms of Britain, the overall population statistics are revealed in Table 1 below.

Nearly ninety-five percent of the population is of white ethnic origin, while the remaining five and a half per cent make up the so-called 'ethnic minority' communities. Of this, approximately 1.2 million can claim to be of African descent (if we take into account the 'Other-other' category which the Commission for Racial Equality statistician did not). This figure accounts for people directly from the African continent, African Caribbean and those of African mixed origin descent.

Table 1 also shows how difficult it is to classify people into particular 'racial' groups. Indeed, terms such as 'Black-other' and 'Other-other' reveal the complexity in the way racial categories more often confuse rather than clarify the racial origin of particular social groups. For instance, the 'Black-other' category is more explicit than the nebulous 'Other-other'. Yet it at least gives an indication that the census is categorising persons of African mixed origin descent. What can be stated here, however, is the fact that those persons who are designated within the racial groups that are clearly 'not white' are effectively regarded as 'ethnic minorities' by the official census data in the UK.

Therefore, in regard to understanding racism in the contemporary UK context, it is necessary to first acknowledge the various racial groups which make up the 'minority communities'. Apart from the obvious cultural differences between the diverse minority groups in the UK, it has also been found that their experience of racism in British society can be qualitatively contrasted.[20] Moreover, due to the small numbers of Black groups within the UK, some Asian groups have adopted the term 'Black' as a political label, rather than a cultural one, in order to fight racism.[21] However, for the purpose of clarity, this chapter refers to the term 'Black British' as to those persons who can claim African heritage.

Table 1: 1991 Census Ethnic Composition of the UK Population[22]

Ethnic Group	No.	%
White	51,873,794	94.5
Black Caribbean	499,964	0.9
Black African	212,362	0.4
Black - other	178,401	0.3
Indian	840,255	1.5
Pakistani	476,555	0.9
Bangladeshi	162,835	0.3
Chinese	156,938	0.3
Other Asian	197,534	0.4
Other - other	290,206	0.5
Total ethnic minority population	3,015,051	5.5
Black Ethnic groups	890,727	1.6
South Asian	1,479,645	2.7
Chinese and others	644,678	1.2

People of African descent have been present in Britain, at least, since the Romans invaded in AD 43.[23] They also settled in Britain during the era of the European slave trade. In particular, it was the seaport cities such as Liverpool, Bristol and Cardiff that saw the development of Black communities in the eighteenth and nineteenth centuries. Black presence was further increased with World War I and II and the involvement of Black troops, seaman and munitions workers from Britain's colonies. They came to fight for Britain and many settled in the UK once the wars had finished.

It was, however, the post-World War II era that saw a major increase in Britain's Black population. The increase was primarily due to there being a need for labour in Britain in regard to the post-war economic boom. In order to keep the cost to a minimum, Britain drew the labour supply from its former colonies. A. Sivanandan deems this Black migration into Britain, between the late 1940s and early 1960s, as the 'reserve army of labour'.[24] He maintains that Black people provided the cheap labour for the "shit" jobs that the indigenous white working class would not do. For example, they were employed primarily on the London transport system, with the underground railway and buses. They also took up menial posts in the National Health Service.[25] Racial discrimination, therefore, manifested itself within the labour market in the UK. Black people also found it very difficult to obtain housing due to the racism of white British landlords.[26]

Therefore, the Black experience in Britain has been characterised by a high degree of racism and discrimination. This pattern of racial discrimination should be viewed from an historical perspective. As argued earlier, it is futile to understand racism as something that is merely a contemporary social phenomena. Rather, it is necessary to examine the deep-rooted nature and development of British racism. Indeed, from a British context this involves seeking knowledge into how and why people of African descent became enslaved, colonised and neo-colonised.

It also requires us to examine how racism has impacted in various times and places. In addition, we need to know how it appears to have an almost insuperable quality in terms of trying to eradicate it from modern Western societies. Is it because there is a failure by those in power to fully acknowledge the historical legacy of racism and deal with it accordingly? Indeed, in reading the comments made by the European Union's leaders regarding the launch of the '1997 Year Against Racism in Europe', there appears to be a distinct denial of Europe's fundamental role in the enslavement process and the subsequent (1884/5) European nation-state 'scramble for Africa'.

EUROPE AND ITS 'HISTORICAL AMNESIA'

When one considers the European slave trade, and the subsequent colonisation of Africa, parts of Asia and the 'New World', it is difficult to take seriously Jacques Santer's statement that: "Racism is against all that Europe stands for in protecting human dignity and promoting mutual respect and understanding". To be sure, there is an implicit political silence in regard to Europe's past involvement in the development of racism and the subsequent racialised exploitation of peoples of African and Asian descent. For instance, albeit in different forms, the Portuguese, Spanish, British, French, Belgians, Dutch, Germans and other European nations each have a history of colonising and subjugating African peoples sometime or other over the past five centuries. Yet, in the current political rhetoric, this history is not alluded to in any concrete sense. In fact, it appears that 'racism' is viewed as something 'foreign' to Europe - an aberration!

Specifically in relation to Britain and its Empire, on an intellectual level, and, in hindsight, considering the '1997 year against racism' that openly confirmed the contemporary adverse aspect of it throughout Europe, there should be an acceptance of the role it has played historically in disseminating dubious racial theories. After all, it is this legacy of such racist ideologies that impacts so negatively, at present, in the contemporary world. Crucially, this form of 'historical amnesia' that the European Union appears to suffer from, will contribute little to the long-term removal of racism from its member states.

Indeed, not to admit to the past development of European racism is tantamount to a doctor refusing to trace or recognise a patient's past illness when diagnosing the treatment for a persistent and related disease. In other words, the doctor needs to get to the root of the present illness to adequately treat the patient. That usually entails examining the health history of the patient (e.g. to establish if there is a family history of cancer) to gauge whether there is a pattern of illness. This, then, gives the doctor a better understanding of the disease in the present context, and facilitates a more relevant prognosis for the patient's recovery. Often it is fatal to the patient if the doctor does not explore the history of the specific illness.

Writing from the perspective of education, and with prophetic insight into the problems the contemporary world faces with the seemingly permanent spectre of racism, W.E.B. Du Bois (1868-1963), a gifted African American and Ghanaian scholar, too often ignored by his white counterparts, stated over fifty years ago:

> This insistent clinging to the older patterns of race thought has had extraordinary influence upon modern life. In the first place, it has for years held back the progress of the social sciences. The social sciences from the beginning were deliberately used as instruments to prove the inferiority of the majority of the people in the world, who were being used as slaves for the comfort and culture of the masters. The social sciences long looked upon this as one of their major duties. History declared that the Negro had no history. Biology exaggerated the physical differences among men. Economics even today cannot talk straight on colonial imperialism. Psychology has not yet recovered from the shame of its 'intelligence' tests and its record of 'conclusions' during the first World War.[27]

It is in this "clinging to the older patterns of race thought" that persists today in Western European society. In line with W.E.B. Du Bois, Ashley Montagu has described the social significance of dividing humanity into 'races' as: "man's most dangerous myth".[28] It is difficult to disagree with such a sentiment at the outset of a new century. Yet, in my opinion, apart from superficial political statements condemning racism, Europe has failed to fully appreciate the deep-rooted aspect of the problem. Moreover, as patterns of racial discrimination manifest themselves openly throughout Britain and the rest of Europe, there will continue to be a need to consider tackling, vigorously, the legacy of racist ideologies that are often concomitant with modern forms of racism. This will take not only a European initiative, for the attack on racism in all its various forms, needs to be global in scope.

Europe, with the '1997 Year Against Racism' behind it, has, in a sense, prompted further debate and action regarding its evil prevalence in modern societies. The next stage in the process ought to involve Europe coming to terms with its past involvement in the enslavement and colonisation of many millions of Africans and Asian peoples. Britain, in particular, needs to make a stand in this direction by formally apologising to those peoples whose ancestors suffered tremendous human indignity under the British Empire (US President, Bill Clinton, in 1997, considered offering an apology to the African American community regarding the enslavement of their ancestors). Indeed, for those victimised by racial discrimination in the modern era, to see the current stance against racism as authentic, there should be a formal apology, if only to show the British government's commitment to eradicating racial discrimination. Otherwise, the cancer of racism will inevitably continue to fester in the social body of the United Kingdom and the rest of Europe.

CONCLUSION

The aim of this chapter has been to examine the '1997 Year Against Racism in Europe'. It also adopted an historical analysis in relation to the origins of racist thought and practice primarily against peoples of African descent, within a British colonial heritage context. This was to give some depth to the discussion and to show how racism against Black people in Britain has deep roots in British history. Using the examples of some key white British thinkers from the eighteenth and nineteenth centuries, it was suggested that racist ideology became ingrained within the consciousness of the British people. This was at the height of the era of the British enslavement of Africans and the colonisation of Africa and the 'New World'. Each fed into the other, racism and the British Empire.

Particularly in terms of the '1997 Year Against Racism in Europe', until there is a significant political change in the way the European Union tackles racism from the origins of its development, it seems unwise to respond to it in a rather contemporary and superficial sense. Indeed, having a 'year' designated to grapple with the social problem of racism in European society may be a step in the right direction. However, there will inevitably be a need for a follow-up program of action that sustains the work now being done in the member states well into the twenty-first century. In point of fact, there should be a long-term plan that enables member states to deal with the growing problem of racism more effectively. Too many lives have been, and are, destroyed by the negativity of racist practices, both on the institutionalised and individual levels. Surely now, at the dawn of a new a millennium, there needs to be genuine recognition given to the past racial discourse that helps destroy so much of humanity in the present context. Papering over the cracks of an ugly history, as Europe appears to be doing, will only create further misunderstanding and poor 'race relations' in the future. Indeed, to remove a weed from harming the landscape of a garden, there is a need to get to the root of it. Cutting down to the surface of the root may take it away from sight for a while, but in due course the weed will certainly grow back. Racism is something that needs to be removed fully from the earth.

NOTES AND REFERENCES

1. European Commission. Cited in a newsletter for the *European Year Against Racism* (1 May 1997) p. 9.
2. In alphabetical order, the nations which accounted for the European Union in 1997 were: Austria, Belgium, Denmark, Finland, France, Germany, Greece, Ireland, Italy, Luxembourg, Netherlands, Portugal, Spain, Sweden and the United Kingdom.
3. Cited in the UK's Commission for Racial Equality *Quarterly* (Spring, 1997) p. 3.
4. Ibid.
5. European Commission. (above, Note 1) pp. 2-3.
6. Ibid.
7. See Institute of Race Relations. *Roots of Racism* (book one) (London: IRR, 1982); and Fryer, P. *Staying Power: The History of Black People in Britain* (London: Pluto, 1984) chapter 7.
8. For example, Eric Williams in his book *Capitalism and Slavery* (New York: Capricorn Books, 1966; first published 1944) p. 7, writes: "Slavery in the Caribbean has been too narrowly identified with the Negro. A racial twist has thereby been given to what is basically an economic phenomenon. Slavery was not born of racism: rather, racism was the consequence of slavery. Unfree labour in the New World was brown, white, black, and yellow; Catholic, Protestant and pagan." See also Cox, O. C. *Caste, Class and Race* (New York: Monthly Review Press, 1970; first published 1948).
9. Primarily, it was sugar, cotton and tobacco plantations which required the thousands of white indentured servants and indigenous Caribs initially, before millions of Africans were enslaved. Eric Williams, ibid., sees the 'plantation economies' in the seventeenth and eighteenth centuries as providing England with the profits to boost and promote its Industrial Revolution at home.
10. See Walvin, J. *The Black Presence: A Documentary History of the Negro in England: 1555-1860* (London: Orbach & Chambers, 1971) p. 115.
11. Long, E. *History of Jamaica, vol. II* (New York: Arno Press, 1972; first published 1774) pp. 351-383.
12. Walvin, J. *The Black Presence...* pp. 115-116.

13.   See Yeboah, S. K. *The Ideology of Racism* (London: Hansib Publications, 1988).

14.   Thomas Carlyle cited in Walvin, J. *The Black Presence...* p. 142.

15.   Fryer, P. *Staying Power...* p. 172.

16.   Ibid.

17.   Trollope, A. *The West Indies and the Spanish Main* (New York: Hippocrence Books, 1985; first published in 1859) p. 47.

18.   Ibid.

19.   Cited in Cashmore, E. (ed.) *Dictionary of Race and Ethnic Relations, 4th Edition* (London: Routledge, 1996) p. 370.

20.   See Modood, T. et al *Ethnic Minorities in Britain: Diversity and Disadvantage* (London: Policy Studies Institute, 1997).

21.   Again, this indicates how 'race' is a socially constructed phenomena rather than something that is biologically determined.

22.   Table 1 is taken from the Commission for Racial Equality *Roots of the Future: Ethnic Diversity in Britain* (London: CRE, 1996) p. 38.

23.   Fryer, P. *Staying Power...* chapter 1.

24.   Sivanandan, A. *A Different Hunger* (London: Pluto, 1982).

25.   Ibid.

26.   See Miles, R. *Racism and Migrant Labour* (London: Routledge Kegan & Paul, 1982); James, W. and Harris, C. (eds.) *Inside Babylon: The Caribbean Diaspora in Britain* (London: Verso, 1993); and Donald, J. and Rattansi, A. (eds.) *'Race', Culture & Difference* (London: Sage, 1992).

27.   Du Bois, W.E.B. cited from 1944 in Dan S. Green and Edwin D. Driver (eds.) *W.E.B. Du Bois on Sociology and the Black Community* (Chicago and London: University of Chicago Press, 1978) p. 299.

28.   Montagu, A. *Man's Most Dangerous Myth: The Fallacy of Race, 4th Edition* (Cleveland and New York: The World Publishing Company, 1964).

Chapter Four

BLACK POLITICAL CONSCIOUSNESS AND EMPOWERMENT: THE 20th CENTURY COGNITIVE BASIS OF AFRICAN AMERICAN POLITICS

William E. Nelson, Jr.

IN THEIR book, *Black Power: The Politics of Liberation in America*, Stokely Carmichael and Charles V. Hamilton, advance the provocative proposition that "Before a group can enter the open society it must first close ranks".[1] This thesis is important because it calls attention to the fundamental linkage between group cohesion, political consciousness, and the process of political mobilisation. Literally translated, Carmichael and Hamilton's thesis means that before Black people can begin to operate in the political system, from a position of strength, they must unite in order to attain a sense of consciousness of the kind requisite for the realisation of their full power and potentialities in the American political process. This observation cogently underscores the crucial psychological basis of Black liberation politics. In the context of ethnic and racial politics in America, group consciousness is a pivotal political resource.

The issue of group consciousness for Black people grows directly out of the character, content and contours of American political life. In the United States, Black people have been the victims of a hierarchical system of racism that has subordinated Black interests to white interests and subjected Black people to considerable social and economic misery and psychological trauma. This is not a recent phenomenon but has its roots buried deeply in the soil of the history of slavery and nineteenth century systems of peonage labour.[2] Racism and oppression have forced Black people to mount insurgency movements to make real the promises of American democracy.

The assumptions about the legitimacy of the democratic process that underpin Black movements are distinctly different from those that served as the pivotal touchstone of white-led movements such as the temperance campaign, the women's suffrage movement and the twentieth century movement of organised labour. Black movements have often taken the form of protest campaigns. They have moved from the assumption that official laws and institutions are arrayed against the Black community. Thus, Black movements have sought to loosen the shackles of racism through protest and confrontation. In doing so they have been compelled to flaunt established laws to bring into existence new laws that will serve the cause of social justice and racial uplift.

The process of Black insurgency is a complicated one involving profound psychological adjustments. As a precondition for physical mobilisation, Black insurgents must grapple with psychological forces leading to group consciousness, or what Doug McAdam terms "cognitive liberation".[3] Hubert Blalock further illuminates important dimensions of the psychological basis of minority politics in America when he notes that minority political mobilisation requires an assessment of the strength of group goals and the perceived probability of achieving those goals.[4] This means that before substantial Black protest action can take place, Black people must do a substantive assessment of their situation and conclude that the goals or objectives are meaningful and important and that the probability of obtaining them is quite high.

McAdam contends that the likelihood of a Black insurgency action is greatest when the structure of political opportunities is most positive and when the available group resources, especially organisational resources, are strongest.[5] This essay expands McAdam's analysis to consider external threats to group interest as a major factor underpinning the emergence and expansion of Black consciousness in the process of political insurgency. Indeed, I am prepared to argue that external threats are capable of stimulating insurgency campaigns fuelled by the momentum of surging Black consciousness during periods when structure of political opportunities for the Black community is not very encouraging. This chapter suggests that the social forces underlying the emergence and constructive utilisation of political consciousness as a Black political instrument, are far more complex than those presented in McAdam's political process model. My reading of Black political history in America strongly indicates that not only do threats to Black interests play a role in the construction of group goals, but the character and effectiveness of Black leadership, the responsiveness of society to that leadership, and the prevailing track record of victory and defeat, are all key factors in the determination of whether or not the Black community will be ready and willing to move in the direction of cognitive liberation.

ELITE VERSUS MASS-BASED POLITICAL MOVEMENTS

Doug McAdam's *Political Process and the Development of Black Insurgency, 1930-1970*, represents a careful, and often brilliant, theoretical treatise of the origins and impact of Black political movements in America. The volume is not flawless. One of its main imperfections is the failure to come to grips with the contradictions of Black political development. McAdam properly locates the decline of Black political power in the first decade of the twentieth century in the political compromise of 1876; this compromise resulted in the election of Rutherford B. Hayes as President of the United States and the withdrawal of federal troops from the South that had been used in the post-slavery era to protect and preserve Black political and social rights. McAdam contends that the compromise, in a large sense, represented an economic rapprochement between northern industrialists and southern planters that facilitated the vigorous flow of cotton from the South to the North, a process that had been seriously interrupted by the growing political empowerment of Black people during the Reconstruction period.

Negative repercussions emanating from this compromise were extensive and enduring. Seeking to strategically position themselves to take advantage of the return of the southern planter class to power through the vehicle of the Democratic Party, white leaders of the Populist movement – a coalition of Black and white farmers – abandoned the cause of racial uplift, and joined in a reactionary campaign to strip Black people of their political and human rights by institutionalising a comprehensive campaign of Black disenfranchisement. These acts of betrayal were buttressed and supported by political compromises reached between southern Democrats and northern Republicans that saw the wholesale abandonment of the Republican program of racial reform, including the prosecution of election-related court cases in the South under the Enforcement Act of 1870-71.[6]

Arguably, the most crucial blow to Black social, economic, and political advancement was delivered by the Supreme Court. In a series of reactionary rulings, including decisions in the Civil Rights Cases of 1883 and Plessy vs. Ferguson in 1896, the court essentially ripped the heart out of 14th Amendment provisions intended to provide constitutional protection for Black civil and political rights.

Clearly, as Black people walked into the twentieth century, the structure of political opportunities for the Black community in American politics was not promising. McAdam contends that during the first two decades of the twentieth century, the political environment for the Black community did not markedly improve. Passive involvement by the federal government in the undermining of Black rights changed to aggressive legislative and executive attacks under the administration of Woodrow Wilson who promised Americans new freedoms while endorsing policies that lead to the establishment of widespread segregation in federal departments in Washington, D.C.[7] Over a period of less than forty years, McAdam maintains, the federal government was transformed from "an advocate of Black equality into a force buttressing the southern racial status quo".[8] In McAdam's construction of Black political history, the structure of political opportunities did not become favourable for the Black community until the decades of the 1930s, 1940s and 1950s. This was when Black political power in the South began to grow because of factors such as the decline of King Cotton, the great migration to the north and the expansion of the Black vote, the electoral shift of Black people to the Democratic Party, and increasingly favourable government action.[9]

The theoretical exposition presented by McAdam is troubling in several respects. First, it strongly suggests that Black political insurgency is dependent for its emergence on positive opportunities for Black political advancement. Second, it appears to locate the incentives for such insurgency in mass-based political action rather than the leadership impact of Black political elites. I contend here that both assertions represent a startling misreading of Black political history, one that leads to the papering over of huge chapters in the political development of the African American community. A correct interpretation of Black political history shows that Black people were not paralysed by the downward turn of American racial policies at the turn of the twentieth century. On the contrary, many courageous Black politicians viewed the reactionary drift of American politics on racial issues as both a challenge and an opportunity. Black political consciousness found expression in the work of a strategically sagacious Black political elite that confronted the hostile political climate produced in the broader environment with a rich variety of institutional formations and innovative political strategies. Attacks on Black voting rights, coupled with physical assaults on Black people in the form of racial lynchings, served as poignant mechanisms for strengthening the salience of groups' goals and stimulating Black political behaviour reflective of high political consciousness. The most immediate response to these threats to continuing Black progress was the mounting of insurgency campaigns by Black radicals who refused to succumb to the siren song of Booker T. Washington's accommodationist approach.

As early as 1887, T. Thomas Fortune stepped forward to establish an organisation to fight for social, economic and political rights for the Black community. Fortune's organisation was the National Afro-American League. This organisation embraced an extremely progressive platform. Its six-point program, adopted at the first annual convention in 1890, included the securing of voting rights; the combating of racial lynchings; the waging of a fight against state school funding formulas that discriminated against Black people; reform of the southern penitentiary system; campaigning against discrimination in railroad and public travel conveyances; and campaigning against discrimination in public places and hotels.[10] The existence of a hostile racial climate, a conservative political establishment committed to segregation and Black subordination, and an economic recession that inspired nativist attacks against Black people and European immigrants, did not prevent Fortune from deriving sufficient cues from his social and political world to prod him in the direction of radical protest action. A journalist and the editor of the *New York Age*, Fortune was, in fact, a militant spokesman for the cause of collective Black protest in the American political system. His commitment to social justice for African Americans was unflagging. Labelled by the white press as an agitator, Fortune used his pen and his oratorical skills to roll back the barriers of racial oppression produced by the system of social segregation operating in the North and the South. In strident terms, Fortune urged Black people to no longer accept in silence "a condition which degrades manhood and makes a mockery of our citizenship".[11]

Leadership is obviously a key factor in the generation of Black political consciousness. The leadership model crafted by T. Thomas Fortune established the mould for a dominant brand of political action to be found in the political styles of a number of twentieth century Black politicians including one of the early supporters of the Afro-American league, W.E.B. Du Bois. Like Fortune, Du Bois was deeply disturbed by the rapidly deteriorating social and economic position of the Black community. He sincerely believed the one major remedy for the Black condition was the mobilisation of Black strength in the political arena. Du Bois's formal career as a political activist was significantly influenced by the emergence of Booker T. Washington as a towering figure in American politics. Through a variety of actions, Washington had made it clear that he opposed the use of protest strategies as political strategies in the service of racial uplift. Du Bois accused Washington of not only blocking Black progress, but of using his influence with powerful whites to build a personal political machine.

Du Bois led the effort to construct a political organisation composed of Black professionals as a countervailing force to Washington's power in the Black community. Responding to an invitation from Du Bois, twenty nine Black activists met in 1905 on the Canadian side of Niagara Falls to form the Niagara Movement. In clear, unmistakable terms, the members of the Niagara Movement sent out a clarion call for Black protest:

> We repudiate the monstrous doctrine that the oppressor should be the sole authority as to the rights of the oppressed. The Negro race in America, stolen, ravished, and degraded, struggling up through difficulties and oppression, needs sympathy and receives criticism, needs help and is given hindrance, needs protection and is given mob-violence, needs justice and is given charity, needs leadership and is given cowardice and apology, needs bread and is given stone . . . we do not hesitate to complain and to complain loudly and insistently. To ignore, overlook, or apologise for these wrongs is to prove ourselves unworthy of freedom. Persistent, manly agitation is the way to liberty.[12]

W.E.B. Du Bois and William Monroe Trotter, a Boston Black leader and editor of the *Guardian*, emerged as the guiding spirits of the Niagara Movement. Internal conflict and dwindling patronage led to the disintegration of the Niagara Movement in 1910. On the heels of this disintegration, Du Bois joined forces with an interracial group of political activists to create The National Association for the Advancement of Colored People (NAACP). The NAACP quickly became the premier institutional force in America committed to the cause of achieving social and economic uplift for Black Americans through aggressive political action. The social advancement agenda adopted by the organisation during its first decade of operation was very impressive: lobbying Congress to pass anti-lynching legislation; campaigning for Black voting rights and equal educational opportunities; opposing the assigning of Blacks in the military to segregated units; filing suits in courts on behalf of Black victims of employment and housing discrimination; defending Blacks accused of rape and other serious crimes. Du Bois served as editor of the *Crisis*, the official publication of the NAACP, and used this position as a public platform to editorialise against white oppression and to cement his reputation as a militant freedom fighter.[13]

How can we explain the expressions of high political consciousness by Black leaders and organisations in the absence of accompanying favourable conditions or positive structures for political opportunities? Apparently, political consciousness develops in response not only to positive stimuli but negative stimuli as well. Studies of slave protest campaigns have clearly shown that under crisis conditions, Black people will organise to challenge the main instruments of their oppression.[14] Stanley Elkins' line of analysis not withstanding, most enslaved Africans were not 'Sambos'.[15] Forms of extreme oppression tend to produce rebellion not submission.[16]

In the case of African Americans, Black political leaders have the capacity to draw upon a host of cultural, ideological, spiritual and intra-psychic forces, especially in the formation of their assessments of the importance of group goals. Professor V. P. Franklin's important book, *Black Self-Determination* provides important cues to the identity of the forces involved. Franklin identifies five key values that have provided an overarching spirit of self-determination in African Americans. These values are survival with dignity, resistance against oppression, freedom, education and advancement. Recognition of the existence of these values has immensely important political implications.[17]

The struggle for political power, waged by early freedom fighters like Fortune, Du Bois and Trotter, can only be properly understood in the context of a cultural inheritance that emphasises survival with dignity, resistance against oppression, freedom, education and advancement. Thus, even in the dark and dismal days when Du Bois was often ridiculed by members of the NAACP Executive Board for suggesting that Black people should build and profit from their own co-operative economic market, Du Bois felt compelled to press on because he was driven by a desire for Black freedom and the goal of laying a firm foundation for the promotion of Black resistance to oppression. McAdam's failure to examine the internal value system of the Black community leads him to discount the importance and efficacy of many forms of Black resistance and insurgency that are clearly visible to the naked eye.

MARCUS GARVEY AND BLACK SELF-DETERMINATION

The Marcus Garvey Movement also raises serious questions regarding the adequacy of the structure of opportunities proposition. Garvey's major contribution was the building of a mass organisation that went beyond civil rights agitation to produce a well thought out program for Black liberation. Garvey's Universal Negro Improvement Association was established in 1918. By 1925, the UNIA had established 725 branches in the United States and 271 branches outside the United States.[18] Eventually, the organisation would create a vast array of economic enterprises including restaurants, laundries, a printing plant, and a steamship company called the Black Star Line. Garvey attracted into his organisation millions of grassroots Black people who had never before participated in political struggle. In part, the spectacular growth of his organisation was due to his success in tapping into the growing militancy of the Black community after World War I as that community became urbanised and began to respond emotionally to events like the East St Louis race riots of 1918. Garvey preached a gospel of racial solidarity that helped to forge a new political consciousness and a new commitment to social activism on the part of masses of Black citizens. His teachings were reinforced by the writings of intellectuals associated with the Harlem Renaissance. Garvey himself was an established poet; his artistic contributions to this awakening of Black consciousness were by no means insignificant.

Garvey's message of Black solidarity continued to resonate strongly in Black political circles long after he had been deported from the United States. This message became the catalytic agent in a new commitment to public demonstrations and other forms of public protests made by Black political activists in the 1940s and 1950s. Garvey's political philosophy also became the backbone, the critical ideological foundation, of the Black nationalist movement of the 1960s.

The Garvey experience demonstrates the importance of charismatic leadership in the generation of political consciousness. A mass movement must be organised around a central purpose or interest. Garvey was the critical force that held his movement together. Millions of Black people were ready to invest in his steamship line and contemplate moving to Africa because they believed in him. In this regard, it should be noted that Garvey had the ability to transfer many elements of his cognitive assessment process to his followers. They became committed to the values of freedom and resistance against oppression because of their faith in his ability to deliver many of the benefits they considered important to their survival. The Garvey movement also underscores the importance of timing in the process of mass political mobilisation. Little in the way of transfer will take place if the masses are not ready. Clearly, the success of the Garvey movement was intimately tied to the migration of massive numbers of Black people to the cities. The sense of alienation the city experience produced, and the sense of disappointment many new Black city citizens felt when they realised that the trip from the South to the North would not insulate them from the sharper edges of racism, prejudice, and bigotry, was profound.

BLACK POLITICAL CONSCIOUSNESS
AND THE CIVIL RIGHTS MOVEMENT

An examination of the issue of political consciousness provides us with an opportunity to make a more realistic appraisal of the origins of the civil rights movement. McAdam contends that the civil rights movement in the United States grew out of the convergence of a number of forces.[19] One force was the shift of the Black population from the South to the North, creating strong political power bases in Northern cities. In reality, the strength of Black electoral power in the North, in the decades before the advent of the civil rights movement, was weakened by the control exercised over the Black vote by urban political machines. McAdams also points to the growth of chapters of the NAACP in the South as a key factor.

Again, we must issue a caveat, in that the effectiveness of NAACP chapters in many Southern states was inhibited by the declaration of the NAACP as an outlaw organisation by many law enforcement agencies. McAdam further contends that the favourable reaction to Black issues by the Roosevelt administration translated to the Black community a sense of hope and inspired Black people to move aggressively towards the implementation of a civil rights agenda. In truth, Roosevelt did very little to accommodate the interest of the Black community during his administration. Roosevelt's top priority was clearly that of getting white America back to work, and to construct a financial floor to support the long-term growth of white industrial concerns, white corporations, and white-owned farms..

Aldon Morris has done a superior job in chronicling the role of local organisations and movement centres in the implementation of the civil rights agenda in the 1960s.[20] The pivotal question that this study does not answer is what factors inspired local poetical actors to become involved in civil rights activity in the first place. It is my contention that the principal factor underpinning the psychological commitment to civil rights struggle was the victories achieved by the NAACP in the courts in the 1930s, 1940s and the 1950s. These victories emerged in the wake of strategies mounted by lawyers for the NAACP, especially Thurgood Marshall, Charles H. Houston and William H. Hastie. For instance, they chipped away at the 'separate but equal' ruling of the Plessy vs. Ferguson case of 1896, and by challenging state rules and statutes that prevented Black people from enrolling in predominantly white colleges and universities. The first opportunity for the NAACP to test this strategy came in 1938 in the case of Missouri Ex Rel Gains vs. Canada. In this case, the NAACP was successful in overturning a Missouri law that required Black students to seek graduate education outside of Missouri because state institutions were racially segregated. The Supreme Court ruled that the fact that Missouri was willing to pay for the education of Black students out of state did not satisfy the equal protection of the laws clause of the 14th Amendment.[21]

The NAACP scored a similar victory in 1950 in the case of McLaurin vs. Oklahoma State Regents for Higher Education. This case involved a Black student who was admitted to study at the University of Oklahoma but required to sit at a designated desk outside the classroom and a designated desk in the library. In a unanimous decision, the Supreme Court ruled that the segregated conditions under which the student was required to study deprived him of his personal right to the equal protection of the laws.[22]

On the same day the McLaurin case was decided, the Supreme Court ruled in the case Sweatt vs. Painter that a Black student must be admitted to the law school at the University of Texas, rather than being forced to attend a makeshift law school set up overnight by the Texas legislature to avoid coping with the issue of integration.[23]

Collectively, these victories gave a psychological lift to Black people across America because they suggested that the court was abandoning its commitment to the 'separate but equal' principles of Plessy vs. Ferguson. These cases were also seen as a prelude to the declaration of segregation in elementary and public schools as unconstitutional.. That decision was finally rendered in 1954 in the case of Brown vs. Board of Education Topeka. The Brown case pushed the level of political consciousness among Black Americans to unprecedented heights.

This decision was broadly interpreted as meaning that the walls of segregation would come tumbling down in all aspects of American life. Black jubilation over the court's ruling was short-lived; joy turned to sorrow when it became clear that white public officials had no intention of following the court's mandate. In the wake of this realisation, high Black political consciousness was converted into militant protest action.

The protest phase of the civil rights movement began in 1953, with the initiation of a municipal bus boycott movement by Black people in Baton Rouge, Louisiana. In 1955, the protest movement swept into Montgomery, Alabama. The Montgomery campaign marked the birth of the Black revolution, a revolution that would profoundly alter the strategy, the participatory base, and the goals of the civil rights movement. Under the leadership of Dr Martin Luther King, Jr, the approach to the civil rights question changed from one of legal manoeuvring in the courts and quiet negotiation in the conference room, to street-level demonstrations centring on the strategy of non-violent civil disobedience.[24] The function of the new Black leader was no longer that of speaking for his people but of encouraging the Black masses, through their bodies and the force of their commitment, to speak for themselves.[25] As a consequence, the civil rights movement was transformed from one dominated by an elite establishment, to one involving the participation of the masses in social and civic action on their own behalf.[26] This transition had enormous consequences for the development of racial pride and political consciousness.

The involvement of the Black people of Montgomery in a crusade against southern segregation, stirred the emotions of Black people throughout the country; their success was viewed not just as a triumph for local residents, but as a solid victory for all Black people. Montgomery represented for all strata of the Black population an assertion of their manhood – an affirmation of their worth as human beings and their determination to remove the yoke of racism whatever the cost. After Montgomery, a new Black mood came alive; in its wake, the apathy and sense of hopelessness which had paralysed both the energies and the emotions of the Black masses, began a swift and final dissipation.[27]

The new Black mood after Montgomery found its clearest expression in the spread of the protest movement throughout the South. Moreover, in the transition of protest strategy from persuasion to bargaining from a position of strength.[28] A pivotal stage in this transition was the integration of Central High School in Little Rock through the use of federal troops. The presence of federal troops in support of Black rights in Little Rock symbolised a developing foci on power rather than persuasion as the key strategic variable in the civil rights struggle.[29]

Taking their cues from this new motif, Black college students, beginning in 1960, escalated the strategy of protest to the level of confrontation through direct action. In contrast to previous non-violent protests, the student sit-ins were launched not merely to challenge the validity of existing practices and laws, but to provoke confrontations in order to compel white officials to bargain with them. Protest activity thus became a power resource by which concessions could be obtained through the use of force rather than persuasion.[30] As concessions were made, and the symbols of southern white supremacy came tumbling down, Black people throughout America learned a lesson of enormous political import: power, when strategically applied, can produce results in situations where all the efforts at persuasion in the world will have little, if any, effect. The success of the Black revolution in the South created among Black Americans a high sense of political consciousness and a keen sense of their power potentialities.[31]

The student sit-ins and the white violence heaped upon Black people in Birmingham, Alabama, during 1963, did much to weld Black people together into a common group responding to common threatening symbols and acts of white oppression. Large numbers of Black people were shaken out of their apathy and their isolation from events in the South by the use of dogs, cattle prods and water hoses on non-violent protesters in Birmingham. And the tragic church bombing incident in Birmingham, in which four Black girls were killed, created tensions of crisis proportions in practically every Black community in urban America.

These events implanted a new militancy and a new compulsion to become involved in the psyche of rank and file northern Blacks. As was probably inevitable, given this fact, the strategy of coercive public protests spread to the North, focused on defacto-segregation of the public schools and drew into the civil rights movement thousands of the urban poor. With the shift of the Black movement to the North, a parallel change in its basic theme took place. In the South, the primary aim of the protest movement was freedom, an objective fashioned into a slogan signifying the urgency of the demand: "freedom now".

BLACK POWER

In the North, it became apparent that Black freedom required for its procurement and preservation the ability of Black people to control resources and institutions affecting their social, economic and political status in American society.[32] The Northern translation of the theme of the Black revolution, therefore, became 'Black Power'. This theme symbolised the group consciousness of Black people and their frustration with the slow pace of their social and economic progress in the face of rising aspirations to enter the mainstream of American life. It represented a growing sense of community, of common situation and of common fate. It connoted a rejection of white power and a categorical repudiation of white paternalism. This meant, on the one hand, releasing the fetters of white institutions on the economic, social and political lifelines of the Black community, and, on the other, the establishment in their place, of Black economic self-help organisations and politically viable Black organisational structures which were independent from white dominance.

In resounding terms, Black Power invoked a feeling that Black people ought to control communities in which they were the main ethnic group. Even more, it represented the abiding conviction that they would control them. Above all, it constituted a call for group solidarity in politics, "an appeal to Negroes to build strength around the vote".[33] In this sense, Black Power denoted the use of colour consciousness to build unity of action among Black people in the political process. It also prescribed independent political action – the organisation of cohesive voting blocs by Black people and their expeditious employment to elect public officials dedicated to the overall progress of the Black community rather than individual achievement.

These various dimensions of Black power, Black pride, Black unity, self-determination, and cohesive political action, have all played major roles in laying the attitudinal foundation essential to the political mobilisation of Black people in city politics.

POLITICAL CONSCIOUSNESS AND THE NEW BLACK POLITICS

By way of a conclusion, the collapse of the civil rights coalition in the 1970s resulted in the shift of the centre of gravity of Black political activity from protest to politics. Coming to power in this process was a new breed of Black politician with the organisational skills and political savvy to translate political consciousness spawned by the civil rights movement into electoral power. In Gary, Indiana, for example, Richard Hatcher was an active participant in both the local and national civil rights movement. He was able to catapult himself into the Mayor's office by evoking themes of Black pride and Black unity. Hatcher was able to take advantage not only of the Black political consciousness generated by the civil rights movement, but the political consciousness in Black voters he stimulated through his work as both a civil rights activist and member of the Gary City Council. It is clear that Hatcher's image as a dynamic, committed, responsible and trustworthy public servant was a major factor underlying the decision by many Black Gary voters to cast a ballot in a mayoral election for the first time:

> A lot of people paid close attention to the way this man conducted himself in those council meetings and how he really fought for the issue he believed in. Not necessarily the way we thought it should have gone, but the man stuck to his convictions … Mr Hatcher would stand alone and fight for the things people needed in this city. I never will forget one council meeting when the people of Brunswick told him in no uncertain terms not to even run for 'dog catcher' again in this town because he wouldn't be elected. But Mr Hatcher still fought for open occupancy while all the other Negro councilmen backed down. He was a man who stood on honesty and integrity.[34]

In recent years, civil rights activists like Hatcher have been replaced by Black mayors who do not manifest a high degree of race consciousness. These mayors have often won their positions in close elections where the white community has traditionally held the balance of electoral power. To assure electoral victory they have run de-racialised campaigns designed to appeal to the policy preferences of a multiracial constituency. These campaigns are in sharp contrast to the Black insurgency campaigns run by the first generation of Black mayors; these insurgency campaigns were characterised by challenges to the prevailing power structure and explicit racial appeals to Black voters.[35] The second generation of Black mayors have specialised in practising the politics of racial reconciliation. Although often publicly supportive of policies of racial uplift, they have tended to fashion governing coalitions committed to delivering major benefits to powerful non-Black constituents.[36] The political alliance between the new Black mayors and the corporate community has been very strong. Deeply committed to pro-growth, corporate-centred, urban development, the new Black mayors have warmly welcomed the direct involvement of the business sector as permanent and influential participants in the local policy-making process.

A major casualty of these developments has been the psychological link that fused the hopes, aspirations and goals of the Black community with the symbolic and administrative roles of local public officials, especially Black mayors. The reality of this phenomenon finds ready expression in low turnout rates by Black voters in local elections and the organisational collapse of neighbourhood groups and associations.

Unlike the 1960s, Black citizens today cannot draw psychological strength from the national political environment because the activist wing of the national civil rights movement has disappeared.[37] In addition, responses to Black needs by state and federal officials have been discouraging. Black people across America suffered a major psychological blow when President Clinton decided to sign the Welfare Reform Act against the wishes of national leaders of the NAACP, Urban League, and Children's Defense Fund. The decision by the leaders of both national parties to deliberately polarise the electorate around the issues of race, rights and taxes represents an ominous development with the potential of leaving most Black Americans stranded on the extreme left wing of the political spectrum.[38]

There is no doubt that today the Black community has reached another era of political crisis. What is obviously required is a re-education and re-mobilisation of the Black community for political purposes. Once again, the development of political consciousness looms extraordinarily large as a precondition for Black insurgency, mobilisation, and empowerment. Just as they have done in the past, I am confident Black leaders will rise up to meet this challenge. They can only do so successfully if they are willing to adhere to the logic and imperatives of traditional African American values. At the dawn of a new millennium, the struggle for Black liberation needs again to be fought on the terrain of survival with dignity, resistance against oppression, freedom from want, and education for advancement.

NOTES AND REFERENCES

1.   Carmichael, S. and Hamilton, C. V. *Black Power: The Politics of Liberation in America* (New York: Vintage Books, 1967) p. 44.

2.   Kovel, J. *White Racism: A Psychohistory* (New York: Vintage Books, 1970) pp. 12-22; and Kardiner, A. and Ovesey, L. *The Mark of Oppression* (New York: World Publishing, 1962) pp. 38-47.

3.   See McAdam, D. *Political Process and the Development of Black Insurgency, 1930-1970* (Chicago: The University of Chicago Press, 1982).

4.   See Blalock, H. *Toward A Theory of Minority Group Relations* (New York: Wiley Publishers, 1967).

5.   McAdam, *Political Process...* pp. 40-43.

6.   Ibid. pp. 71-72.

7.   Ibid. p. 72.

8.   Ibid. p. 73.

9.   Ibid. pp. 73-90.

10.   Cruse, H. *Plural But Equal* (New York: William Morrow, 1987) p. 9.

11.   Thornbrough, E. L. 'T. Thomas Fortune: Militant Editor in An Age of Accommodation', in Franklin, J. H. and Meier, A. (eds.) *Black Leaders of the Twentieth Century* (Urbana, Illinois: University of Illinois Press, 1982) p. 27.

12.   Rudwick, E. 'W.E.B. Du Bois: Protagonist of the Afro-American Protest' in Franklin, J. H. and Meier, A. (eds.) *Black Leaders of the Twentieth Century* (Urbana, Illinois: University of Illinois Press) 1982) p. 69.

13.   Ibid. pp. 73-75.

14.   See Harding, V. *There Is A River: The Black Struggle for Freedom in America* (New York: Harcourt Brace Jovanovich Publishers, 1981).

15.   Stanley Elkins contends that the oppressive nature of American slavery fundamentally suppressed Black protest. He draws a similar conclusion regarding the Jewish experience in the concentration camps of Europe during World War II. See Elkins, S. *Slavery: A Problem in American Institutional and Intellectual Life* (Chicago: University of Chicago press, 1968).

16. Harding, *There Is A River...*
17. Franklin, V. P. *Black Self-Determination: A Cultural History of the Faith of the Fathers* (Westport, Connecticut: Lawrence Hill and Company, 1984).
18. Martin, T. *Race First* (Dover, Massachusetts: The Majority Press, 1976) p. 15.
19. McAdam, *Political Process...* pp. 73-145.
20. Morris, A. *The Origins of the Civil Rights Movement* (New York: The Free Press, 1984).
21. Davis, A. L. and Graham. B. L. *The Supreme Court, Race and Civil Rights* (Thousand Oaks, California: Sage Publications, 1995) p. 79.
22. Ibid. p. 80.
23. Ibid.
24. Bennett, L. *Confrontation Black and White* (Baltimore, Maryland: Penquin, 1968).
25. Killian, L. M. *The Impossible Revolution? Black Power and the American Dream* (New York: Random House, 1968) pp. 47-57.
26. Ibid. pp. 47-48.
27. Bennett, *Confrontation Black and White*, pp. 199-204.
28. Killian, *The Impossible Revolution...*, pp. 73-77.
29. Ibid. p. 71.
30. Ibid.
31. Ibid. pp. 111-115.
32. Ibid. p. 113.
33. Danzig, D. 'In Defense of Black power' in Commentary Vol. 42 (July-December, 1966) p. 41.
34. Gary Interview. Quoted in Nelson, Jr., W. E. and Meranto, P. J. *Electing Black Mayors: Political Action in the Black Community* (Columbus, Ohio: Ohio State University Press, 1977) p. 219.
35. Persons, G. A. 'Black Mayoralities and the New Black Politics' in Persons, G. A. (ed.) *Dilemmas of Black Politics: Issues of Leadership and Strategy* (New York: Harper Collins Publishers, 1993) p. 45.
36. Reed, Jr., A. 'The Black Regime: Structural Origins and Constraints' in Smith, M. P. (ed.) *Power, Community and the City* (New Brunswick, New Jersey: Transaction Books, 1988) p. 160-164.

37.   Ibid. pp. 160-169.

38.   For an extremely thoughtful discussion of the race policy agenda of the major parties See Edsall, T. B. and Edsall, M. D. *Chain Reaction: The Impact of Race Rights and Taxes on American Politics* (New York: W.W. Norton and Company, 1991).

PART II

Social and Cultural Markers

Chapter Five

AFROCENTRICITY AND THE DECLINE OF WESTERN HEGEMONIC THOUGHT: A CRITIQUE OF EUROCENTRIC THEORY AND PRACTICE

Molefi Kete Asante

AFROCENTRICITY, as a theory of human liberation and intellectual critique, was initially a project of practical social reform for highly industrialised, complex, heterogeneous nations[1] – Western nations, such as the United Kingdom, the United States, and Canada where there are increasingly large numbers of Africans faced with the reality of mutual living spaces and the continuation of white racial hegemony over all symbols and social systems.

Afrocentricity is presented as one way out of the impasse over social and cultural hegemony: the positioning of the agency of the African person as the basic unit of analysis of social situations involving African-descended people is a critical step in achieving community harmony. It becomes absolutely necessary to accept the subject position of Africans within the context of historical realities. Simultaneously, the eradication of the hegemonic blanket of white Western ideology is necessary for complete liberation of the African mind. The United States of America, because of its role as a former slave economy, had depended upon the degradation of the African world-view, the denial of African humanity, and the ignoring of African achievements in civilisation in order to enhance its own rationalisations for the enslavement of millions of Africans. With the end of the Great Enslavement in 1865, there were nearly four and a half million African refugees in the United States. Within the next thirty-five years, the literacy rate would jump from five per cent to nearly fifty per cent. In one generation it was one of the most remarkable expressions of educational interest in the history of the world. This was generated by a period of 'Reconstruction' from 1865 to 1877. It would barely last twelve years, but during that time it would mean that the African people could exercise freedoms that had been denied for nearly 250 years.[2]

During Reconstruction, the African population voted and ran for political office and once in office created many innovations such as public schools and public highways. However, with the signing of the Hayes-Tilden Compromise that allowed the rebellious southern whites additional privileges, the Union Army that had protected the four million Africans of the southern states was withdrawn from the South and a reign of terror literally set back the clock of social progress for generations. Whites organised vigilante groups to pursue, hound, and harass Africans out of government offices. The Ku Klux Klan organisation was born with the express purpose of terrorising any

African who had the courage to register to vote, or who voted, or ran for office. The southern landscape was littered with the corpses of Africans who simply attempted to express the right to vote. Such harsh measures meant that soon Black people had been completely eliminated from legislative and administrative posts in the South.[3]

An entire league of African reformists sought remedies and relief but was met with even more lynchings and brutalising of African people. In the United States, the top of the twentieth century was devoted to the campaign against mob rule and the denial of citizenship rights. By the time Martin Luther King, Jr and his comrades started the Montgomery Bus Boycott in 1955, many religious African Americans had come to believe that it was possible for whites to reform their actions and change their racist behaviours. Of course, there has always been those in our community who believed that history demonstrated an unwillingness of whites to share space with any other people. Indeed, King's strategy was to appeal to the principal documents in which white Americans believed – the Bible and the American Constitution. Some change was brought about and the results were that King was considered a hero to many Americans. Yet the final results would reveal the hollowness of the victory of that romantic age, the decade of the 1960s.

There was a growing sentiment after Malcolm X, and perhaps in response to him, that what was needed among African Americans and Africans in general was a more self-defining and self-determining attitude about all social, economic, political, and cultural issues. It was understood that reform was necessary, but the reform was to be of the African person. In fact, it was to be an intense interrogation of the African person's concept of space and time. Being was held to the light of history and it was revealed that for five hundred years African people had been moved off all terms. We were operating, so to speak, on someone else's intellectual space and within someone else's time frame. This meant that we could not actively pursue our own course of agency and direction for African people without conflicting with the received idea that whites would have to change before progress was made. The Afrocentrists redefined the meaning of progress, charged the receivers of violence and oppression with as much complicity as the ones who carried out the initial crimes, and went on the warpath. To change one's situation it would be necessary to change one's self, became the dictum of a new generation of scholar-activists, after the publication of *Afrocentricity* in 1980 I think it is important that we have a clear understanding of how Afrocentricity emerged as a paradigm of theory and practice in the arena of African American Studies.

By way of distinction, Afrocentricity is not Afrocentrism. The term 'Afrocentrism' was first used by the opponents of Afrocentricity. Their aim was to assign religious signification to the idea of African-centredness. However, it has come to refer to a broad cultural movement of the late twentieth century that has a set of philosophical, political, and artistic ideas that provides the basis for the musical, sartorial, and aesthetic dimensions of the African personality. On the other hand, Afrocentricity, as I have previously defined it, is a theory of agency, that is, the idea that African people must be viewed as agents rather than spectators to historical revolution and change. To this end, Afrocentricity seeks to examine every aspect of the subject place of Africans in historical, literary, architectural, ethical, philosophical, economic, and political life. Afrocentricity precedes Afrocentrism, that is, it is older as a term in the intellectual discourse.

Afrocentricity enters the critique of European hegemony after a series of attempts by European writers to advance critical methods of the construction of reality in the context of Europe itself. But Europe has been unable to critique itself from outside the racist, hegemonic paradigm established as the grand narrative of the European people. It is here that Afrocentricity provides the first deep analysis of the social and political situation inherent in hegemonic societies. It is as if we cannot learn from Europe in the area of human relations because everywhere Europe has been, it has been the destroyer of humanity. In no place where Europe has appeared with non-European people, has Europe sought to live in mutual peace with other people. Everywhere, Europe has sought domination, defeat, ethnic cleansing, and conquest. All European ideologies, from dialectical materialism to post-modernism, protect the ruthless Eurocentric idea of white triumphalism and hegemony.

What remains problematic with European thought is its inability to allow space for other cultures and therefore it becomes self-absorbed in some notion of Europe as the categorical universal for the world. Such self-centredness has left the rest of the world searching for a theoretical corrective. Among the principal ways that Europe has approached its own rendezvous with destiny has been the establishment of schools of thought that have answered some of the questions of displacement, economic inequality, fragmentation, universalism, grand narratives, and ethical issues. In order to ascertain how and where Afrocentricity enters the picture in the context of the Western world, I will discuss some of the relevant Eurocentric approaches and suggest how they differ from Afrocentricity.

DIALECTICAL MATERIALISM

It was the European concern with industrialism and capitalism that gave birth to dialectical materialism.[4] We must never forget that these concerns were not expressed the same way, universally. Other nations arrived at industrialisation in different ways. In fact, Karl Marx was very much Eurocentric in his focus. There was no global idea to his initial formulations. One might even say that there is a bias against modern notions of culture, whether as cultural relativity or cultural materialism, because there is simply a fascination and intense concern with the position of Europeans in the world. I am not criticising this inasmuch as I believe that what the dialectical materialists sought was the revivification of Europe. This was their task because they saw it as their obligation to Europe itself. When one reads the *Communist Manifesto* one grasps the ideas of Marx and Engels clearly when they say, "The history of all past society has consisted in the development of class antagonisms".[5] In a later edition, Engels corrected this idea when he wrote that the notion "all past society" should be the "history of society" since the evolution of the state. Engels wrote the book, *The Origin of the Family, Private Property and the State*, which was the centrepiece of Marxian social thought for nearly thirty years.[6]

In 1877, Lewis Henry Morgan had written *Ancient Society*[7] and had influenced works by Engels and Marx. They thought that they had seen in Morgan a corroboration of the materialist conception of history. Yet *Ancient Society* was interested in causality as much as germ ideas and natural selection. The idea of trying to impute causality to original germ ideas demonstrates how Eurocentric writers have periodically been fascinated with an interest in essentialist theories, yet quite ironically it is the Eurocentrists who now try to demonstrate that Afrocentrists are essentialists. As African American ancestors often said when the hounds of the slave owners would be trying to track those who ran away, "they are barking up the wrong tree".

Engels never transcended the limitations of Morgan and his book, *The Origin of the Family, Private Property and the State*, is now seen as flawed in its methodology. There was no attempt to provide an infrastructural explanation for the development of the clan lying at the heart of village and chiefdom social structure.[8] The reason for this inability of dialectical materialism to deal with some of the issues outside of Europe is because the work falls in line with the entire narrative of European history where anything that is pre-capitalist, non-European, and external to the capitalist system is literally outside of history.

The key contribution of dialectical materialism is its understanding and appreciation of the infrastructure, the material conditions of society. To the degree that dialectical materialism establishes theoretical principles that undergird the primacy of material conditions, it is distinguished from Afrocentricity which argues that the constant interplay of infrastructure and structure, the material conditions and matter, so to speak, is the proper way to understand society. It is like nature or the relationship between lovers.

Thus, Afrocentricity is the answer to questions that are left open by dialectical materialism's fascination with the industrial realm in European development. In saying this, I am not suggesting that Afrocentricity is the opposite of dialectical materialism, as the dialectical materialists might say, but rather stating that Afrocentricity must not be seen as a counter to Eurocentricity. The idea behind Eurocentricity in its most vile form, whatever its theoretical manifestation, is that Europe is the standard and nothing exists in the same category anywhere. It is the valorisation of Europe above all other cultures and societies that makes it such a racist system. On the other hand, there should be nothing incorrect about European people wanting to have motifs, ideas, narratives and concepts that are derived from their history. That is to be expected, but what is not to be expected is the idea that Europe somehow has a right to hold a hegemonic banner over all other people. Afrocentricity does not seek African hegemony; it seeks pluralism without hierarchy. We will replay this discussion in a different light when I return to the dangers of avoiding structure or content in symbols, society, infrastructure and text.[9]

STRUCTURALISM

While dialectical materialists were having a problem maintaining the character of their work on a consistent basis, the French intellectuals, under the guidance of Claude Levi-Strauss, were actually defining the most influential Western system of analysis, structuralism. Most of what we read in the social sciences in the West in the 19th and 20th centuries is influenced by structuralism, whether it is a support of it or a rejection of it. Structuralists are fundamentally anti-positivist, ahistorical and idealist. But like all theorists, each structuralist would have a commentary to make on the type of structuralism practised. For example, there are those who argue that they are not idealists because they accept the idea of infrastructure as primary in analysis. Idealism normally makes everything consist in ideas, denying the grounds for material bodies, and in the extreme having belief in nothing except percipient minds and ideas. Yet Levi-Strauss, the founder of the theory of structuralism, had said that he wanted to deal with superstructures that Marx had not dealt with, namely, the psychological structure of socio-cultural systems. He saw ethnology as psychology.[10] Where this type of structuralism and ethnology impact on Africans is at the level of research itself. If you assume that there are certain moulds that must fit some societies, hence, people, and other moulds that must fit other people, you are likely to establish a hierarchy of moulds. This is what the Eurocentric writers did in following Emile Durkheim's idea that society is a conscience collective, collective consciousness or collective conscience, all meaning the same thing in French, is identified as a set of exterior ideas that have a coercive force over individual thought. Durkheim may have given the classic essentialist position when he wrote:

> The collective consciousness is the highest form of the psychic life since it is the consciousness of the consciousness. Being placed outside of and above individual and local contingencies, it sees things only in their permanent and essential aspects, which it crystallises into communicable ideas.[11]

As I have tried to indicate in previous works, structuralism in some of its guises raises questions that Afrocentrists are interested in because they question the psychological mode of thinking, the collectivity of

Europe as a creator of images, and the motivations behind the actions that destroy, maim, and stifle human personality and community. But Afrocentricity is not structuralism; it is more than structuralism because like dialectical materialism, structuralism does not answer the issues the Eurocentric ground creates itself. For example, while I share structuralism's interest in developing a system that considers 'superstructures', Marx's 'infrastructures', that are not evaluated in dialectical materialism such as the psychological or even cognitive structures of society, I have a problem with the inability of structuralists to self-analyse. This lack of self-analysis leads to a paralysis of interpretation, explanation, and meaning whenever the structuralists are confronted with white racial supremacy.

It is more complicated when the ideas of white racial supremacy are inherent in the discussion of social confrontations among people who are presumably defining themselves as whites. The structuralists and almost all European theorists have a loss of words when it comes to properly explaining white racial supremacy. Starting from this idea as a normative idea means that Africans are automatically thrown into the categorically other. The Afrocentrists reject this notion and therefore understand that structuralism cannot handle the contradictions of white racial supremacy anymore than the dialectical materialists or their relatives, the cultural materialists. They are blinded by a white racial ideology that is only a little more sophisticated than that of the socio-biologists.

MODERNISM AND POST-MODERNISM

Of all the European narratives on society, post-modernism is the most difficult to define and locate because of its continuing flux in areas of art, music, film, literature, sociology, communications and technology. Those who call themselves post-modernists know that Europe is in a deep cycle of social danger and they are thrusting around for another venue for explanation and sense having found most of their social theories abandoned after the Nazi Holocaust, the interminable hatreds of Ireland, the Balkans, and ethnic rivalries in numerous nations of Europe. This flux in social and political life appeared constant, and so, after the 1960s, with the decade-long sorting out of values, we found European writers, mainly literary scholars, attempting to create some new response to the crises of culture and identity. Even without a formal definition it is possible to view it as a set of ideas about literary, artistic and social life that emerged during the decade of the 1980s. Was it intended as a counter to the newly found voice of African agency with the emergence of Afrocentricity in the 1980s, or was it by chance that these two approaches to social phenomena arose to compete in the African arena?

Post-modernism emerges out of modernism's aesthetic sensibilities, and in some ways, may be seen as a reaction to the twentieth century ideas of European art forms. Modernism was a movement of the visual arts, drama, literature, and music that transcended the Victorian rules of what constituted art. There was a period of 'high modernism' between 1910 and 1930, taking in the disintegrating period of the First Great European War (1914-18). At this time, as Europe sought to redefine its own value systems on the battlefields, the writers Rilke, Joyce, Eliot, Pound, Proust, Mallarme, Woolf, and Kafka undertook a radical alteration in the way people viewed poetry and fiction. Europe's literary modernists must include these writers as among the founders of twentieth century modernism. They held in their minds, and put on their pages, the seeds of post-modernism.

Among the leading characteristics of post-modernism are fragmentation, reflexivity, a rejection of high and low cultural forms, and an intense subjectivity that allows for self-consciousness in writing. In some senses these were also the elements of modernism as seen in the stream-of-consciousness and highly subjected forms of modernist writers such as e.e. cummings and Rilke. The difference between modernism and post-modernism relies on ways of viewing the decentred, destructured, and destabilised state of our existence. Post-modernists would not rely on works of art to produce anything of value, certainly not a more stable, or a better society. The modernist view was that art could bring stability, unity, and a degree of coherence to human society. A rejection of this view has enthroned post-modernism as the principal literary mode of the European experience at the dawn of the new millennium. Thus, the attack on grand narratives remains in full force and constitutes the major assault on the works of African scholars, poets, and novelists seeking to bring about a revolutionary change in society.

It is extremely important to appreciate the source of post-modernism's uncertainty, its lack of place, and fear of anything solid, certain, either as belief or as fact. I suggest that it can be traced back to the ghastly war fought in Europe in the late 1930s. and 1940s, to the reconstruction of the German economy by the West; to the dispersal of European Jews to Israel; to the unsettling of the Roma; to the continuing drive of the Anglo-Germanic elements to define a separate identity from the rest of Europe; and to the inability of Europe to agree on a 'collective consciousness' in the Durkheimian sense.

In short, what this meant was that the uncertainty of persons created alienation, unrest, insecurities, and a sense that stability was not only fleeting but useless. If people knew who you were, then they could bring danger to you, harm your family, resurrect some old crime, entangle you in a web of red tape and Kafka-esque bureaucracy, so why not be someone today and someone else tomorrow?

The African writer, Manthia Diawara in his recent book, *In Search of Africa*, claims as much for himself. He is a Parisian, New Yorker, Guinean, or Malian, according to him, in a most post-modern expression.[12] This is precisely the problem as the Afrocentrist would see it. One can live in many places, but one's identity, basic personality structure and all the elements that go into culture, whatever culture it is, remains with you regardless of your venue. Indeed, the Jew cannot escape his Jewishness by claiming that he is an American citizen. He simply adds a layer onto his identity. He could be a citizen of France, Britain, or Germany, but he remains a Jew.

The problem here is just as the African has found identity after five hundred years of moving Africans off centre, the West announces through post-modernists that there is no longer any warrant to discuss identity. Afrocentricity rejects this as a false position, one that is intended to stunt the growth and development of African people while maintaining the dominance of Europeans as Europeans in a solid and stable place. The English is no more going to give up Englishness than the Tiger is giving up Tigerness. Suggesting the death of identity or the end of essentialism or the completion of the search for stability is nothing less than a betrayal of the oppressed.

Therefore, since we cannot find any intellectual support in the major avenues of European thought, we must seek closer to home, that is, to the traditions that have helped to make African thought what it is today. Thus, I sought to discover, in the reading of several African authors, their understanding of Africa, African culture and linkages to Afrocentricity.

LINKAGES TO AFROCENTRICITY

If Afrocentricity is a response to Europe, it is only so as a response to the conditions of African people at the hands of European oppression for five hundred years; it is not a response to European intellectual theory and does not find its energy in any European system of thought. Critics sometimes speak of the Afrocentrist's use of European languages and the use of logical arguments as indications that the Afrocentrist is really incapable of abandoning European influences. Even the suggestion is an attempt to place Europe at the centre of all discourse. To discuss anything intellectually, they would claim, means that one has to be doing European discourse.

There are several responses that can be made to such a charge but the important one, particularly as it relates to language, is that English and French are increasingly less English and French. In fact, English has been changed permanently by the Black speakers of the language and there are more people who are non-English speaking the language now than there are English speakers of it. The same holds true for French where the French speakers of French are among the minority speakers. English and French are truly contested languages. Beyond this fact, however, is the fact that the Afrocentric discipline protects the Afrocentrist in the matter of language choices.

This was one of the initial developments in the Afrocentric theory development because I understood that the first liberation had to be language liberation. A considerable literature has grown up around this particular point and I do not need to repeat it here except to say that Afrocentrists are aware of this charge regarding language. You will never read an Afrocentrist writing of "Black Africa", "African tribes", "primitive huts", "Africa, South of the Sahara", and such expression because of the discipline.

The statement about logical argument is less serious. Logic is not the exclusive purview of any people. Indeed, logical argumentation itself, as far as actual presentation of arguments is concerned, goes back to Khun-anup's *Defence Before the Judges*, often called by Europeans "The Eloquent Peasant".[13] Khun-anup's piece appears more than a thousand years before the existence of Thales of Miletus, the first Greek philosopher. Using logic is a human activity and to set one's arguments in a certain fashion is not following Europe but Africa. Just as when Europeans use introductory greetings at the beginning of their speeches, they are following the patterns of the ancient Nile Valley Africans.

Three intellectual currents are directly linked to Afrocentricity: Negritude, Diopian historiography, and Kawaida. While each influenced the early work in Afrocentric theory, the development of Afrocentricity itself must be seen as linked to each one differently. Afrocentricity shares with Negritude its promotion of African agency, though Negritude was unable to deliver African centredness. Afrocentricity and Diopian historiography share the same epistemology, but Afrocentricity is much broader in its reach in an effort to shape the discourse around the African world. Afrocentricity and Kawaida share the same epistemology but have emphasised different theoretical and philosophical methods. Kawaida is much more concerned with ethical aspects of actions than Afrocentricity which is more concerned with the structures that encourage moral decisions.

NEGRITUDE

The main proponents of Negritude were Leopold Sedar Senghor, Aimé Cesaire, Jean Rabemananjara, and Leon Damas. It was a school of thought that emerged in Paris in the 1930 and 1940s as a reaction to the totalising idea of culture as presented by the French scholars. To the French, in the European fashion, Africa was without culture, that is, without self-conscious art or an artistic tradition. As students in Paris, the young continental Africans and South American and Caribbean Africans came together to defend their own historical tradition as legitimate and valid within the world context. They were the first line of resistance to the virulent racism of white supremacy in the area of art, particularly in poetry, drama, and literature. On the fringes of this movement, Cheikh Anta Diop, Alioune Diop, and Pathe Diagne operated as fellow travellers, encouraging the Negritudinists, writing historical essays, and creating spaces for writers to assemble and publish.

Senghor wrote 'Negritude and Humanism' as one of the central essays in the definition of the movement. It was Senghor who unfortunately characterised the African as concerned with emotion and the European with reason. Widely misunderstood and badly interpreted, Senghor could never live down the dictum, "L'emotion negre, la raison Hellene". Of course, Senghor knew, if any one did, that all human beings shared emotion and reason and he was simply trying to place an emphasis on the degree to which Africans and Europeans had distanced themselves from each other as one embraced and the other distanced life.

Cesaire has grown over the years as the greatest poet of African peoples, as his work in *The Return to My Native Country* is called the best poetry of the Negritude period.[14] He is, at once, serious, playful, surreal, symbolic, and culturally sensitive to the various moods, directions, contours, and crevices of the African condition. As a voice of Africa, Cesaire remains, at least in his poetry, clairvoyant.

From Negritude, Afrocentricity learned the constituents of resistance to oppression were action and agency, although Negritude itself did not give us the kind of agency that would be revealed in the work of the Afrocentrists. In fact, Afrocentricity was a much broader paradigm than Negritude which depended upon Africanity much more than Afrocentricity to thrust its place in the discourse of social change. Africanity is not Afrocentricity. One can have an appreciation of African cultural behaviour, participate in it, and still not be Afrocentric. One is a state of being; the other is a state of consciousness. The value of one is that it is what we might be doing existentially, but the other allows us to see what is possible, even in the area of consciousness. Afrocentricity establishes a window on African culture but does not see the culture merely as a good photograph; it must be a moving picture that takes into consideration all of the ways African people express agency. It is not simply about poetry, or about Blacks in poetry, or about beautiful Black women in poems, but about a way of viewing the images that move in and out of our sight as we carry out our lives.

DIOPIAN HISTORIOGRAPHY

Cheikh Anta Diop, the late Senegalese scholar, who had written for the Negritudinists, went beyond their work with a new historiography of Africa. Indeed, Diop may be considered the most significant African scholar of the century because of his demolition of the European construction of ancient Africa. He did it almost single-handedly, without African or European support, when he initially started his research. In the end, he established conclusively that the ancient Egyptians were black-skinned Africans and that the origin of civilisation must be traced to the Nile Valley. A school of historians calling themselves Nile Valley historians arose to lend support to his thesis.[15]

Among the principles in this discussion and debate were the African Egyptologists, Theophile Obenga[16] and Maulana Karenga.[17] Obenga had been a protégé of Diop since the 1970s and after Diop's death Obenga continued his work in the United States, initially at Temple University, in the midst of the Afrocentrists, and then at San Francisco State University as Professor of African American Studies. At Temple University, the first graduate class in the Ancient Egyptian Language and Culture was organised and taught by Theophile Obenga and myself. Karenga, a Professor of Black Studies at California State University, Long Beach, organised the first conference around the Diopian methodology and founded the Association for the Study of Classical African Civilisation. In addition, he published several key books on ancient Egyptian civilisation that gave direction to a new field of research culminating in his second dissertation, a comprehensive study of Maat, ancient Egyptian ethical system, written for the University of Southern California.

Although it is true that Afrocentricity borrows from Diopian historiography in the arena of historical epistemology and methodology, Afrocentricity is much more far-reaching than a discussion of history. As we used to say in the late 1960s, African American Studies and history are two different disciplines. You cannot limit Afrocentricity to Diop's historiography anymore than you can limit soccer to a ball and soccer shoes; these are necessary tools but one must have all the other elements, rules of play, field, etc., to make the game. The Afrocentric idea engages all sciences, social sciences, family sciences, and arts and consequently must be viewed as an innovative paradigm in the discourse around African people. At Temple University the first graduate class in the Ancient Egyptian Language and Culture was organised and taught by Theophile Obenga and myself. But we were not simply reproducing Diop; he had already done his work. The scholarship of Miriam Maat Ka Re Monges,[18] Troy Allen, Mohammed Garba, Cynthia Lehman, James Naazir Conyers,[19] Katherine Bankole and others actually follow in the academic line created by Diop, but have added Afrocentric dimensions that articulate the best methods and practices of Afrocentric theorists.

KAWAIDA

Maulana Karenga, while in graduate school, proposed the theory of Kawaida as a corrective for what he observed were cultural problems within the African American community. In Karenga's view, any examples of alienation, degradation, dysfunctionality, self-hatred, and criminal activity were directly related to a misplaced consciousness. How to regain a sense of culture or to introduce a sense of national culture into a community that had abandoned its best ideals in the face of oppression and white racial supremacy, was the challenge confronting Karenga.

Contending that the cultural crisis was the main element in the dysfunctionality of many in the African American community, the philosophy of Kawaida expressed an orientation toward corrective action that included the reconstruction of cultural values on the basis of African traditions. It was to be a reconstruction, in the sense that what Africans had lost in the five hundred years of involvement in the West. Yet it was also a rediscovery, in the sense, that what was possible existed within the epic memory of the people themselves and only had to be appealed to in ways that the masses would respond to with action.

Kawaida was dependent upon collective action. Karenga perceived the truth of the organic relationship of leadership to community and articulated a belief in the possibility of mass education resulting in mass revolution in the sense that people would do better if they knew to do better. The real revolution, he was fond of saying, had to be in the mind of the people or else no other revolution was possible. His appreciation of the role of the masses in all modification of society was a major contribution to the radical movement of humans from a condition of dependence to one of liberation.

The tenets of Kawaida were prescriptive; the concepts of Afrocentricity proved normative in terms of what was happening in the African American community. Afrocentricity sought to use the Kawaidan critique of culture as a starting place for suggesting African agency in two radically different kinds of phenomena. In the first place, agency must be sought in all human behaviours influenced by the environment, large or small, in any given situation. This meant that the superstructure or infrastructure along with the structure or content had to be seen as loci for agency. What is the role of the African in such-and-such a story? How are we to examine the position of the African person during the Constitutional Debate in Philadelphia? Did the enslaved African have a choice in his or her enslavement? What role did Africans play in resistance against oppression? These are questions that get at the phenomena of the infrastructure and structure, but what of phenomena that is more mental? What about the thoughts and emotions we experience within our heads? I mean, what is to be done with the researcher's silent questions regarding phenomena that seem racist, white supremacist? To explain the mental processes of the African people in Brazil, Jamaica, Ghana, the United States, Britain, or any other nation, means to have some idea of the symbols, myths, motifs and concepts that exist within those cultural realms. Even so, the explanation can only be partial since it is not possible to reproduce the behavioural processes or mental processes of any people with one hundred percent certainty. We can only speak of plausible approximations. Yet I know enough as an Afrocentrist to know that an African in Britain, say, would have different things going on in his or her head than an ordinary white Britisher during a discussion of racism in the workplace.

WE ARE FREE AT LAST!

The escape from the Western hegemony is not easy and just as we have announced our escape we recognise that the Fortress West is not going to let us leave the mental plantation without a struggle. Afrocentricity seeks to obliterate the mental, physical, cultural and economic dislocation of African people by thrusting Africans as centred, healthy human beings in the context of African thought. Every conceivable concept, movement, institution and office will be placed at the disposal of those who would argue against the self-determination of African people. To be for one's self is not to be against others; this is the most authoritative lesson that can be learned from the Afrocentric school of thought. Only when there is an effective mass movement of Africans from the margins of Europe to the centre of their own reality, in a self-conscious way, can there be a true revolution. This would, of course, mean the end of white world hegemony.

NOTES AND REFERENCES

1.   Asante, M.K. *Scream of Blood: Desettlerism in Southern Africa* (Princeton: Sungai Books, 1999); and my earlier work: *Afrocentricity* (Trenton, N.J.: Africa World Press, 1987).

2.   Asante, M.K. *African American History: A Journey of Liberation* (Maywood, N.J.: Peoples Publishing Group, 1993).

3.   Asante, M.K. and Mattson, M. *African American Atlas* (New York: Macmillan, 1998).

4.   Harris, M. *Cultural Materialism* (New York: Vintage, 1980).

5.   See Marx, K. and Engels, F. *Communist Manifesto*, in Feurer, L. (ed.) *Marx and Engels: Basic Writings on Politics and Philosophy* (New York: Doubleday, 1959) p. 23; see also Marx, K. *Capital: A Critique of Political Economy, Vol.1* (New York: International Publishers, 1975).

6.   Engels, F. *The Origin of the Family, Private Property and the State* (New York, International Publishers, 1972).

7.   Morgan, L. H. *Ancient Society* (New York: Holt, Rinehart, 1877).

8.   Harris, M. *Cultural Materialism*, p. 161.

9.   Asante, M.K. *The Afrocentric Idea, Revised Edition* (Philadelphia: Temple University, 1998).

10. Levi-Strauss, C. *The Savage Mind* (Chicago: University of Chicago Press, 1966) p. 131.

11. Durkheim, E. *The Elementary Forms of Religious Life* (Translated by J. W. Swain: London: Allen & Unwin, 1915) p. 444.

12. Diawara, M. *In Search of Africa* (New York: Oxford University Press, 1999).

13. Asante, M.K. and Abarry, A. *The African Intellectual Heritage* (Philadelphia: Temple University Press, 1999).

14. Cesaire, A. *The Return to My Native Country* (Paris: Presence Africaine, 1954).

15. See Diop, C. A. *The African Origin of Civilization* (New York: Lawrence Hill, 1976); and by the same author, *Civilization or Barbarism* (New York: Lawrence Hill, 1990).

16. See Obenga, T. *African Philosophy in the Context of World History* (Princeton: Sungai Books, 1997).

17. See Karenga, M. Kawaida (Los Angeles, CA: University of Sankore Press, 1997).

18. See Monges, M. *Kush: The Jewel of Nubia* (Trenton, N.J.: African World Press, 1996).

19. See Conyers, J. (ed.) *Essays in African American Biography* (New York: Sharpe, 1998).

Chapter Six

THE BLACK INTELLECTUAL/ ACTIVIST TRADITION: NOTES ON THE PAST, PRESENT AND FUTURE

Mark Christian

Men make their own history, but they do not make it just as they please: they do not make it under circumstances chosen by themselves, but under circumstances directly encountered, given, and transmitted from the past. The tradition of all dead generations weighs like a nightmare on the brain of the living.

Karl Marx[1]

The farther the Negro gets from his historical antecedents in time, the more tenuous become his conceptual ties, the emptier his social conceptions, the more superficial his visions. His one great and present hope is to know and understand his Afro-American history in the United States more profoundly.

Harold Cruse[2]

THE INTENTION of this chapter is to provide an outline in the tradition of the Black[3] intellectual within the context of the West[4] and its academy, mainly from the 1960s up to the late 1990s. A number of critical questions will be considered regarding this theme. One, how much space does respect and preservation of tradition allow for critique and revision? Two, what types of Black intellectuals exist today in the US and UK? Three, where is the current post-modern, jargon-layered, analyses of Black history and culture heading? And finally, four, does the Black intellectual tradition have a future? However, in order to comprehend the significance and impact of Black scholarship and social activism, there first ought to be recognition of the social backdrop to its development.

Particularly since the nineteenth century, it is a tradition that has brought forth a number of Black intellectual giants: David Walker, Martin Delaney, Edward Wilmot Blyden, W.E.B. Du Bois, Carter G. Woodson, Marcus Garvey, C.L.R. James, George Padmore, Kwame Nkrumah, Paul Robeson, Frantz Fanon, Amilcar Cabral and Walter Rodney, to name but a few (the role of Black women intellectuals deserves special mention and this will follow below).

Although many of these scholar/activists differed in philosophy and practice, they each espoused a profound Pan-Africanist vision within their respective intellectual works and activism. That is, they each endeavoured to unite both theory and practice in the liberation struggle of Africans on the continent and in the

Diaspora. It is this foundation in the intellectual tradition that has informed and sustained much of Black scholarship and political activism since the 1960s.

The struggle for human dignity and self-respect has involved the vast majority of African-descended peoples, directly or indirectly, throughout the globe since about the fifteenth century and up to the present. In short, the nature of this mental and physical struggle has essentially involved overcoming the European dehumanisation of peoples who can claim African ancestry. Primarily, this has been due to the philosophy and practice of white supremacy,[5] and through its varied growth and usage during the eras of African enslavement, colonisation, segregation and, the more recent and endemic form of social exclusion, second class citizenship. In a general sense, this is the social backdrop to the emergence of the modern Black intellectual tradition – specifically from the eighteenth to twentieth centuries.

IMPORTANCE AND CRITIQUE OF THE
BLACK INTELLECTUAL TRADITION

To acknowledge and give respect to the predecessors of the Black intellectual tradition is both morally and academically correct. However, this does not mean that one should romanticise in assessing this tradition. Indeed, the need for a constant and critical examination of the past and present Black intellectual tradition is imperative to both the legacy and future of what I prefer to deem an African-centred paradigm of scholarship and practice.

In addition, it is important to point out that Black intellectual activism is neither monolithic nor homogeneous. On the contrary, it has produced a range of schools of thought from Marxist-orientated (e.g. C.L.R. James, Paul Robeson, Eric Williams, Angela Davis and Walter Rodney) to right-of-centre conservative-orientated discourses (e.g. Booker T. Washington, Thomas Sowell and Shelby Steele). There has also been the Black nationalist and Pan-African visionaries (e.g. Edward Wilmot Blyden, Martin Delaney, Marcus Garvey, Kwame Nkrumah, Cheikh Anta Diop, John Henrik Clarke, Malcolm X, Maulana Karenga, Ivan Van Sertima and Molefi Asante). Sometimes there is an overlap between the schools of thought and the particular Black intellectual/activist. For instance, Marcus Garvey was both a Pan-Africanist and a capitalist, while Kwame Nkrumah was both a

Pan-Africanist and a scientific socialist. Therefore, to evaluate the Black intellectual tradition holistically is also to acknowledge the breadth and scope of its contradictions.

In terms of a specific critique of the Black intellectual tradition, it is fair to suggest that the majority of the historically known Black intellectual personalities have been male. This, from the vantage point of the twenty-first century, may seem understandable given the historical predominance and nature of the Western patriarchal global social structure. Nevertheless, the next generation of Black scholars should not fail to seek out the many constructive roles women of African descent were and are playing in the Black intellectual tradition. For instance, we would not have the *Philosophy and Opinions of Marcus Garvey*[6] had it not been for the sterling editorial work of Amy Jacques Garvey.

Moreover, the present and future generations of Black scholars should not forget the efforts of Anna Julia Cooper, who was a strong advocate for the rights of women and Black peoples. She published the classic *A Voice from the South* in 1892 and was one of the first women invited to speak at the 1900 Pan-African Conference held in London; organised primarily by Henry Sylvester Williams, and attended by a youthful W.E.B. Du Bois.

Other Black women who have not been given enough credit for their intellectual work and social activism include Mary Church Terrell and Ida B. Wells-Barnett. Along with fighting for the rights of women in general in the late nineteenth century and early twentieth century, they each played significant roles in the fight against the lynching of African Americans. Crucially, in the sense of discovering more about the role of Black women intellectual activists, there is still much work to be done by the next generation of scholars.[7] It is therefore important to give respect and to preserve the foundations of the Black intellectual tradition, but it is equally significant for the next generation of Black intellectuals to critique and revise what has gone before in order to improve what is produced in the present and future.

THE CONTEMPORARY BLACK INTELLECTUAL SCENE IN THE USA

In looking at the contemporary Black intellectual scene in the USA, Cornel West, the 'elite' Harvard-based African American professor, argues that there are three distinct types of Black scholars: the race-distancing elitists, the race-embracing rebels, and the race-transcending prophets.[8] West describes the first type of Black intellectual as being usually located in the "dominant and more exclusive universities and colleges", for example at Harvard University. In a rather incongruous critique, given the fact that he is also part of the contemporary 'Black intellectual establishment', he states:

> They [the race-distancing elitists] pontificate about standards of excellence, complexity of analysis, and subtlety of inquiry – yet usually spin out mediocre manuscripts, flat establishmentarian analyses, and un-creative inquiry. Even so, they prosper – though often at the cost of minimal intellectual respect by their white colleagues in the Academy.[9]

It is not clear who Cornel West is specifically alluding to as he offers no examples of the 'race-distancing elitists'. What is an underlying point, however, is the notion of 'white approval' in the Academy. To put it another way, how important should the existence of respect from white intellectual colleagues in the Academy be in the creative output of a 'race-distancing' Black intellectual? If it is a key factor then they should be regarded as 'seeking-white-approval' Black intellectuals. An underlying motivation of this sort is unlikely to produce authentic Black intellectual creativity, only imitations of European-centred epistemology. At bottom, one cannot expect to gain intellectual respect by seeking it. This is the wrong approach to intellectual work as it limits the potential for exploration and innovation.

The second type of Black scholar, the race-embracing rebel, is depicted by West as falling into the trap of 'reverse racism'. It appears to be a thinly-veiled condemnation of prominent contemporary Afrocentric scholars such as Molefi Asante, based at Temple University, and Leonard Jefferies, based at New York City College (the fact that Afrocentrist scholars are diverse, and offer varied philosophical perspectives in African-centred discourse, is also overlooked). West again states:

> . . . race-embracing rebels express their resentment of the white Academy (including its subtle racism) by reproducing similar hierarchies headed by themselves, within a black context. They

rightly rebel against the tribal insularity and snobbish civility of the white Academy (and the first type of black scholars), yet, unlike Du Bois, their rebellion tends to delimit their literary productivity and sap their intellectual creativity . . . Much, though not all, of Afrocentric thought fits this bill.[10]

This is a rather harsh and selective critique as West offers no evidence of the writers or rather, as he suggests, the non-writers who fit this bill. There is also an assumption implying that all white scholars write and publish – and this is not the reality. In fairness to West, it can be said that some contemporary Afrocentric or African-centred scholar/ activists have not produced much creatively in terms of writing, but this cannot be claimed in regard to all or most of them. For example, Molefi Asante, Maulana Karenga, Wade Nobles, Diedre Badejo, William Nelson, Ivan Van Sertima and John Henrik Clarke have each produced scholarship from an African-centred perspective that is both manifold and international in scope. Alongside this, they have maintained a high level of grassroots work with Black communities across the globe. In view of this, West is incorrect to state above: "Much, though not all, of Afrocentric thought fits this bill." Certainly without providing clear evidence of what is good and bad in the African-centred field of scholarship and activism. In addition, it seems that he is too keen to dismiss the virtue of 'race-embracing' and the reason why it is such a necessary component in the development of a mentally and physically healthy diverse global Black community. Especially given the fact that African humanity and heritage has been so viciously maligned.

West's third type of Black scholar, the race-transcending prophet, is characterised in the mould of the late James Baldwin: self-taught and self-styled. This type of Black scholar, according to West, is "beholden to no white academic patronage system" and can therefore create with autonomy. West, however, fails to point out that Baldwin, albeit an outspoken social critic, still had to deal with white patronage within the publishing world. Moreover, white patronage is something that has been an integral aspect of Black creativity in the western hemisphere. In point of fact, the majority of the Harlem Renaissance writers relied heavily on patronage, mainly from white homosexual backers.[11]

Interestingly enough, in terms of West himself, in his analysis he leaves it up to the reader to assess where he himself fits within this three-type schema of Black intellectuals – but implicitly we are left with the sense that he regards himself also as a 'race-transcending prophet'. Beyond this underlying megalomania, West summarises his understanding of the contemporary Black intellectual scene by providing a rather pessimistic view concerning the present generation of Black scholars. Fundamentally, he suggests that there is presently a profound crisis in Black intellectual leadership in the US.[12]

THE CONTEMPORARY BLACK INTELLECTUAL SCENE IN THE UK

Turning to the contemporary scene in the UK, among the most celebrated Black scholars in the British Academy are Stuart Hall and Paul Gilroy. It is fair to presume here that both Hall and Gilroy would not be too keen in being associated with the term 'Black intellectual'. Also, it would be wrong to associate them with the tradition of Black intellectual activism as they are merely 'Ivory Tower' scholars. For them it would be playing the essentialist race card to be regarded as a Black intellectual activist. For instance, in relation to Black identities, Hall discusses what he terms as the growth of "new ethnicities". He argues that he has come to the realisation of the "end of innocence" whereby the sense of "an essential black subject" should now be deemed as moribund. Indeed, for Hall, the term 'Black' is essentially a "politically and culturally constructed category"[13] that emerged during the 1960s 'Black cultural revolution'. In regard to the diverse nature of the Black experience, he states:

> What brings into play [regarding the analysis of Black culture] is the recognition of the immense diversity and differentiation of the historical and cultural experiences of the black subjects.[14]

According to Hall, then, what it is to be a Black intellectual is in contestation, and how one articulates from a Black perspective also depends, to a large extent, on the social background of the given Black scholar. This, in my opinion, is a post-modern analysis and amounts to noting the dynamic hybridity involved in Black culture and experience. Yet most thinkers would agree that the Black experience differs from within and beyond national boundaries. The point here is that regardless of the unique differences in the way the global Black world has been shaped, it would be facile to overlook the obvious similarities of what 'being Black' entails. Indeed, is this not one of the key reasons why Pan-Africanist thought and practice developed in the African Diaspora, in order to link the diverse, but similar, African global struggle against white political, socioeconomic and cultural supremacy?

Take, for example, Francophone and Anglophone African intellectuals located in the Diaspora prior to the actual independence struggles. They each had different analyses to explain their specific African continental experiences under the respective colonial oppressors, France and Britain. Nevertheless, overlooking the fact that they each had a different colonial language to master, there was still far more in common in terms of liberating their African nations and collective minds from the physical and mental grip of the white European, cultural imperialist, stranglehold.

The same can be stated in relation to the experience of peoples of African descent connected via the Diaspora. For instance, in the African Caribbean experience, there has historically emerged Black intellectuals (Hall is an expatriate of Jamaica) with a radical edge not, I would argue, surpassed in other parts of the Diaspora. For example, Edward Wilmot Blyden, Marcus Garvey, Frantz Fanon, Malcolm X, Kwame Ture and Louis Farrakhan all have cultural roots emanating from the African Caribbean region. Therefore, although Hall is right to articulate the uniqueness and obvious diversity of the Black world, he is off course to simply fragment this diversity to the point whereby there is no viable commonality in the global Black experience.

Yet it is not suggested here that the Black experience is unchanging and static. What is being stated is the reality that the struggle against white supremacist thought and practice has been and continues to be an overriding social fact in the global Black experience. This social fact is being under-played at present by cultural theorists in the UK who are, sadly, 'policing' Black intellectual enterprise via an 'arty-farty' post-modern, jargon-layered, 'race-transcending', analysis of Black history and culture.

In this regard, Paul Gilroy exemplifies the contemporary Black intellectual post-modernist trend in the UK. He makes it apparent in his essentially Africaphobic dialogue in *The Black Atlantic*. This is insidiously evident at the very outset of the text as he sets the reader no difficulty in understanding his underlying craving to be an 'accepted' European first, and Black second. As he states: "Striving to be both European and Black requires some specific forms of double consciousness."[15] Gilroy's use of the word, 'striving' is laden with connotations relating to a struggle, a desire, a hope for acceptance. Interestingly, Gilroy does not explicitly reveal why he is at first 'striving to be European and black' and not, conversely, an African and European. Does this matter? I think it does depending on the context of the discussion. Throughout Gilroy's *The Black Atlantic* he is at pains to stress the debt African Diasporan humanity has, in a cultural sense, for its five hundred plus years association with white European peoples. Gilroy contends that this cross-cultural relationship is inextricably linked to, and characterised by, the enslavement of Africans in the Diaspora. In turn this has produced a melange of Black cultures – a hybrid form of cultures that are interwoven with European, African, Caribbean and other influences. Because of this, Gilroy suggests that it is wrong to think merely of an African-centred experience. For him, the Black Atlantic is identified through an interconnection of historical and cultural forces that have produced "mongrel cultural forms".[16]

This post-modern analysis by Gilroy et al is the standard 'Black intellectual' offering in the UK at present. Yet this perspective rarely tackles head-on how the notion and practice of white supremacy still maintains a hegemony over peoples who are distinctly 'not White'. Without a doubt, African, European and Asian peoples and their specific cultures have intermingled during the eras of enslavement, colonisation and beyond. Yet often this has had little bearing on how white supremacy fundamentally operates. To be sure, in some regions, the intermingling of peoples and cultures was employed in order to further divide and conquer. This was most visible in South Africa before and under apartheid, and in the British Caribbean colonies. Indeed, 'skin-tone' effectively determined the social stratification of society. Thus, accounting for the contemporary post-modern analyses by Gilroy and others from an African-centred perspective, one can suggest that this is neither original nor something to culturally celebrate. That is, in the way post-modern cultural theorists are suggesting we do in their spurious, avant-garde, hybridity theories.

Other post-modern 'Black' intellectuals based in the UK include Kobena Mercer and Issac Julien. They maintain that it is academically correct to express the social construction and modality of all idiosyncrasies relating to humanity's inhumanity, but the social fact of a universal and common African, racialised, historical oppression is out of bounds.[17] In other words, it is now the vogue in academia to understand the plight of the homosexual, the lesbian, the drug addict, the homeless and the myriad other members of 'outcast' social groups. However, and ironically, it is an essentialist sin to express a view that proposes to link 'the fact of Blackness' via all its varied global struggle and social complexity.

As with some of the leading US Black intellectuals, it appears that being of African descent has gone out of academic fashion. African-centred discourse is summarily dismissed as 'kitsch' or essentialist and struck off the reading lists of cultural studies courses. Thus, often there is not even room for a critical dialogue and exchange of views – African-centred scholars are simply dismissed as ideological or political. In short, to try and understand a world-view from an African-centred perspective, is to be considered narrow-minded and inward-looking in scope. To be recognised in the UK as a broad-minded Black scholar by the leading cultural theorists, you have to show evident signs of embracing every oppressed group that walks the earth. Regardless of the fact that at the core of African-centred philosophy is anti-oppression.

In view of this lack of understanding there is a dire need for more dialogue and debate among Black scholars. Indeed, if it is 'inward-looking' to claim to be an African-centred thinker that seeks first and foremost to understand the diversity, through commonality, of African-descended peoples in the Diaspora, we need to discuss why this is so. It is unfair and intellectually short-sighted of 'Black' post-modern theorists to confine African-centred scholars to an 'essentialist sin-bin' and lampoon them as 'race-rebels' without a cause. Historical evidence clearly indicates a need for African-descended peoples to unite in their respective struggles. This is not inward-looking, just plain sensible.

WHERE DO WE GO FROM HERE?

If the contemporary state of Black intellectual production is in crisis, then what is the solution to it? Where do we go from here (to use a phrase from Dr Martin Luther King, Jr)? Given the ascendancy of post-modernist discourse in the academy, the future does look particularly bleak, as West points out above. Indeed, the average post-modern analysis of Black history and culture is inaccessible to the average reader. What is often regarded as sophisticated scholarly inquiry merely amounts to esoteric semantics that offer little in terms of a constructive clarity of analysis. In a prescient statement relating to his conclusion of European culture at the dawn of the 1960s, Frantz Fanon inadvertently speaks to the 'Black' post-modern theorist of the late twentieth century:

> . . . We today can do everything, so long as we do not imitate Europe, so long as we are not obsessed by the desire to catch up to Europe.

He continues:

> Europe now lives at such a mad, reckless pace that she has shaken off all guidance and all reason, and she is running headlong into the abyss; we would do well to avoid it with all possible speed.[18]

It would be wise to take heed of Fanon's insight, as today it appears that many of these post-modern Black intellectuals are uncritically obsequious to European canons of knowledge and creativity. Rightly so, each of us should have the option to follow what we consider an epistemology that is correct for him or her. Yet, given the history of Europe's blatant exploitation of African-descended peoples, and especially in terms of their exclusion from being able to read and write in the African Diaspora during the enslavement era, we need to be critical and not lose sight of the role European education has played in the dissemination of not only racialised pseudo-science, but of an insidious cultural hegemony.[19] To think of this as something ancient and not worth considering today, is to be critically naïve. So what is the alternative? Is it necessary to have thinkers that think Black today? Let us briefly consider these questions via the ideas of a quintessential Black intellectual activist, Walter Rodney.

WALTER RODNEY AND THE THEORY/PRACTICE IMPERATIVE

Unlike many of the post-modern Black intellectuals today, Walter Rodney was able to analyse and critique the global plight of people of African descent from both an historical and contemporary perspective. In this sense, his intellectual and political activism was historically grounded with an understanding of the imperialist bourgeois exploitation of the masses, particularly in the Caribbean region. But what makes Rodney important to the struggle of Black people today is the fact that his analysis was not parochial. In other words, Rodney linked the socioeconomic problems of the masses in the Caribbean and Africa to that of the Black masses in the US, UK and all over the world. In short, he deemed the predicament of Black people in a global sense. It was for him important to analyse specific regions of the Black world in their own right, but he was always looking for the macro linkages that could unite Black peoples. Rodney did, for example, employ a class analysis in his search for the way in which capitalism exploits the many while profiting the few.

As it was for a number of his Black intellectual predecessors, Rodney was influenced by Marxist philosophy and the notion of 'praxis': an action-orientation mode of scholar/activism. However, unlike orthodox Marxism, he maintained that one could not deny or underestimate the variable of 'race' in the analysis of the global struggle for Black liberation. Indeed, as a Black intellectual, he linked both the concepts of 'race' and class to an overall economic determinist perspective in his historical understanding of racism and the oppression of Black people in the modern world.[20]

THE ROLE OF THE BLACK 'GUERRILLA INTELLECTUAL'

Walter Rodney employed the term 'guerrilla intellectual' to define the role of the potential progressive Black intellectual functioning in the Western academy. In order to transform the existing 'mental incarceration', Black intellectuals should find ways of breaking out of it.[21] Put another way, the guerrilla intellectual has to be conscious of the class element of his/her position within mainstream, bourgeois, educational institutions.

Black scholars, for instance, located at Harvard, Yale, Cambridge or Oxford, if they are agreeable enough to have been recruited by those who hold power, ordinarily should seek to advance an ideological perspective conducive to the Black masses. But more often than not the intellectual output is merely destined for a minority bourgeois Black or white populace. For Rodney, then, the major task of the intellectual is the 'struggle over ideas'. In relation to the progressive intellectual, it should be realised that the artificial distinction between mental and manual labour was not their creation, but that of the bourgeois element in the academy. In order for the Black intellectual to achieve a viable and worthwhile existence in the academy, he or she needs to transcend the separation between 'ideas and labour' by 'breaking the pattern that entrenches such a distinction'.[22]

If there is to be a genuine attempt by Black intellectuals to break the hegemony of the bourgeois academy, an understanding in the function of Western discourse is imperative. Rodney pointed to the fact that not everyone can be a 'Che Guevara', and that often this type of strategy adopted by the progressive intellectual could be detrimental in the long term struggle. He proposed it was more useful to expropriate bourgeois knowledge and transform it to the benefit of the Black masses. However difficult this may be, the reality is that bourgeois institutions of higher learning have the 'facilities and possibilities for the elaboration of knowledge'.[23] In this way, the role of the guerrilla intellectual is to find ways of mastering that knowledge so that it can be of use to the Black masses in their mental and physical liberation from a relatively oppressive system. Only time will tell whether or not there will emerge a cadre of guerrilla intellectuals out of the next generation, but the signs at present appear ominously bleak.

CONCLUSION

This chapter has briefly discussed the Black intellectual tradition within the confines of the Western academy. Although it is a rather impossible task to try and wade through and summarise the various schools of thought, a major theme that unifies the Black intellectual tradition in the West is in regard to the struggle against white supremacist thought and action. Focusing on the current output of Black scholarship in the US and UK spheres, there was an attempt to give some examples of the current generation. The model-types of Black intellectuals proposed by Cornel West provided the foundation for this part of the discussion.

It was contended that the post-modern discourses offer nothing substantial in providing a continued assault on white supremacy. This is primarily due to the discourses being relatively inaccessible and turgid analyses of Black history and culture.

Writing essentially from an African American perspective on intellectual activism and artistic expression, Harold Cruse, in his classic text, *The Crisis of the Negro Intellectual*, called upon the African American intellectual community not to commit the mistakes of the past by being historically short-sighted.[24] Over thirty years on, Cruse's analysis still makes sense in regard to some of the work being produced by contemporary, post-modern, Black scholars. In regard to the Harlem Renaissance writers, Cruse felt that they had sold-out the possibility of cultural self-determination to the whim and fancy of white liberal, middle class, patronage. As he states:

> . . . the Harlem intellectuals were so overwhelmed at being 'discovered' and courted, that they allowed a bona fide cultural movement, which issued from the social system as naturally as a gushing spring, to degenerate into a pampered and paternalised vogue.[25]

Cruse put forward an analysis that urged a new generation of Black intellectuals in the late 1960s to synthesise the integrationist and nationalist social forces that propelled the history of African America via politics, economics and culture. This, he contended, would usher forth a new 'social theory of action' that was imperative to halt the retrogression of Black intellectual creativity. As we reflect on this proposition from Cruse at the dawn of a new millennium, it still appears to be a relevant and significant suggestion.

As a designated and proud member of the next generation of Black intellectuals, the task involved in synthesising the tradition is immense. Yet, it has to be done and if we can heed the advice of Cruse, by not falling into the trap of white patronage, then we have a hope in developing a body of scholarship that will be more conducive to the uplift of the global Black community. Indeed, the world is a far smaller place than it was thirty years ago, and now more than ever we have the technology and educational expertise to compare and contrast the African continental and Diasporan experiences. This is something that should be seized upon by Africana Studies Departments. After all, it is in these departments that many of the future Black intellectuals will be produced.

Finally, I would envisage that the next generation of Black intellectuals will involve more Black women than ever there was in previous generations.[26] This fact is very positive in terms of the future empowerment of Black communities. Indeed, without Black women at the forefront, there will be no genuine progress for the African Diaspora. When the input of Black women is at the forefront in the various struggles, one can confidently expect results for the good of a whole society and not just a few of its members. This is a major challenge for the next generation of Black intellectuals who will want to establish a dynamic approach to Black liberation discourse and practice in the new millennium.

NOTES AND REFERENCES

1. Taken from Karl Marx' *The Eighteenth Brumaire of Louis Bonaparte* (1852) and cited in Lewis S. Feuer (ed.) *Marx and Engels: Basic Writings on Politics and Philosophy* (London: Anchor Books, 1989) p. 320.

2. Cruse, H. *The Crisis of the Negro Intellectual* (New York: Morrow, 1967) p. 565.

3. The term 'Black' refers to persons who can claim to have African heritage and to those that are ordinarily socially defined as Black in the Western world.

4. The term 'West' in this sense refers to both the Northern European and North American development of academic canons and its white ethnic colonial, settler, heritage in Africa and the 'New World'.

5. The term 'white supremacy' is defined by Fredrickson as ". . . attitudes, ideologies, and policies associated with the rise of blatant forms of white or European dominance over 'non-white' populations." I employ the term in the same sense; see Fredrickson, G. M. *White Supremacy: A Comparative Study in American & South African History* (Oxford: Oxford University Press, 1981) p. xi. See also, Martin Luther King, Jr. 'Racism and the White Backlash' in *Where Do We Go From Here: Chaos or Community?* (Boston: Beacon Press, 1989; first published in 1967) pp. 67-101.

6. See Garvey, M. *Philosophy and Opinions of Marcus Garvey* (edited by Amy Jacques Garvey, New York, Antheneum, 1969).

7. This is not to suggest that work has not already taken place, indeed Maulana Karenga's, *Introduction to Black Studies, 2nd Ed.* (Los Angeles, CA: Sankore Press, 1993) provides a good outline in the recent development of 'Black Women's Studies', pp. 38-43. For a more in-depth analysis see Hudson-Weems, C. *African Womanism: Reclaiming Ourselves* (Troy, MI: Bedford, 1993).

8. West, C. 'The Crisis of Black Leadership' in *Race Matters*, (New York: Vintage, 1994) pp. 64-66.

9. Ibid. p. 65.

10. Ibid.

11. See Watson, S. *The Harlem Renaissance: Hub of African-American Culture, 1920-1930* (New York: Pantheon, 1995).

12. West, C. Race Matters, p. 66.
13. Hall, S. 'New Ethnicities' in J. Donald and A. Rattansi (eds.) *'Race,' Culture & Difference* (London: Sage, 1992) p. 254.
14. Ibid.
15. Gilroy, P., *The Black Atlantic: Modernity and Double Consciousness* (London: Verso, 1993) p. 1.
16. Ibid. p. 3. See also, Paul Gilroy. 'Roots and Routes: Black Identity as an Outernational Project' in H. W. Harris, H. C. Blue and E. E. H. Griffith. (eds.) *Racial and Ethnic Identity: Psychological Development and Creative Expression* (London: Routledge, 1995) pp. 15-30.
17. This point is substantiated by the fact that as implicitly acknowledged 'Black intellectuals', Kobena Mercer and Issac Julian tend to promote and elevate the 'essence' of homosexuality and/or the analysis of masculinities over and above being Black in white culturally-dominated societies such as the UK and USA. Though they would probably not overtly admit this contradiction. A good text for an understanding of the current anti-African-centred discourse is Gina Dent's (ed.), *Black Popular Culture* (Seattle, WA: Bay Press, 1992) part V. It is odd that collectively these authors are ill at ease with being Black, yet sell their product with a clearly Black marketable title. This suggests that 'Black' as a term is socially useful when selling a product, but not when it comes to creating solidarity among the diverse global African-descended communities.
18. Fanon, F. *The Wretched of the Earth* (New York: Grove Press, 1968) p. 312.
19. See Fryer, P. *Staying Power: The History of Black People in Britain* (London: Pluto Press, 1984), Chapter 7.
20. Marable, M. *Race, Class and Democracy: Walter Rodney's Thought on the Black American Struggle* (London: Friends of Bogle, 1988) p. 4.
21. Rodney, W. *Walter Rodney Speaks: The Making of an African Intellectual* (Trenton, N. J: African World Press, 1990) p. 112.
22. Ibid. pp. 113-114.
23. Ibid.
24. See Harold Cruse's *The Crisis of the Negro Intellectual*, note 2 above.

25.   Ibid. p. 52.

26.   In terms of the US, the fact that the 'Million Woman March' that took place in Philadelphia, Pennsylvania, 25 October 1997, is again testimony of the profound influence and presence of African-descended women in the liberation struggle. Along with the 'Million Man March', Washington, D.C., 16 October 1995, it also shows that there is potential for an organised, grassroots assault on the oppressive forces that beset the overall community. Time will tell.

Chapter Seven

AFRICAN-CENTRED SOCIAL WORK: CONCRETISING ETHICAL PRINCIPLES OF EQUALITY AND SOCIAL JUSTICE FOR A NEW MILLENNIUM

Mekada Graham

SOCIAL WORK interventions with Black[1] families and children have been the source of controversy, conflict and disquiet for many decades. Research evidence continues to indicate that Black communities are over-represented in those services that involve social control functions, for example, the juvenile justice system in its dealings with young Black people, compulsory admissions to psychiatric units, and child protection. Black families are under-represented in receiving preventative and supportive aspects of service delivery.[2] Black communities and Black professionals in the field continue to voice their general dissatisfaction with social work interventions and with the disabling effects of the social work process.[3]

The Association of Black Social Workers and Allied Professions (ABSWAP) provided compelling evidence to the House of Commons Select Committee in 1983 highlighting the plight of Black children in the care system and was active in identifying the need for a legislative framework which addressed race, culture and language in the provision and delivery of services.[4] Despite the introduction of the 1989 Children Act, and in particular, Section 22 (5) (C) which clearly requires local authorities to give due consideration to "the child's religious persuasion, racial origin and cultural and linguistic background" in the provision of services and service delivery, Black children of all ages and both sexes continue to be over-represented in the public care system (the statistics for the over-representation of Black children in the public care system refer to children of African Caribbean origin and African children of mixed origin).[5]

Institutional racism has been identified as one of the key factors in the continued oppression of Black families within society and its effects compounded by 'the system' of social welfare.[6] Scholars, such as Dominelli and Ahmad,[7] have provided a well-documented exposition of racism in social work and of the continuing need to construct anti-racist strategies that are incorporated into social work practice rather than merely offering an understanding of the nuances of racism in the wider society.

The primary response of social work in addressing the needs of Black people has been to adapt existing models of social work with special attention given to racism and cultural differences. The ethnic sensitive model in the US and anti-discriminatory practice (which now incorporates anti-racist practice) have emerged as the most appropriate paradigms that can assist and best meet their needs. However, although these models include important areas that must be addressed, they fall short of using social work designs that reflect the worldviews and cultural values of diverse communities in British society.

Anti-racist and ethnic sensitive models of social work fail to consider that Black and white people have historically been placed in vastly different positions in the mechanics of social oppression. Moreover, the infusion of the Black perspective/experience is articulated as an adaptation or modification that serves to mask more fundamental theoretical deficits inherent within the ethnocentric nature of social work knowledge.

Traditionally, Black scholars and researchers have been locked into Eurocentric philosophy in shaping a frame of reference that became the context for analysis of the Black experience. Over the past decades, a new generation of Black scholars has advocated an alternative social science paradigm that affirms the traditions, history and visions of Black people. There is now a large body of academic literature that articulates African-centred epistemology. This conceptual framework locates African people at the centre of analysis rather than as objects of examination and research.[8] The Afrocentric paradigm is based upon African-centred worldviews that reflect the social philosophy of ancient and traditional Africa to interpret a distinctive African school of thought. These cultural antecedents form part of interpretative frameworks that emerged from Black communities to explain and resolve social problems. These cultural value systems provide the theoretical base to develop new social work practice models.

Alternative worldviews, such as Afrocentricity, have been largely ignored or marginalised as the bases for social work theories and models of practice. By establishing the legitimacy of an alternative system of knowing, African-centred worldviews present a powerful challenge to the hegemony of Eurocentric social theories in demanding equal standing across the spectrum of human knowledge.

The purpose of this chapter is threefold: one, to examine the theoretical deficits apparent within existing social work paradigms; two, to explain and discuss African-centred worldviews as a conceptual framework for social work; and three, to define the meaning and contours of Afrocentric social work as an alternative means through which human problems can be understood and solved in contemporary

Britain. The chapter, therefore, seeks to expand the philosophical base of social work to promote alternative worldviews and advance the fulfilment of humanitarian social work goals to ensure the profession's participation in its commitment to equality and social justice.

THEORY AND SOCIAL WORK PRACTICE
WITH BLACK FAMILIES

In response to the growing awareness that traditional social work models have been ineffective and oppressive in addressing the needs of African people, ethnic-sensitive social work practice in the US and anti-discriminatory practice (which now incorporates anti-racist practice) in the UK have been proposed as the way forward in providing the 'blueprint' for good social work practice with Black people. The model of anti-racist social work is predicated upon theories drawn from the sociology of race relations to provide an understanding of the source and impact of different kinds of inequality and oppression.

Dominelli, Thompson and Ahmad, each define racism as an ideological social construct that involves social and political meanings,[9] culminating in what Audre Lorde described as "the belief in the inherent superiority of one race over all others and thereby the right to dominance".[10] The social effects of racism are manifested in disadvantage that permeates areas of social life, housing, employment, education, etc. Thus, the understanding of the social construct of race and racism becomes central to the anti-racist discourse as a tool to organise for social change.

The dominant anti-racist and anti-discriminatory practice focus and parameters of this model are expressed as follows:

* understanding how racism, oppression and discrimination have created barriers to opportunities in the wider society, agencies and structures;
* social worker awareness of personal biases, attitudes and stereotypes; challenges to racism within others and institutions.[11]

Anti-discriminatory practice is concerned with limiting the damage within social work practice that preaches the worth of every individual, yet supports institutional and cultural racism at every level. In effect, anti-discriminatory practice tries to put social work's 'house in order' in attempts to combat racism in the system and within the 'professional' subjective judgements of social workers. The underlying knowledge-base of anti-discriminatory practice is confined within the parameters of this essentially reactive stance against racism and oppression. The existing parameters of anti-discriminatory practice do not provide social work models that aspire to support, nurture and understand the emotional, spiritual and developmental needs of Black families to advance the collective interests of African people.

Instead, this social work model promotes damage limitation by infusing a 'Black perspective/experience' which is articulated as an adaptation or modification of existing theoretical frameworks that serves to mask more fundamental theoretical deficits that are inherent within the ethnocentric nature of social work knowledge. Consequently, this model falls short of creating a social work that mirrors the worldview and cultural values of those who are most often recipients of social work interventions. Moreover, as Karenga maintains, "a people whose paradigms of thought and practice are borrowed from its oppressor clearly have limited human possibilities."[12] Creativity and transformation are available only when the individual is connected to his or her cultural authenticity.

Anti-discriminatory practice offers the potential of a response that is 'free' from discrimination on several levels but falls short of providing a knowledge-base for social work that is engaged in the collective development of the Black community. The ethnocentric nature of the underlying knowledge-base of social work continues to assume that this knowledge has universal application, that is, that one theory, worldview or paradigm, can be used to explain human behaviour among all people and in every culture. Consequently, anti-discriminatory practice inherently promotes existing social work interventions by calling for a form of change, adaptation and assimilation that inevitably supports the collective interests of the dominant culture.

ETHNIC 'SENSITIVE' SOCIAL WORK

The ethnic-sensitive model developed by Devore and Schlesinger[13] proposes the need for 'sensitivity' to cultural differences together with an understanding and appreciation of racial, cultural and social diversity. The model provides specific strategies that include:

- awareness of and sensitivity to cultural differences and value systems of ethnic and cultural groups;
- adaptation to practice skills in response to the differing family patterns and lifestyles;
- an understanding of how cultural traditions and values influence family functioning and consider these nuances in planning social work interventions.

The concept of 'ethnic reality' is placed within a social work knowledge base, which is inherently ethnocentric:

> Theory builds a series of propositions about reality; that is, it provides us with models of reality and helps us to understand what is possible and how we can attain it.[14]

In other words, the 'reality' of Black people is placed within the realities of others who have constructed their own theories and models of practice as the basis for solving people's problems. Somehow, it is assumed that these will provide the principal remedies for Black oppression and for problems within Black families and communities. In line with Karenga[15], Asante asks the poignant question, "how can the oppressed use the same theories as the oppressors?"[16]

The levels of adaptation of prevailing models of social work practice to the infusion of the ethnic reality, is the key theme in social work literature; the fact that the prevailing models of social work practice are an expression of the hegemony of Eurocentric knowledge is ignored. The ethnic-sensitive approach uncovers several flaws that contribute to a projected image of 'universality' of existing social work paradigms and, more importantly, the establishment of the social work knowledge-base as the norm. This model maintains a subtle form of cultural oppression in negating the legitimacy of other worldviews as the basis for social work theory and practice.

As Schiele argues, cultural oppression "is achieved by imposing one group's culture onto another's in a manner that marginalises and devalues the culture of another."[17] In other words, the knowledge validation and hegemony in information dissemination cannot be separated from social, political and economic hegemony within British institutions and the wider society.

Western thought and culture provide the epistemologies that dominate the social sciences shaping the contours of social work knowledge. Theories of human behaviour are inextricably bound and located within Western philosophical assumptions about human beings and their relationship with the world.[18]

Leading Afrocentric scholars, Nobles and Goddard, identify the control element propagated within traditional social science paradigms:

> The most efficient way to keep Black people oppressed and powerless is to provide them with ideas that justify and certify our status and condition. A powerful approach to the empowerment of marginalised groups is to work together to develop critical consciousness, to develop together the tools to critique frames of reference, ideas, information, and patterns of privilege.[19]

The hegemonic nature of social work knowledge propagates the belief that Eurocentric precepts are primary in the analysis of social problems because they are presented as devoid of cultural impositions that effect the theorist and theorising – thereby suggesting objectivity in the understanding of human behaviour. This expression of cultural oppression in social work fosters the belief that Black people lack the skills and abilities to develop social work designs. These beliefs must be challenged by Afrocentric social work educators and other critical theorists in order to gain cultural inclusion. The existing parameters of ethnic-sensitive practice and anti-racism in social work reflect a Eurocentric project that fails to understand, recognise or respond to Black autonomy. Therefore, an anti-racist model in social work must consider how race and gender are implicated in ways of knowing and of knowledge itself to ensure the profession's participation in its commitment to equality and social justice. Thus, what is required, therefore, is a broader remit of anti-racist social work where a multiplicity of worldviews provide legitimate strategies for social work.

SOCIAL WORK'S COMMITMENT TO EQUALITY AND SOCIAL JUSTICE

The hallmark of the social work profession has been its emphasis upon promoting humanitarian values. The core foundations of social work embrace a commitment to equality, social justice and place emphasis upon self-determination as an integral part of its professional ethos.[20] The central maxims of professional social work are, one, the belief in the inherent dignity and worth of human beings and, two, the belief in the capacity of self-determination in human beings.

Weick's discussion of the philosophical origins embedded within social work ethics refers to the overlay of culture expressed in the socialisation of individuals that functions to create a homogeneous view of the world.[21] Thereby, the capacity of people to develop within their own cultural reality is often denied. This is because the shared views about the nature of reality are invariably built upon the definitions of others. She argues that recent human liberation movements provide new insights that can bring conceptual depth to the belief structure of social work. As Weick proposes, "to even imagine that one has the capacity to create a new definition for oneself is a radical act."[22] This radical act is exemplified in the collective knowledge of liberation movements that the definitions of others could be challenged. The essence of these ideas was the belief in their inherent value and worth as human beings. Thus, alternative worldviews, such as Afrocentricity provide the vehicle that:

> ... self knows itself as not enslaved, but free; not repulsive, but desirable; not helpless, but licensed and powerful; not history-less, but historical; not damned, but innocent; not a blind accident of evolution, but a progressive fulfilment of destiny.[23]

Therefore, the interrogation of the nature of social work knowledge as a hidden source of cultural oppression, provides the context in which Afrocentric worldviews can initiate conceptual frameworks for new practice models.

AFRICAN-CENTRED WORLDVIEWS: NEW PHILOSOPHIES FOR SOCIAL WORK

The unique feature of our culture is that its root and base is Africa. To acknowledge its origins is also to identify the unchanging seam which is common to all Black cultures in the Diaspora.[24]

African-centred worldviews are social philosophical models based upon traditional philosophical assumptions in pre-colonial Africa. Over the past two hundred years, eminent Black scholars (such as Diop, Obenga, Du Bois, Asante, Fanon, Nobles, Rodney, Blyden and Garvey), and a long line of activists, have been instrumental in defining an African-centred intellectual school of thought. Black scholars – notably, Asante, Akbar, Nobles, Hilliard, Diop, T'Shaka, Karenga, Clarke and Ani – have engaged in a process of reclaiming ancient African philosophical systems to interpret a distinctive African school of thought.

Africa is the source and historical beginnings of African people throughout the Diaspora. These historical beginnings contain the template of philosophies, belief systems, family values, knowledge of self and the world. This worldview reflects elements of a core African value system that existed prior to, and independent of, racial oppression.[25] The African-centred worldview has a core philosophical foundation derived from classic African civilisations of Kemet, Nubia, Kush and Axum as its baseline for conceptions of human beings and the universe.[26]

The term 'African-centred worldview', or 'Afrocentric/Africentric worldview', has been used to describe the cultural values of people of African origin and African descent throughout the world. Although it is important to acknowledge the cultural diversity of African peoples, as Mbiti contends, there are underlying commonalities and affinities in the thought systems of all African (Black) peoples.[27]

Widely respected Black scholars have detailed the existence of traditional African-centred worldviews, and certain distinguishing cultural characteristics and beliefs that are prevalent.[28] These generalised worldviews are consistent with cultural value systems that are cited at a deep structural level. Traditional African philosophical assumptions – significant ways of knowing and understanding the world survived the physical uprooting of African people through enslavement to remain an essential part of their ethos.[29]

There are two main issues that have generated controversy surrounding the legitimacy of Afrocentric worldviews. First, it is claimed that African people within the Diaspora are now so far removed from African cultural values and traditions (because of their forced removal from Africa and the experience of 400 years of enslavement) that they have become fully acculturalised. As a result of this process, they have developed their own modern 'identities' based upon their lived experiences in Western societies. However, these explanations are all too easy to accept, particularly when African people within the Diaspora have been taught to separate themselves from Africa and Africans. Moreover, historically the cultural defamation of Africa and its people has been a defining feature of British society.

Eminent Black scholars have engaged in identification and analysis of African cultural value retention that are expressed in many forms through, and within, Black existence. This evidence suggests that people of African descent tend to function within African-centred worldviews whatever their geographical location.[30]

Second, it has also been proposed that Afrocentric worldviews are in essence essentialist, which mirror the grand narratives inherent within European modernity. The post-modern discourse has dismissed generalities as incredulous, embracing the notion of increasingly narrow definitions of ethnicity located in the culture of difference. Post-modern constructs have been expressed within social work knowledge as an appreciation of narrative, ambiguity and understanding, shifting the emphasis away from the constraints of a scientific and technical definition of knowledge. However, I agree with bell hooks' observations:

> Racism is perpetuated when blackness is associated solely with the concept concrete experiences that either oppose or has no connection with abstract thinking and the production of critical theory.[31]

The post-modern discourse is, essentially, a product of European social thought characterised by a view of the 'modern' as its frame of reference. What is more, the notion of the modern has historically been used to devalue and oppress indigenous people throughout the world. Cornel West asks the poignant question:

> Does the post-modern debate seriously acknowledge the distinctive cultural and political practices of oppressed peoples? . . . [Can] postmodernism debates cast some significant light on cultural practices of oppressed peoples?[32]

It can be argued, therefore, that Eurocentric hegemony and racial bias extend to the post-modern debate and has been a feature of:

virtually all of the different critical approaches – including critical theory . . . critical post-modernism have been repeatedly cited for their racial biases.[33]

In any event, dominant epistemologies, sources of knowledge are derived largely from Western European philosophical, historical, social, political, economic and cultural development and like all specialised knowledge 'reflects the interests and standpoint of its creator'.[34] Allowing space for other culturally-based epistemology remains somewhat problematic for European thought and can sometimes foster a strategic refusal on the part of some academics to engage in African-centred ways of knowing. However, social work is ideally placed to embrace alternative worldviews such as Afrocentricity in knowledge production and dissemination to promote and concretise its ethical commitment to equality and social justice.

African-centred worldviews move beyond the issues of historical oppression and draw upon historical sources to revise a collective text – the best of Africa to develop social work approaches and patterns which support the philosophical, cultural and historical heritage of African people throughout the world.

African-centred worldviews begin with an holistic conception of the human condition which spans the cosmological (an aspect of philosophy that considers the nature and structure of the universe), ontological (the essence of all things), and axiological (an area of philosophy that considers the nature of values and value preferences in a culture).

African-centred philosophy is an holistic system based upon values and ways of living which are reinforced through rituals, music, dance, storytelling, proverbs and metaphors. Also in the promoting of family, rites of passage, naming ceremonies, child rearing, birth, death, elderhood and values of governance. The principles and values that underpin African-centred worldviews are:

- the interconnectedness of all things;
- the spiritual nature of human beings;
- collective/individual identity and the collective/inclusive nature of family structure;
- oneness of mind, body and spirit;
- the value of interpersonal relationships.[35]

THE INTERCONNECTEDNESS OF ALL THINGS

Within the cosmological perspective of African-centred worldviews, all elements of the universe – people, animals and inanimate objects – are viewed as interconnected. Since they are dependent upon each other, they are, in essence, considered as one.[36] Human reality is unified and we divide unity into parts only because of the limitations of our present knowledge. Molefi Asante expresses unification through a statement credited to the Zulu peoples: "I am river, I am mountain, I am tree, I am love, I am emotion, I am beauty, I am lake, I am cloud, I am sun, I am sky, I am mind, I am one with one".[37]

For Akbar, the unity of "the African cosmos is like a spider web; its least element cannot be touched without making the whole vibrate. Everything is connected, interdependent".[38] These relationships provide individuals with a sense of purpose and connection with families and community. Moreover, the maintenance of harmonious social relationships supports the development of positive self-esteem and social competence. Social problems and human dysfunction arise when people become alienated and disconnected from their independent human relationships.

The interconnectedness of all things sees no separation between the material and the spiritual, 'reality is at one and inseparably spiritual and material' and as all reality (universe) begins from a single principle. Human beings are perceived as an integral part of nature, and living in harmony with the environment helps them to become at one with all reality. The concept of oneness relates to those not yet born and those who have died – all human beings are linked spiritually across time and space.[39] As Schiele also maintains:

> The focus on interconnectedness recognises that people are spiritual (i.e. non-material) beings who are connected with each other through the spirit of the Creator.[40]

The spiritual aspect of human beings transcends the spheres of time and space. The interconnectedness of human beings, spiritually, is translated socially, so that the human being is never an isolated individual but always the person in the community. The community defines the person, as Mbiti explains, paraphrasing an African proverb, "I am because we are; and since we are, therefore I am".[41] Self-knowledge is rooted "on being centred in one's self, one's own experience, one's history".[42] To become aware of the cultural self is an important process that connects a person, spiritually, to others within a culture. Furthermore, self-knowledge within the context of one's connection with others provides the basis for transformation, spiritual development and well-being.

THE SPIRITUAL NATURE OF HUMAN BEINGS

Spirituality forms the cornerstone of African-centred worldviews and is the essence of human beings. Spirituality has been defined as 'that invisible substance that connects all human beings to each other and to a creator'.[43] The spiritual essence of human beings requires a shift in thinking towards valuing human beings above the social and economic status which have been assigned to them. For example, who you are, your personhood, comes about through your relationship with the community. As Maulana Karenga argues:

> . . . personhood [is] a process of becoming rather than a simple state of being. Personhood . . . is achieved not simply by existence but by successive stages of integration or incorporation in the community.[44]

Life is a series of passages – a process whereby a person is accorded the challenge to grow, change and develop to attain moral, intellectual and social virtues within the authenticity and context of community.

COLLECTIVE/INDIVIDUAL IDENTITY AND COLLECTIVE/INCLUSIVE NATURE OF THE TWINLINEAL FAMILY STRUCTURE

The individual cannot be understood separately from other people.[45] The collective nature of identity is expressed in the African proverb "I am because we are and because we are therefore I am".[46] These philosophical assumptions transmit to the psyche a sense of belonging to the collective and of being part of the whole.

From these assumptions of collective identity follows the emphasis upon human similarities or commonalities rather than upon individual differences. The collective nature of human beings entails collective responsibility for what happens to individuals. 'Whatever happens to the individual happens to the whole group and whatever happens to the whole group happens to the individual'.[47]

The collective identity of human beings links the conception of the family and its structures and functioning. The family structure is based upon twinlineal systems incorporating the lineage both of the mother and the father, and also includes members who are not biologically related and an extensive network of cousins.[48] This has immediate implications for social work: as social workers have been confounded in their attempts to describe and define Black families using criteria which have emanated from their own experiences.[49]

The notion of half-siblings prevalent within social work theory and practice, for example, is incomprehensible; it does not exist within an African-centred worldview. Ryan and Walker discuss the increase in family breakdowns:

> . . . some of these relationships eventually end too. As the years progress, there may be a tangled network of full siblings, half-siblings and stepsiblings. It should be remembered that these family networks are neither abnormal nor unusual and it is important for children to understand this.[50]

Ryan and Walker go on to describe a family network as follows:

> Pete and Mary married in May 1980. Pete became Wayne's stepfather, Pete and Mary had two children, Lisa and Alan. Mary told Wayne that Lisa and Alan were his 'half' brother and sister. Annie and Cheryl were Lisa and Alan's half-sisters and Wayne's stepsisters.[51]

The model is then illustrated to indicate complicated family ties, showing circles that overlap each other to help a child understand how the family network developed. The underlying precept of 'half-sibling' becomes a value-based supposition within social work practice that is manifested where contact arrangements with 'half-siblings' may be viewed as less important than those with 'full siblings'. In my experience, and that of many other professionals working in the field of childcare, neither these concepts nor these assumptions reflect the reality of Black children. Thus, the ethnocentric worldview constructs a 'universalism' of social work practice and imposes a value system and construct which compromises the psychological well-being of Black children.

For the same reason, the therapeutic tool of the ecomap does not capture the reality of Black families or of the network of cousins and other family members beyond the 'extended family'. This more complex picture of families which includes members who are not biologically related, is reflected in developing African-centred designs for social work practice where there is an emphasis on being part of a group, spiritually as well as physically, as an essential ingredient of identity. The failure of the social work profession to comprehend this critical proposition is one of the reasons why Black professionals and the Black community were so vociferously opposed to the one-way traffic of transracial placements. The children were considered a loss to the whole community, not just physically but as a loss felt spiritually by the collective, the whole community, worldwide.

African-centred worldviews regard children as the collective responsibility of the community. The African proverb "it takes a village to raise a child" expresses the view that child-rearing is a collective responsibility, rather than falling on individual nuclear families. Children are highly valued in general, as 'of the community' and they therefore cannot be deemed illegitimate.[52]

ONENESS OF MIND, BODY AND SPIRIT AND THE VALUE OF INTERPERSONAL RELATIONSHIPS

There is no division between mind, body and spirit in the African-centred paradigm. They are each given equal value and are believed to be interrelated.[53] The development and knowledge of self, mind, body and spirit are the hallmark of human objectives to seek divinity through Ma'at (truth, justice, righteousness, harmony, balance, order, propriety, compassion and reciprocity) within the self and through reaching a state of optimal health.[54] To promote personhood, optimal health requires optimal emotional health, physical health, intellectual health and spiritual health. It can be attained by achieving harmony with the forces of life. As King explains, "being in harmony with life means that one is living with life – co-operating with natural forces that influence events and experiences while simultaneously taking responsibility for one's life by consciously choosing and negotiating the direction and paths one will follow."[55] Linda Myers writes, "once we realise who we are, we understand that the process of learning more about ourselves becomes who we are, and external knowledge, per se, loses meaning."[56]

African-centred worldviews include the concept of balance. The task of all living things is to maintain balance in the face of adverse external forces. When this inner peace is compromised, the psychological, social and physical well-being of a person is threatened. These attributes that underlie African-centred worldviews promote humanitarian values that are in accord with the core principles of social work. African-centred worldviews offer the opportunity to develop social work designs that are pro-active rather than being reactively bound by the limitations of an ethnocentric knowledge-base. This approach generates empowerment, growth, transformation and development as cultural antecedents, and lived experiences are placed at the centre of analysis. As Karenga maintains:

> Afrocentricity is both particularistic and universalistic; it speaks to the specific liberation needs of people of African descent and to the spiritual and moral development of the world.[57]

THE CONTOURS OF AFROCENTRIC SOCIAL WORK
Afrocentric worldviews emphasise interdependence, spirituality and collectivity as the basis of social work theory and practice that stands in opposition to Western individualist models of humanity that emphasise fragmentation, materialism and conflict.[58]

Schiele discusses several methods of Afrocentric social work that can be utilised in attempts to solve problems associated with oppression and spiritual alienation.[59] First, existing social work models place emphasis upon epistemology that reflects a materialist view of reality. Ways of knowing are based upon the fives senses, which de-emphasises the non-material or metaphysical impact on human behaviour and functioning. This perspective supports a proclivity towards self-worth based upon external criteria (i.e. material objects, prestige and status concerns, looks and so on) that becomes more important than concerns about the quality of interpersonal relationships and the collective well-being of people.

Linda Myers considers this worldview has a tendency towards sub-optimal thinking where fragmentation and segmentation characterise not only realities but also people and genders.[60] This fragmented view promotes difference that manifests to justify the exclusion and oppression of people. Optimal thinking on the other hand is derived from a worldview that promotes holistic thinking and spiritual development. The key values of life, self-worth and happiness are gained from within rather than an emphasis upon external materialism. In addition, there is an emphasis upon how opposites are complimentary and differences being interdependent rather than at conflict. Afrocentric social work seeks to transform people from sub-optimal thinking to optimal thinking.

Second, Afrocentric social work considers that political, social and economic oppression is predicated upon cultural oppression and seeks to strive for equal affirmation and equal contribution of the various groups in society to produce a multicultural society without hegemony. This model advocates cultural inclusion within social work knowledge so that the contributions of all groups and their sources of knowledge are validated.

In addition, this model advocates that there are elements within cultural systems that can be utilised to empower communities. Therefore, it is important not only to identify and build upon these 'strengths' but support and enhance the need for communities to institutionalise their cultural values beyond the scope of family and friends. Schiele asserts the right to self-determination and institutional development:

> ... is nothing more than the formalisation and institutionalisation of a group's values and its political interests by establishing organisations, controlled by that group, that speak to and integrate those values and that promote that group's interests.[61]

Rites of passage programmes have emerged as an important theoretical and practice model of Afrocentric social work. These programmes within Black organisations in the UK and the US have established a network of institutional practices that support individuals, families and the regeneration of communities.[62] Many rites of passage programmes have focused upon the period of adolescence and the culturally specific needs of young Black people.

For most young Black people, the period of adolescence is characterised by experiences of institutional and cultural racism that permeates every aspect of British society. Consequently, many young people are left floundering or embrace 'popular' culture that presents, at best, only a loose and segmented response to the problems they face. Elders and responsible adults have recognised the need for an orderly process of maturation to nurture and develop the physical, intellectual, emotional, spiritual and social needs of young Black people. Historically, this was provided through ritual and ceremony and gave a sense of self, who they were, where they were from, and a sense of their own destiny. This was a time to experience the hidden dimensions of life as each stage was distinguished, and carried with it special meaning for the community and the individual.[63]

Traditionally, elders took a major role in the education and socialisation of young children affirming the adage "wisdom embraces knowledge". They provided the linchpin for generations comprised of adults, children and ancestors to secure the forward flow community life.[64] Diallo and Hall also consider the features of elderhood that contributed to the maintenance and forward flow of community:

> Grandparents form the circle of elders. They represent the world of knowledge and constitute the supreme council of the village. To avoid the anger of the ancestors, with whom they can communicate through rituals and divination, they are supposed to know all the prohibitions and how to remedy any violations of a social taboo. They are wise and move thoughtfully. They are walking books of know how.[65]

African-centred rites of passage offer a positive development paradigm drawing upon cultural value systems inherent within Afrocentric worldviews. African-centred rites of passage are characterised by stages of separation and reintegration into the community. The process of separation from the community offers the opportunity to affirm Black existence through patterns of interpreting realities outside of Eurocentric life models that mostly place Black people within the consciousness of oppression. Afrocentric worldviews view life as a journey – a series of passages characterised by a continuous expansion, in which the physical body, the mind and the consciousness are continually opening and widening. The revival of rites of passage constitutes the reclamation of the best of Africa to provide the contours for a life paradigm adapted for modern society in which harmonious development on a personal, communal and spiritual level can take place.

The rites of passage programme translates the principles enshrined within the African-centred value system through the seven principles of Nugzo Saba,[66] or the cardinal virtues enshrined in Ma'at, the central social philosophical principle of Ancient Egypt, Kemet, both encapsulating the cultural foundations of African thought. The rites of passage programmes provide an opportunity to rediscover and re-establish 'the way' as the basis for a paradigm that places cultural foundations at the centre of its methodology to serve as the basis for the development and psychological well-being of young Black people.

EXPLORING HIDDEN HISTORIES IN SOCIAL WELFARE

Mainstream social work presents an ahistorical approach to the nature of helping, whereas Afrocentric social work, on the other hand, considers the importance of historical connectedness in understanding and solving contemporary problems. This paradigm seeks to reclaim the wisdom and sacred traditions and invaluable helping processes that are grounded within cultural antecedents. I have reclaimed a history of social welfare originating in pre-colonial, ancient Africa to the experience of enslavement and the continuity of presence to the re-establishment of Black communities in post-war Britain.[67] The African heritage in the development of social welfare can be found deep in the recesses of British history and immersed within the layers of welfare ideology characterised by the hierarchical bonds of class, gender and race. The African presence during the 18th and 19th centuries provides a unique opportunity to explore social welfare among a group of people endeavouring to improve their lives starting from a baseline of enslavement and servitude.

Contrary to popular belief, African people – men, women and children – were enslaved in Britain, bought and sold as chattels or commodities, a fact validated by numerous advertisements of the period.[68] The growing African community in London during the 1700s consisted of enslaved and some 'free' African people. The historian, Folarin Shyllon notes that until 1772, most African people were enslaved except for some 'free' African people who evaded recapture.[69] The population of African people was estimated to be in the region of ten to fifteen thousand.[70] According to Michael Banton, towards the end of the 18th century, two per cent of the population were people of African descent.[71]

The enslaved African people brought with them a cultural value system based upon African social philosophy. The unfolding of 'hidden histories' of African-descended people and social welfare, reveals a legacy of Black helping processes that comprise of solidarity, mutuality, collective responsibility, spirituality, and reciprocity and community personhood.[72] The context and source of African solidarity was inextricably bound up in, and expressed within, the resistance and self-emancipation of the African community.

During the 18th century, for example, a group of African men calling themselves the 'sons of Africa', set about planning ongoing resistance through mobilising the African community and establishing political and social gatherings. They were at the forefront of the struggle for the abolition of enslavement in Britain during the 1700s, affirming African humanity and solidarity amid the ravages of deep-seated racism, enslavement and destitution. Moreover, the establishment of clubs to support those who are 'out of place' (the term 'out of place' refers to those without employment, probably enslaved African people who had 'run away') offered support, assistance and sustenance providing evidence of a high level of solidarity and mutuality.[73]

Afrocentric social work establishes the historical connections that bind people of African descent to an African heritage in social welfare. In British society today, the institutionalisation of Black helping processes are apparent within the activities of many diverse Black organisations, from the Black churches to Pan African groups. These organisations vary significantly in the internalisation and demonstration of the cultural ethos of traditional African societies. In addition, the acceptance and pride in Africa as an ancestral homeland.[74]

Nevertheless, in spite of the imposition of European cultural values, they have held onto some of those values and patterns of behaviour apparent within the practice modalities of their communal activities. These helping skills and support translate into the affirmation of African cultural systems that emphasise a communal standpoint. Moreover, these cultural forms of mutual help continue to play an important part in the lives of many Black families and communities. Afrocentric social work seeks to make effective use of cultural history in understanding how Black people have sought to solve problems. In addition, it seeks to examine the long tradition of protest to explore its modalities to effect social change.

CONCLUSION

There has been a renewed debate over the past few years about the efficacy of traditional social work practice models in working with Black families and children. The existing tools for social work practice are grounded within ethnocentric epistemologies and, as the foundation for social work theory and practice, are ill-equipped to serve the needs of Black families. This is evident, for example, in the sustained over-representation of Black children in the care system and in the lack of supportive social work services designed to meet their needs.

The existing parameters of anti-racist and ethnic sensitive social work do not adequately challenge hegemony within social work knowledge itself. Thereby, this incongruity serves to support a hidden source of cultural oppression by negating the legitimacy of alternative worldviews as the bases for social work theory and practice. The expansion of the conceptual framework of social work to include African-centred worldviews, provides the vehicle for dismantling cultural oppression to ensure the profession's participation in social justice and equality. Moreover, the development of Afrocentric social work represents a paradigm shift that reaffirms African-centred worldviews, which have been suppressed or denied within Eurocentric frameworks. This perspective assists social workers to view social work in broader terms involving the contribution of Black people to social welfare and social work and the emancipatory aspects of the profession and its role in social change for a new millennium.

NOTES AND REFERENCES

1. I use the terms African and Black interchangeably to refer to all peoples who trace some ancestral and cultural affinity to continental Africa (i.e. peoples of African descent and all those who define themselves as Black/African). Also, this chapter is based upon an article which appeared in the *British Journal of Social Work*, (1999) 'The African centred worldview – developing a paradigm for social work', 29, 2, pp. 251-267.

2. See Lambert, L. and Rowe, J. *Children Who Wait* (London: British Agencies for Adoption and Fostering, 1982); Skellington, R. and Morris P. *Race in Modern Britain Today* (Newbury Park, CA: Sage, 1992); Barn, R. *Black Children in the Public Care System* (London: Batsford, 1993); Clarke, P., Harrison, M., Patel, K., Shah, M., Varley, M., and Zack-Williams, T. *Improving Mental Health Practice*, (Leeds, UK: CCETSW, 1993); Roys, P. 'Social Services', in Bhat, A., Carr-Hill, R. and Ohri, S. (eds.), *Britain's Black Population, 2nd ed.*, (Aldershot: Ashgate Publishing, 1993).

3. Harris, V. 'Values of social work in the context of British society in conflict with anti-racism', CD Project Steering Group (eds.), *Setting the Context for Change*, (London: CCETSW 1991).

4. Association of Black Social Workers and Allied Professions. *Black Children in Care: Evidence to the House of Commons Social Services Committee*, (London: ABSWAP, 1983).

5. See Lambert, L. and Rowe, J. *Children Who Wait...* (note 2); Rowe, J., Hundleby, M. and Garnett, L. *Child Care Now* (BAAF Research Series 6, London: British Agencies for Adoption and Fostering, 1989); Barn, R. *Black Children in Public Care... (note 2)*; Barn, R., Sinclair, R. and Ferdinand, D. *Acting on Principle: an Examination of Race and Ethnicity in Social Services Provision for Children and Families* (London: British Agencies for Adoption and Fostering, 1997).

6. Mercer, K. 'Black communities experience of psychiatric services' in *International Journal of Social Psychiatry* 30(1/2) (1984) pp. 22-7.

7. See Dominelli, L. *Anti-racist Social Work* (Basingstoke: Macmillan, 1988); and, Ahmad, B. *Black Perspectives in Social Work* (Birmingham, UK: Venture Press, 1990).

8.   See: Akbar, N. 'Our destiny: Authors of a scientific revolution'
     in McAdoo, H. and McAdoo, J. (eds.) *Black Children: Social
     Psychological and Educational Environments* (Newbury Park,
     CA: Sage Publications, 1985); Nobles, W. *Africanity and the
     Black Family* (Oakland, CA: Black Family Institute Publications
     1985); Baldwin, J. 'The psychology of oppression' in Asante,
     M. and Vandi A. (eds.) *Contemporary Black Thought: Alternative
     Analyses in Social and Behavioural Science* (Newbury Park,
     CA: Sage Publications, 1980); Asante, M. *The Afrocentric Idea*
     (Philadelphia: Temple University Press, 1987); Schiele, J. (1994)
     'Afrocentricity as an alternative worldview for equality' in
     Journal of Progressive Human Services 5(1) pp. 5-25.

9.   Dominelli, L. *Anti-Racist Social Work... (note* 7); Thompson,
     N. *Anti-Discriminatory Practice* (Basingstoke: Macmillan
     1993); Ahmad, B. *Black Perspectives in Social Work...* (note 7).

10. Lorde, A. *Sister Outsider* (New York: The Crossing Press, 1984)
     p. 115.

11. Schiele, J. (note 8); and Thompson, N. (note 9).

12. Karenga, M. *Kwanzaa: A Celebration of Family, Community
     and Culture* (Los Angeles, CA: University of Sankore Press,
     1997) p. 34.

13. Devore, W. and Schlesinger, E. G. *Ethnic-Sensitive Social Work
     Practice* (New York: Macmillan 1991).

14. Turner, F. J. 'Theory in social work practice' in Turner, F. J. (ed.)
     Social Work Treatment (New York: The Free Press, 1986) p. 2.

15. Karenga, M. *Kwanzaa* (note 12).

16. Asante, M. (1987, note 8) p. 165.

17. Schiele, J. 'The contour and meaning of Afrocentric social work'
     in *Journal of Black Studies*, 27(6) (1997) p. 803.

18. Sacco, T. 'Towards an inclusive paradigm for social work' in
     Doel, M. & Shardlow, S. (eds.) *Social Work in a Changing World*
     (Hampshire: Arena/Ashgate Publishing 1996).

19. Nobles, W. & Goddard, L. 'Black family life: a theoretical and
     policy implication literature review' in Harvey, A. R. (ed.) *The
     Black Family: An Afrocentric Perspective* (New York: United
     Church of Christ Commission for Racial Justice 1985) p. 27.

20. Banks, S. *Ethics and Values in Social Work* (Basingstoke,
     Macmillan, 1995); and Schiele, J. (1994, note 8).

21.   Weick, A. 'Reconceptualising the philosophical perspective of social work' in *Social Service Review* 61(2)(1987) pp. 218-230.

22.   Ibid. p. 226.

23.   Morrison, T. *Playing in the Dark: Whiteness and the Literary Imagination* (Massachusetts: Havard University Press, 1992) p. 52.

24.   Bryan B, Dadzie S and Scafe S. *The Heart of the Race: Black Women's Lives in Britain* (London: Virago, 1985) p. 183.

25.   Ibid.

26.   Diop, C. *The Cultural Unity of Black Africa* (Chicago: Third World Press, 1978); Hilliard, A. 'Kemetic concepts in education' in *Journal of African Civilisations* 6(2)(1985) pp. 133–53; Williams, C. *The Destruction of Black Civilisations: Great Issues of a Race from 4500 BC to 2000 AD* (Chicago: Third World Press, 1987); Asante, M. *Afrocentricity: The Theory of Social Change*, (Trenton, NJ: Africa World Press, 1988); Abarry, A. and Asante, M. *African Intellectual Heritage: a Book of Sources* (Philadelphia, Temple University Press, 1995).

27.   Mbiti, J. *African Religions and Philosophy* (Garden City, NY: Anchor Books, 1970).

28.   Asante, M. (1988, note 26); Diop, C. (1978, note 26); Nobles, W. (1985, note 8); and Myers, L. *Understanding an Afrocentric World View: Introduction to Optimal Psychology* (Dubuque, I.A: Kendall, 1988).

29.   Herskovitz, M. J. *The Myth of the Negro Past* (Boston: Beacon Press, 1958); Asante, M. (1988, note 26); Nobles, W. 'African philosophy: foundations for black psychology' in Jones, R. (ed.) *Black Psychology* (New York: Harper & Row, 1980).

30.   Herskovitz, M. Ibid.; Mbiti, J. (1970, note 27); Schiele, J. (1994, note 8).

31.   bell hooks cited in Swigonski, M. 'Challenging privilege through Africentric social work practice' in *Social Work* 41 (2)(1996) p. 157.

32.   West, C. 'Black culture and post-modernism' in Kruger, B. and Mariani, P. *Remaking History* (Dia Art Foundation, Seattle: Bay Press, 1989) pp. 91-92.

33.   Scheurich, J. & Young, M. 'Colouring epistemologies: are our research epistemologies racially biased?' in *Educational Researcher* 26 (4) (1997) p. 10.

34. Hill-Collins, P. *Black Feminist Thought* (London: Routledge, 1991) p. 201.

35. See: Akbar, N. 'Rhythmic patterns in African personality' in King, L., Dixon V. and Nobles W. (eds.) *African Philosophy: Assumptions and Paradigms for Research on Black People* (Los Angeles, CA: Fanon Research Development Center, 1976); Myers, L. (1988, note 28); Asante, M. Kemet, *Afrocentricity and Knowledge*, (Trenton, NJ: Africa World Press, 1990); Schiele, J. (1997, note 17).

36. Mbiti, J. (1970, note 27); Nobles, W. (1985, note 8).

37. Asante, M. (1990, note 35).

38. Akbar, N. (1976, note 35) p. 176.

39. Myers, L. (1988, note 28) p. 24.

40. Schiele, J. (1994, note 8) p. 18.

41. Mbiti, J. (1970, note 27) p. 141.

42. Verharen, C. 'Afrocentrism and acentrism: a marriage of science and philosophy' in *Journal of Black Studies* 26(1) (1995) p. 65.

43. Schiele, J. 'Afrocentricity: an emerging paradigm in social work practice' *Social Work* 41 (3) (May 1996) pp. 284-294.

44. Karenga, M. (1997, note 12) p. 37.

45. Myers, L. (1988, note 28).

46. Mbiti, J. (1970, note 27) p. 141.

47. Ibid.

48. See, T'Shaka, O. *Return to the African Mother Principle of Male and Female Equality, Vol 1*, (CA: Pan African Publishers 1995). The author maintains that 'twinlineal' is a new term for African families. It is defined as African family lineages that come from the mother and father rather than only the mother or father as in matrilineal and patrilineal family systems.

49. Akbar, N. (1976, note 35).

50. Ryan, T. and Walker, R. *Life Story Work* (London: British Agencies for Adoption and Fostering, 1993) p. 28.

51. Ibid.

52. Suda, C. 'Street children in Nairobi and the African cultural ideology of kin-based support system: change and challenge' in Child Abuse Review 6(3) (1997) pp. 199–217.

53. Mbiti, J. (1970, note 27).

54. Chissell, J. *Pyramids of Power! An Ancient African Centred*

Guide to Optimal Health, PO Box 31509, Baltimore MD, 21207–8509, (USA: Positive Perceptions, 1994).

55.   King, A. E. 'An Afrocentric cultural awareness program for incarcerated African-American males' in *Journal of Multicultural Social Work* 3(4) (1994) p. 20.

56.   Myers, L. (1988, note 28) p. 20.

57.   Karenga, M. *Introduction to Black Studies, 2nd edition*, (Los Angeles, CA: University of Sankore Press, 1993) p. 36.

58.   See, Schiele, J. (1994, note 8); Asante, M. (1990, note 35); Akbar, N. 'Africentric social sciences for human liberation' in *Journal of Black Studies* 14 (4) (1984) pp. 395-414.

59.   Schiele, J. (1997, note 17).

60.   Myers, L. (1988, note 28).

61.   Schiele, J. (1997, note 17) p. 813.

62.   Graham, M. 'Exploring Black Families: Rites of Passage' (Unpublished practice report, 1987); Graham, M. 'The African centred worldview: developing a paradigm for social work' in *British Journal of Social Work* 29, (2) (1999) pp. 252-267; Hill, P. *Coming of Age: African American Male Rites of Passage* (Chicago: African Images, 1992); Obonna, P. Education of the Black Child Conferences, Rites of Passage Programmes (Manchester, UK: Kemetic Guidance Group, 1996).

63.   Hill, P. Ibid.

64.   Wilcox, D. *The Rites of Passage for African American Youth: Perspectives of Eight Elders* (Unpublished PhD Thesis: Kent State University, Ohio, USA, 1998).

65.   Diallo, Y. and Hall, M. *The Healing Drum: African Wisdom Teachings*, (VT: Destiny Books, 1989) p. 44.

66.   Karenga, M. *Kwanzaa, Origin, Concepts Practice* (Los Angeles, CA: Kawaida Publications, 1977); Perkins, U. *Harvesting the New Generations* (Chicago: Third World Press, 1985).

67.   Graham, M. (2001) The 'miseducation' of black children in the British educational system - towards an African-centred orientation to knowledge in Majors R. (Ed) *Educating our Black Children, New Directions and Radical Approaches*, London, Routledge. See, Graham, M. *Social Work and African-centred worldviews*, (Birmingham, UK, BASW, Venture Press, 2001).

68.   See, Christian, M. 'An African Centred Approach to the Black

British Experience' in *Journal of Black Studies* 28 (3) (January 1998) pp. 291-308; Lorimer, D. 'Black resistance to slavery and racism in eighteenth century England' in (eds) Gundasra, J. & Duffield, I., *Essays on the History of Blacks in Britain* (Ashgate Publishers, 1992); Shyllon, F. *Black People in Britain* 1555-1833 (London: Institute of Race Relations: Oxford University Press, 1977); Fryer, P. *Staying Power: The History of Black People in Britain*, (London: Pluto Press, 1984).

69. Shyllon, F. Ibid.
70. Shyllon, F. *Black Slaves in Britain* (London: Institute of Race Relations, Oxford University Press, 1974).
71. Banton, M. *Racial Minorities* (London: Fontana, 1972).
72. Dei, G. 'Afrocentricity: a cornerstone of pedagogy', *Anthropology and Education Quarterly*, 25 (1) (1994) pp. 3-28.
73. Fryer, P. (1984, note 68) p. 70.
74. Schiele, J. (1997, note 17).

PART III

Nuances in Shades of Black Markers

Chapter Eight

BLACK PEOPLE OF MIXED ORIGINS AND THE POLITICS OF IDENTITY

Stephen Small

THERE IS A scene in the middle of the Spike Lee film, *Get On The Bus* (1996), in which two Black guys, one apparently of mixed racial heritage, one presumably 'unmixed', cross swords on the issue of slavery and preferential treatment for 'mixed-race' people.[1] The unmixed one (nicknamed 'Hollywood' because he is an actor), tells the mixed one (Gary) that he must know what the white bus driver is thinking because the two of them, he says, "share a white thing!". A heartfelt renunciation of 'the white thing' follows, and he maintains he is Black. After an intervention by another passenger who says, "the man's Black", and if this were slavery "old master" wouldn't care if he were 'half white', Hollywood explodes:

> "He would be a house slave pimping round the big house, while the rest of us would be talking about grits . . . this fool would be salting potatoes; he would have the best of chicken, we would have the neck bones, our women would be all blistered up and stinking from picking cotton, his would be all bathed, smelling good, and nine times out of ten the honey he would be hitting skins with . . . she would be a white girl."

Gary retorts, "my lady is not white" and accuses Hollywood of wanting to sleep with a white woman himself. The tension passes, for the moment. Similar portrayals have appeared in other films about slavery in which men and women of mixed origins supposedly received favourable treatment, especially from their white fathers. A particularly interesting example is *Sankofa*, a progressive film that explores the complexities of slavery in the United States, including rape, in empathetic and insightful ways, and yet manages to reproduce all the derogatory stereotypes of Black people of mixed origins. In *Sankofa*, Joe, the 'mulatto', is the product of rape; he idolises and embraces white culture in the form of an excessive devotion to Christianity, deprecates all things African, and makes a libidinal fetish of the Virgin Mary, while refusing to sleep with a dark-skinned woman. Poor Joe despises his African mother, whom he eventually kills. Films that speak to the Caribbean, to Central and South America, and South Africa, reflect similar kinds of issues – preference and privilege, the process of Blancamiento (the whiter your skin, the better your life chances), betrayal and treachery, during slavery and since then.[2] And if the history of Black people of mixed origins in England offers so much evidence that contradicts the stereotype – victimisation, tragedies, atrocities, despicable experiences – so much the better that it is ignored.[3] In contexts across the length and breadth of the African Diaspora, these issues rebound and reiterate themselves, as so many chapters in this book attest.

Most of these issues, especially in film, we might argue, are not fact, truth or evidence, but stereotype, myth and impressions. We cannot expect films to tell us 'the truth', nor do we unreflectively act on what they do tell us. In *Get On The Bus*, the character, 'Hollywood' does not know the facts, and it is suggested that he will never be bothered to find them out. Why should he? He has more pressing concerns, more pressing needs, in the here and now. Moreover, most Black people today have more pressing needs and interests than to spend their time in the tedious labour of uncovering historical fact. But it is also clear that in the United States and Britain, these images continue to shape attitudes and behaviours, especially in the Black community. We should expect academic literature to, at least, provide interpretations that can be supported by evidence. With few exceptions, however, academic literature reinforces such notions.[4] For example, of the legally free Black people of mixed origins in Jamaica, we are told, "Toward the whites they were humble; toward the blacks, contemptuous; towards their own slaves, brutal. The brown population identified with the European side of its ancestry and abjured the African side." We can also learn that enslaved "mulatto and quadroon women were brought into the shade of the great house to perform domestic tasks, while their Black sisters, whether weak or strong, toiled in the fields." And that more generally, Black people of mixed origins achieved their goals on the backs of Black people.[5] Why did this happen? Because whites were outnumbered by enslaved people of African origin and created a class of 'free mulattoes' as a buffer group; because Black people of mixed origins had rich white fathers who gave them preference; and because white men preferred 'half breed' women to 'pure Blacks', for purposes of sex and pleasure.[6]

Any attempt to come to terms with what is usually called 'race mixture' and the question of Black identity requires us to engage in a critical analysis of the history of the European encounter with Africa and Africans. We need information about the complex matrix of racialised formations in the history of European colonialism and slavery, as well as the machinations of identity formation in the Black community. And we need to think about the kinds of images used to portray Black people of mixed origins and their parents – both historically and today. As burdensome as this appears, much progress can be made by those who want to make the first steps. In this chapter, I address the identity of Black people of mixed origins in the twentieth century. In doing so, I am concerned, particularly, with the politics of that identity, the responsibilities presumed to go with Black identity, as they relate to Black people of mixed origins. But this can only be achieved by first taking issue with the images and by revisiting a history which dances like a lively corpse in the lives of the living each day.[7]

THE HISTORICAL BACKGROUND

I want to address three of the stereotypes portrayed in *Get On The Bus*; that Black people of mixed origins have always received preference from whites over Black people presumed to be unmixed; that we are 'sell-outs'; and that most of us do not see ourselves as Black. The first notion arises from the belief that during and beyond slavery, the children of white master-enslavers got preferential treatment, and have used it to their advantage and to the detriment of Black people (of presumed unmixed origins).[8] That they were treated better than Black people, enjoyed preferential job allocations, being kept out of jobs that were laborious, tedious or unhealthy, and channelled into work that was desired or advantageous; that they enjoyed better living standards (such as lower mortality rates), acquired better material goods (food, clothing and medicine) and had a higher social status in the eyes of white people. They were also more likely to access legal freedom. This was particularly the case if they were the children, or the sexual partners, of white master-enslavers.

Most evidence supporting such views comes from official records on enslavement and legal freedom, and from the observations of whites. This is why, in the social imagination, the majority of house servants were Black people of mixed origins, that most Black people of mixed origins were house servants, and that most Black people of mixed origins escaped slavery into legal freedom. It is also why we continue to believe that after slavery they consolidated the advantages they had already enjoyed, took all the powerful positions over Black people, relentlessly vilifying and oppressing them and imitating white culture and values. It is for these reasons that enslaved Black people often held them in fear and/or contempt, and why Edward Wilmot Blyden (the father of Pan-Africanism) and Marcus Garvey, wanted no Black people of mixed origins to accompany them in the repatriation of African Americans to Africa.

However, substantial evidence indicates that these impressions are exaggerated and distorted, and that they harbour many silences. In fact, Black people of mixed origins only enjoyed advantages in certain circumstances – where they had a wealthy white father, where they were outnumbered by Black people and could be given the best jobs, and where white stereotypes operated (for example, that they could not work in the heat of the sun like Black people). Indeed, most Black people of mixed origins had no white father, or if they had one, he was poor; most house servants were not of mixed origins; most Black people of mixed origins were not house servants, and most Black people of mixed origins remained in slavery all of their lives.

In Jamaica, at the start of the nineteenth century, there were 312,000 enslaved people of whom about ten per cent were of mixed origins. It is estimated that about 58 per cent of enslaved people of mixed origins had a white father, which means that around 18,000 had white fathers, but 13,200 had none (their fathers were Black, or Black of mixed origins, and were usually enslaved themselves).[9] Besides, the majority of white men on the island were poor and most of them went from plantation to plantation, raping Black women, and abandoning them and their children. Most whites did not free their mixed children – between 1829 and 1832, at least two thousand children of mixed origins were born enslaved; at the same time, only 796 of them were legally freed.[10] This is also clear from the aggregate figures – in 1832 there were over thirty thousand Black people of mixed origins, enslaved, and about 24,000 legally free. So while significant numbers enjoyed legal freedom, the majority remained enslaved. While Black people of mixed origins occupied many house jobs, they were outnumbered, nine to one, by Black people who occupied the majority of house jobs. Consequently, many of them found themselves in the fields. As Edward Long pointed out: "And as for the lower rank, the issue of casual fruition, they, for the most part, remain in the same slavish condition as their mother; they are fellow-labourers with the blacks, and are not regarded in the least as their superiors."[11] On top of all this, if these white men had a white wife, she was usually openly vindictive towards both the women and the children, punishing them, torturing them, and even selling them.

If Black people of mixed origins enjoyed some advantages, they also faced unique difficulties. White men did not rape women at random, they chose those that were young, and whom they found sexually desirable. White men were more inclined to rape women of mixed origins. Nor does it stop there, as certain unique atrocities were reserved for Black women of mixed origins, including incest. White men raped Black women, and then raped their own daughters by these women. This theme has been more common in novels and poems than in social scientific and historical research, but there is some evidence.[12] In these circumstances, there is little doubt that it was Black people that offered emotional support to the victims of these atrocities.

Sharing common circumstances, and a common kinship, Black people, and Black people of mixed origins, often worked together, as in one of the most famous cases of fugitives from slavery, the Ellen and William Craft story. Ellen Craft had a phenotype that enabled her to pass for white, while William had a physical appearance that clearly identified him as an African. They escaped by her posing as a white man, wearing a scarf to hide her face, pretending she had pneumonia so she did not have to talk, and placing her arm in a sling so she would not have to write (she was illiterate). With William posing as her man-servant, they boarded a train in Georgia, escaped to Boston and on to England, lecturing in Liverpool, and publishing their tale, *Running a Thousand Miles to Freedom*. Nor was this unique; Black people and Black people of mixed origins in Savannah worked together with common circumstances and priorities, and goals prevailed.[13] Neither Frederick Douglass nor Booker T. Washington got any social privileges from their white fathers, each worked tirelessly to promote Black community interests, while Douglass described some of the sexual violence targeted against light-skinned women. Even in San Domingo, while many Black people of mixed origins fought with the French, still others fought alongside Toussaint L'Ouverture.

After the enslavement era in the US, common circumstances and common priorities again led to collective activities. Many Black people of mixed origins, that could have passed for white, stridently rejected that option. In Georgia, the Hunts were a prominent family of mixed origins, leaders in the Black community, especially after the Civil War, and had extensive relations with whites. Several, including Henry Hunt, were associates of the renowned 'mulatto', yet profoundly Black, W.E.B. Du Bois. Hunt opted for a Black identity rather than becoming "the white man that his skin colour and features so obviously declared him", suggested Du Bois. White racism was central here, but so too was the element of deliberate choice. The main reason for this choice 'responsibility and love' arose from kinship ties and ties to the Black community.[14]

Other African American intellects of the early twentieth century, Anna Julia Cooper, Mary Church Terrell, Charles Chestnutt and James Weldon Johnson, could all have passed for white but none chose to do so. So many of the prominent writers of the Harlem Renaissance were of mixed origins. Many thousands did, however, pass for white, but the majority, hundreds of thousands, continued to live their lives as they always had done, as an integral part of the Black communities in which they lived and loved.

Besides, whatever arguments might be made about unfettered privilege under slavery in what became the Americas, the same cannot be said about the United Kingdom. Historically, most Black people of mixed origins in Britain had Black fathers and white mothers, parents who were usually working class, poor and powerless. Both they, and their children were reviled and ostracised by whites.[15] There were no rich white fathers to confer advantages, no jobs specially reserved for them, no gifts heaped upon their Black mothers. Instead, it was a life of hardship and struggle, as it was for most working class whites, but exacerbated by prejudice, discrimination and stereotypes. Once again, it was in the Black community, including the white mothers that resided there, that such children found solace.

The second accusation is that Black people of mixed origins have usually put their own interests before those of the Black community, during slavery and since. That they used their 'advantageous' position to get food, jobs, education, political positions, to escape white violence, and stay out of jail. Who is going to deny this? Not me. Not if this meant that they helped themselves and their families. There is a certain tendency for people to look after their own interests, as they perceive them, and Black people of mixed origins are no exception.

Only someone guilty of an arrogant naivete would suggest that most people do otherwise. But while many Black people of mixed origins put themselves and their families first, it is easy to show that this is rubbish for the majority. Black people, and Black people of mixed origins, share far too much in common for it to be otherwise: family and kinship, economic and political predicaments, cultural values (religion and spirituality, language, music, and folklore) social denunciation and ostracism, shared visions and aspirations. The structures of white supremacy were central here, along with the continued vilification of those that share a common African heritage, and they continue to be crucial today.[16] If the impression is to the contrary, then the problem is with our impressions, and how they arose, which is to say, we need to re-investigate the historical record, posing questions that we think are important. Do not be surprised if it provides a very different outcome.

The third stereotype is that we do not see ourselves as Black. This is the litmus test. Once, while working at the *Weekly Journal* in London, I was asked whether I was really an academic or an activist. I said that I was both, an answer that made them uneasy. The issue here is how one is to identify oneself, and the presumption is that you have merely one identity. The issue is, what is it you stand for, and the assumption is that you stand primarily for one thing. The issue is also whether you respect me? And, finally, the issue is why should I not have what I think you have? (This is the issue for Hollywood in *Get On The Bus*). These questions are based on false assumptions that we only embrace one identity, and that both the identity and the responsibilities that arise from it are clear and unambiguous. This suggests a single Black identity, and a single white identity. Both are fleeting illusions. Do you think William Wilberforce and John Brown shared the same identity? Even though both had a commitment to abolition? Do you think Edward Long and Governor Eyre shared the same identity? Even though they shared a commitment to white supremacy? Similarly, do you think Nat Turner and David Walker shared the same identity? Even though they were committed to abolitionism, by any means necessary? What about Nanny and Harriet Tubman? Or Anna Julia Cooper and Ida B. Wells Barnett? Do you think Bernie Grant and Lord John Taylor share the same identity, or Baroness Amos and Linda Bellos? Even though they all proclaim to be fighting for equal opportunities? Little surprise, then, the Black people of mixed origins do not all share the same identity either. As I argue below, identity and what you do about it, for it, or because of it, depends on far more than racialised group membership; including kinship and family, community and nation, and the old, never to be escaped, contours of class, gender, religion and language.[17]

IMAGES AND DISCOURSES TODAY

Films are just one arena in which images about the experiences and attitudes of Black people of mixed origins (and their parents) are communicated. These images, the ways in which people talk about them, how they are discussed in the public realm, and thought about in the social imagination, are far more varied, far more complex today than in the past. No single image prevails, no single identity is promoted, and no single motivation can be specified. Instead, there is a range of institutions and organisations, that mention, highlight, or allude to these issues. And they do so for their own reasons. In both Britain and the United States it is possible to identify several social arenas in which ideas and images about Black people of mixed origins are in systematic ways. These include the media, romance and sex industries, the state (in particular the agencies responsible for the Census) and right wing groups.[18]

Images of Black people of mixed origins are prevalent in the media (including film, adverts, music, television, and literature), where the primary motivation is to sell goods and advertising space via the promotion of a youthful and/or affluent lifestyle. The most common image is simply one in which people from different racialised groups interact with one another, particularly in sexual and amorous ways. This is common in movies like *Wild Wild West*, where Will Smith and Salma Hayek flirt with one another; more complex images were presented in *Mona Lisa* and *The Crying Game*; and in music magazines like *Vibe* and *Jet* which celebrate marriages and dating across racialised groups including people like Robert De Niro, and his Black spouse, Grace Hightower (previously it was girlfriend Naomi Campbell and *The Sun* 'page three girl' Gillian De Terville).

In the romance and sex industry, including certain tabloid newspapers, raunchy novels and magazines, pornography, prostitution and sex tourism, images of innate, irrepressible sexuality are dominant.

Black men are represented as over-sexed and over-sized. Ready, willing, and able to perform like athletes. Black women are naturally lascivious – they do it because it is their nature to please, to serve, to deprave. They are mainly portrayed as prostitutes and sluts. This area stretches the whole gamut from sex toys such as Black vibrators, sex-for-sale cards that adorn the interiors of telephone booths across central London, sexual fantasy books, adverts in newspapers for sexual partners of a different colour and culture, and for prostitutes. Somewhat entangled in this arena was Hugh Grant's street manoeuvres in Los Angeles, in which a rich, white, desirable male, with a beautiful, intelligent, white girlfriend, just had to get the 'forbidden fruit' attributed to Black causality.

Seeking, particularly, to emulate the achievements of the 'Mixed Race Movement' in the United States, similar groups in Britain invoke the principles of freedom, equality and democracy to push for acknowledgement, respect, identity, and inclusion. Securing a 'mixed race' category in the Census is a major way to achieve this, and after that, other goals will follow. Seeking to prevent the achievements of the 'Mixed Race Movement' in the United States, are the various agencies of the State in Britain. Concerned with a cost-effectiveness, bureaucratic containment and holding back a tidal wave of infinitely expanding Census categories, the bureaucrats work through management, memos and meetings, to ensure that public service is done, and a Census is carried out, timely and economically. Extreme white groups express another discourse of 'race mixture' and this is the discourse of 'racial purity'. Once, when walking through Petticoat Lane Market in London, I came across a member of the British National Party (BNP) selling their newspaper with the loud refrain: "We do not all want to end up coffee coloured". Their press officer made their position clear that "mixed-race relationships" are "not a good idea", and that "they end up with half-caste children who do not fit in . . . a happy relationship is born out of relating to people who are the same as oneself".[19] Members of the BNP, and other groups, articulate opposition to 'race mixture' as the basic responsibility of good, decent (read white) British citizens. Here, good old-fashioned racism (biological truth, 'racial purity', and the avoidance of mongrelisation) motivates its supporters to seek the ascendancy of the white race, and the preservation of white civilisation. Using legal and illegal methods, pushing for laws to expel the 'alien' presence, and prevent copulations of this kind, along with the extermination of inferiors, white supremacy is a language of violence and terror.

While these trends are evident in both nations, they share much in common, though Britain continues to borrow more than it lends, they each have their own unique aspects. In the United States, the 'Mixed Race Movement' is far more prominent than it is in Britain, with organisations, magazines, student groups and the ephemeral prominence of Tiger Woods. Whereas in the UK, the incidence of sexual relationships and the numbers of people of mixed origins is one of the highest in the West, while the debate on trans-racial adoption has a far higher profile. Around 25 per cent of African Caribbean men, and 14 per cent of African Caribbean women who are married (or have a partner), have partners who are non-Black (compared to less than 3 per cent of African American men, and 2 per cent of African American women in the US).[20] Portrayals of prominent British 'mixed racial' couples such as Lenny Henry and Dawn French, Frank Bruno and his wife, remind the British public that such practices are common. And the disproportionate number of children of mixed origins in need of foster care and adoption, as reflected in the photographs which continue to shame the pages of the Black press, continues to fuel interminable debates about politicians and policy-makers, over the complexity of Black identity.

Consideration of these institutionalised idioms demonstrate that ideas about 'race mixture' remain central in both nations, continue to rely on notions that are long since outdated, and are articulated in relation to other ideologies, like individualism and free choice. This means far more diverse images circulate, that a greater array of motivations underlies them, and that far more options appear attainable. We can also expect far more diverse images to be promoted across Black Diasporic communities, including more accurate, realistic ones that reflect the variety of experiences and identities. This diverse array of images will be less stereotypical and restrictive in the long-run. But attitudes towards identity are not just shaped by impressions of history; today's social context, community dynamics, values and aspirations, along with personal experiences, are indispensable factors in the matrix of identity.[21]

THE PROCESS OF IDENTITY FORMATION

What does a Black identity mean? There is, of course, no single identity, and it is far from monolithic, as so many chapters in this book attest. Some of these chapters address many of the dynamics involved and highlight the diverse variables that go into the formation of a Black identity. While indicating the salience of skin colour and African ancestry, they also question the assumption that such an identity is ever 'pure', is ever based exclusively on something called 'race'. Collectively, they show that Black identity has many manifestations across the Diaspora, is shaped by diverse, even divergent factors and is never finally achieved. It is in a constant state of change. Nowhere is this more evident than in Britain, where people from India, Pakistan and Bangladesh often embrace a Black identity.[22] But let us restrict the discussion to people of African origin for our purposes here. I suspect that when people talk of Black identity it usually means to express through attitudes or behaviour and identification with people and cultures of African descent. This might be a Diaspora identity or it might be an African one. Nor is it uncontradictory – one might embrace a Black British or African American identity, and yet deride Africa or the Caribbean. There are, of course, important variations by gender.[23] Expressing interest in this way, is not uni-dimensional. I am sure Lord Taylor and the late Bernie Grant identified themselves as Black. So, too, Baroness Amos or Black Conservative councillors. And in the US, Louis Farrakhan, Al Sharpton and Jessie Jackson, along with Black women of opposite political extremes. Black organisations also reflect a variety of extremes from the National Association for the Advancement of Colored People (NAACP) to the Nation of Islam. So much that is left implicit becomes troublesome when you explore it further. To people in the community, expressing a Black identity might mean behaving in radical political ways. But it is not always clear, and the matter of who is to decide what a Black identity actually is, who is to adjudicate over what behaviour it might entail, is also far from clear at the dawn of a new millennium.

I regard 'Black', 'white' and 'Black of mixed origins' identities as examples of racialised identity, not 'racial' identities.[24] To say that a relationship or identity is 'racial' is to make it appear that this is a biological fact, and that it is the most important aspect of that fact. To say it is 'racialised' is to say that ideas and notions about race, including different racisms, are one aspect of that relationship or identity, and may not be the most important one. In the case of people of African origin, it is both the 'fact' of Blackness, as Fanon calls it, and the knowledge of African ancestry that have been the pre-eminent factors. My premise is that 'race' does not have an independent existence, that ideas about 'race' are only one issue that people draw on to construct their identity, and they are often not even the major issue. Other issues include class, gender and nation, along with ethnicity (including religion and language) and other aspects of culture. We can also add to this sexual orientation.

When most Black people came to Britain, they were invited not because of their Black heritage, but because their labour power was needed. When the lead character in the film *Mona Lisa* was a prostitute, with a lesbian orientation, the fact that she was a woman was central, more so than the 'fact' of her African ancestry. The same might be said about sexuality in *The Crying Game*. When John Taylor was made a Lord, it was in large part because of his political values, rather than the fact that he is Black. When Bob Marley was given the Medal of Honour, it was because he was of Jamaican origin, not because he was Black of mixed origin. When Nigerians and Kenyans, or Jamaicans and Barbadians, disagree over politics, or music, or religion, it is in large part because of their national and cultural upbringing rather than their Black identities. When conflict occurs between Somalis and so-called 'Liverpool-born Blacks', or Nigerians and 'Liverpool-born Blacks', it is often because of age, and issues around immigration and belonging, and perceptions of discipline and respect, rather than Black identity *per se*.[25]

Black people are attacked and abused, and discriminated against because they are Black. But if they live in Hampstead, rather than Clapham, they are more likely to be able to do something about it, and to get more attention. What this means is that racism, or ideas about race, might always be present, and might be the most decisive factors shaping a situation, especially where skin colour is the foremost indicator of African ancestry. But whether they are or not, cannot always be taken for granted, it must be proven so. I have outlined the theoretical and conceptual issues in far more detail elsewhere.[26] What many chapters in this book show is that African ancestry and skin colour remain decisive.

The important factors in the shaping of Black identity have been relatively consistent, even if the ways in which they interact, and the relative strength of each one for different individuals, usually varies. The research I did with young Black men in London in the 1980s, demonstrated that social experiences in Britain, along with language, music, dress, religion and expressed identification with the Caribbean, were indispensable to a Black identity. Gender and masculinity were indispensable. Recent studies indicate similar findings.[27] A central aspect is regional identity, where the general bias towards London becomes obvious.[28] Factors that shape Black identity in London operate in other cities, too, but do so in different ways. Which other city has a concept equivalent to 'Liverpool-born Black' asks Mark Christian?[29]

Yet we do not have to go to academics to find out about how Black identity is shaped, and what is expected of it. We can find that among Black organisations, in the Black press, television and among Black comedians. These are what might be called the cultural arbitrators of Black identity, that is, the public figures that observe, comment on, and urge what a Black identity might be. Buj'u Banton's 'Me love me car, me love me bike, me love me money and t'ing, but most of all me love me Browning!' says more to the shaping of identity in people's lives, than do fifty academic studies. In 1993-1994, I visited over thirty-five comedy shows across Britain, and undertook a number of interviews with Black professional comedians.[30] Through mockery, mimicry and commendations, they let Black people know how they are supposed to eat, drink, walk, talk and behave, including the music they should listen to, where they should live and who they should date. It is also clear what their political views should be. Pride in the Caribbean, in reggae and calypso, were key themes, respect for family, studying Black history, speaking Patois or Creole, dressing according to cultural codes, working for Black organisations and living in Black neighbourhoods, were all part of this package of Black identity. A positive Black identity also required people to work for or support Black community organisations, including Black businesses, and voting Labour. One aspect of this was hostility to dating across racialised groups. Ruth Harper, herself of mixed origins, said, "The only thing a white boy is good for, is to introduce me to a Black man." While Angie Le Mar commented on the nasty looks she gets while walking down a London street with a co-worker who happens to be a white man.

Identity formation for Black people of mixed origins follows similar vectors to identity formation for Black people (presumed to be unmixed), but can often become more convoluted. Some of the variables are more intricate, and there are other kinds of social pressures to take into account. Once again, context is critical, as Mark Christian has shown in his consideration of South Africa, Jamaica and Britain.[31] Partners and children in relationships that cross racialised group boundaries have to negotiate between both sets of families, and their opposition to the relationship; they have to circumvent stereotypes about the sexual motivations of Black men with white women, and what that says about Black men's attitudes towards Black women, often including their mothers; they have to negotiate how the white women in such relationships are seen as social outcasts at best, prostitutes usually, and the presumption that something must be wrong with them if they want a Black boyfriend.[32]

There are also the nasty names, the offensive stereotypes, the expectations that one must prove how Black you are; as in 'half-caste' and 'half-breed', the presumption of biological degeneracy, the questioning of your political commitment.[33] The history of Black people of mixed origins in Liverpool, and Britain's other seaports, provides sufficient evidence of the trauma that has frequently been an inescapable component of a mixed identity in Britain.[34] Enough people in Liverpool have hurtful experiences of travelling to Bootle, or Scotland Road, or Halewood (predominately white neighbourhoods) to meet white uncles and aunts to know that this is real. That these issues have persisted in recent decades is strikingly obvious, as 'Coffee Coloured Children' attests.[35] It is a creatively brilliant example of the vortex of racialised identity for people of mixed origins in Britain. Similarly, there are innumerable examples of the determination to prevail, to insist on one's priorities and, as I have said elsewhere, to refuse a victim mentality even if victimised.[36] It would be so easy if they could – as so many people have so effortlessly urged – simply be Black. But that is not the case, never has been, almost certainly never will be.

Which leaves the issue of transracial adoption. Adding yet another typhoon to the vortex of identity, is the matter of people of mixed origins who are transracially adopted. Given how important the variables that shape identity are, is it little surprise in British culture, that such folks are likely to live a far more turbulent adolescence, and face far more perplexing choices? The evidence is complex and far from clear. The almost despotic insistence of policy-makers, politicians and many academics that these children be given a 'free choice', reflects a naivete and arrogance that is only slightly less offensive than their claim that they are impartial and unbiased. Is it not just a little relevant that those white academics that piously preach this are, so frequently, the very same people who have adopted kids of mixed origins?[37] So much for impartiality. But this matter is far more complex than I can attend to here.

In 1991, I introduced the phrase 'Blacks of mixed origins' in place of nasty little terms like 'half-caste', 'quarter-cast', 'mixed-race', to name but a few.[38] I wanted to highlight what Black people of mixed origins and Black people (presumed to be unmixed) shared in common, while also recognising some of the distinctive problems which confront Black people of mixed origins. It was to suggest that the power of whites to define racialised identities was important, and their tendency to impose what they see as an inferior identity on people who are not 'milky white', was often the most decisive factor.[39] This is still largely true, but not exclusively. I want to continue with that concept. But to that analysis I would add that white impositions and power are no longer the pre-eminent factor, nor should we allow them to be so. As with Black identity formation there is more fluidity now for people to choose an identity. There is less pressure to choose Black, more options to choose an intermediate category (especially with so many more people of this status). Even if we continue to shape identity under the shadows of the continued vilification of Black people that is so pervasive in the British media, from *Eastenders* to *Brookside*, in books and advertisements, from *Little Black Sambo*, to the Robinson's jam jar 'gollywog'. The evidence from studies of young people of mixed origins in Britain shows a distinct trend towards choosing a mixed over a single identity.[40]

In addition, it is clear that white mothers have played a significant role, in particular, where they have become estranged from the Black father of their child. But there is also considerable evidence that many 'mixed' people are comfortable with a Black identity, prefer it, and embrace it ardently, and the city of Liverpool Black experience is just one prime example.[41] And, as is usual with academics and the press, we have far more research and testimony of the squeaking wheels that attract attention, with their own class bias towards the formally educated and professionals (for example, press headlines claiming that the former British athlete, Daley Thompson said that he is not Black) than we do on the majority that just live their daily lives. As Ifekwunigwe has pointed out, we still lack evidence on working class identities, and Christian has argued in relation to the city of Liverpool that there is a lack of evidence on the ways in which Black families shape identities.[42]

In these complex processes, kinship is an indispensable factor in the matrix that shapes identity. For Black people of mixed origins more so. Black family can be the focus of attacks, some times with good reason – especially domestic violence. But also it is in the family that we find the strengths and reinvigoration. Many studies show that the family is a major site that shapes identity, particularly for people of mixed origins, along with community, friends and media. Little surprise that kids raised with white mothers in all-white neighbourhoods, estranged from their Black fathers, and/or from other Black family members, might be ambivalent or openly hostile towards Black identity. Little surprise, too, that kids raised in a Black or mixed neighbourhood, with the Black and white parent present, and sustained contact with other Black family members, are less ambivalent. This means that Black people of mixed origins, like Black people, Asians, white people, in fact any social group, will continue to embrace a diversity of identities, cultural traits and political values. Let us accept that as a fact, and figure out how to get most of them, for that matter, most Black people and non-Black people, to embrace a sense of community that goes beyond the excesses of individualist selfishness.

BLACK MIXED ORIGINS AND
THE POLITICS OF IDENTITY

Identity and the attitudes and actions that follow from it, including socialising, community involvement and commitment, formal politics at the local, national and international level, and a whole array of responsibilities in other arenas, have always been central to the debate about who and what are people of mixed origins. In societies like Cuba and Haiti, Jamaica and Guyana, and in Brazil and Argentina, a particular politics has usually followed from a 'mixed' identity. One is characterised by cultural and political distance from Black people. That has followed from the social formations of those societies from the point of European colonisation and slavery – very few whites, the majority Black people, and intermediate positions for people of mixed origins. But in countries like the US, the UK, France and Canada, and elsewhere, no necessary politics follows from a so-called 'mixed-race' identity. The structure of these societies is not conducive to a distinctive identity, majority whites, and small numbers of people of colour, usually in highly concentrated geographic and urban areas.[43] The situation is far more fluid, and there are far more options. This remains always and everywhere necessarily so, because racialised identity is just one aspect of identity. Whether you have a university education and a well-paying job in a multi-racialised workplace; whether you are male or female; whether you were born and raised in England, or elsewhere, and have the accent to prove it (or otherwise); whether you speak English or do not; whether you are Muslim (which precedes racialised identity), or Christian (which claims to do the same); all these will directly shape your identity, and the prominent aspects of your expressed identity. If you do not believe me, go and ask Louis Farrakhan, Ward Connerly, Foxy Brown, Dennis Rodman, and RuPaul; or Oona King, Lenny Henry or Mel B, to name only a few of the more obvious examples of the complexities involved. And let us not forget the growing numbers of Black people of mixed origins who have a Black parent and an Asian parent (*pace* Tiger Woods).

As I have just argued for slavery, whether Black people of mixed origins identified with Black people or not, depended on their parentage, whether they were centrally involved in relationships with immediate family members of colour, where they worked, their phenotypical appearance (did they look white?) and how whites treated them. The ways in which these factors interacted, produced a divergent range of outcomes. They were always ultimately constrained by the context of plantation slavery in the Americas or servitude in Britain, and by the dominance of white supremacy, whether crude or subtle, but these constraints still allowed for a range of options. Similarly today, these same factors exercise tremendous influence, though the media plays a far more important role than in the past, and the options available are far more varied in today's social climate. Given that so many more organisations and social groups have vested interests in appropriating and reproducing images of racialised sexual relations, and for an array of motivations, the patterns that develop cannot be predicted with certainty. However, I believe that the identities of the majority of Black people of mixed origins will continue to be influenced decisively by the community in which they grow. To the extent that they live outside Black communities, we can expect far less identification with the Black community. But that should not divert us from continuing to embrace Black people of mixed origins in the Black community, or to diversify and strengthen our notion of Black identity. Patterns of racialised inequality and racism are still decisive, as is skin colour.

Politics is the issue here. I care more about political attitudes and social involvement, than I do about identity. There are a lot of Black people of mixed origins I do not want in my circles, or in any organisations or groups I am involved in, or in research or studies I am doing, or associated with me in any way. A lot of Black people, too. And that is because of how they express their political views, their cultural views, and how they act towards social justice and community improvement. But do you think I care that Bernie Grant had a white partner? Or that Lord Taylor has a Black one? Do you think I care that Clarence Thomas has a white wife? Or that Jessie Jackson has a Black one? The fact that Cheikh Anta Diop, Frantz Fanon and Jomo Kenyatta had white wives does not stop me from appreciating their writings and politics. Nor does the fact that Maya Angelou was married to a white man stop me from enjoying her intellectual, critical and creative insights or performances. Do you think I lose sleep over the fact that Jerry Rawlings or Paul Boateng or Oona King are of mixed origins? And I doubt that anyone refuses to listen to Bob Marley because of the same fact. Yes, it might amuse me to discuss these facts with some friends over a cappuccino and a croissant in a Berkeley Bistro, but they are hardly prominent in my mind when I want theoretical or political insights, or think about how to combat racism of various kinds. Or how to invigorate Black communities or mobilise a sustaining Black politics against the ravages of political conservatives, white extremists and global profits. I doubt that those issues are at the centre of most people's minds in Britain when they think of similar issues. No, the more salient issues of what you stand for, what you advocate, what your involvement is, these are most important to me.

Let me quote someone who can say it more persuasively than I ever could:

"The race question is subsidiary to the class question in politics, and to think of imperialism in terms of race is disastrous. But to neglect the racial factor as merely incidental is an error only less grave than to make it fundamental."[44]

Even though C.L.R. James said it decades ago, and was speaking about a time and place centuries ago (the rebellion in San Domingo in the eighteenth century), I believe it has a relevance today that is compelling. In the 1960s, Carmichael and Hamilton said the same thing: having Black people in positions of power does not mean Black Power. Black power only occurs when mechanisms are in place to ensure the fundamental changes in the operation of economic, political and social institutions, and the majority of the Black community benefits.[45] Others have said the same thing recently. And do not get them wrong. They do not mean that 'race', or skin colour, or African ancestry, is unimportant. And nor do I. But that it is always linked to other things, and they are often more important. I seek to embrace a similar approach, even while I have argued elsewhere that racism and racialised identities can be more important. Which one is more salient can be answered in the abstract with no more certainty than the question: what time does it get dark at night? It all depends on the context, the space, the place, the time of year. But it is not all arbitrary. Even while 'race' questions do not have the law-like patterns of gravity and the movements of the planets, they do follow broadly routine, recurrent and consistent patterns, as I have tried to show in this chapter.

Besides, we need more than an opposition to white racism to sustain our collective interests. This was always the case in the twentieth century. More so now, with structural, cultural and political values among people of African descent growing. What are the criteria that say people of African origin must embrace a Black identity? Because whites first introduced that requirement? I do not think so. Because people believing themselves to be of exclusive African origin say so? I do not think so. Because, ultimately, if there is a 'race' war, whites will reject them? Crying wolf like this will not work any longer. Besides, in the final analysis, we will all be dead. Because we have no other choice? Look again, there are choices, and many. Is it because of family, kinship, community and common goals? Now we are talking.

CONCLUSION

A lot has been said about Black people of mixed origins. Far less has been written. And much of what has been written is riddled with errors. At the present time, there is more than a climate of mutual suspicion, resentment, distrust and hostility. The situation is complex, with important variations across contexts. I have placed this discussion about the identity of Black people of mixed origins alongside the issue of Black identity, generally. The power of whites to define and constrain is significant, but no longer overwhelming, as are the pressures of capitalist individualism, which preaches individual freedom and personal choice, even as it restricts and repudiates those who make the wrong choice. But still, there are too many options available for us to expect Black people of mixed origins to continue to choose a Black identity in ways that they seem to have done in the past.

I have shown that our beliefs about history continue to shape our attitudes. How we think about Black people of mixed origins and their identity, today, is shaped first and foremost by popular images of them, especially historically. We cannot accept the images of Black people of mixed origins in slavery because they are based on a small, unrepresentative sample, and from evidence largely compiled by whites. Many Black people of mixed origins enjoyed real advantages, but only in circumstances that were conducive; that is, where they had a wealthy white father, and benefited from stereotypes that proclaimed their inability to work in the fields. Most Black people of mixed origins were not in those circumstances. Most of them usually had a poor white father, who often abandoned them, or had no white father at all; they usually remained enslaved and working in the fields, or, if in the house, they were subject to hostile circumstances from the master-enslaver and mistress-enslaver. Many suffered unique atrocities, including the physical and psychological pain of incest. In these circumstances, Black people of mixed origins and Black people (presumed to be unmixed), related by family, community, or a common predicament and similar goals, worked together, lived and ate together, played and socialised together, and worked for political and cultural advancement. We will only learn more about this when we begin to pose broader and different questions, and collect more varied evidence, than those that have dominated the agendas of academics thus far.[46] We are as likely to get a full picture of all Black people of mixed origins from the narrow, unrepresentative group which so dominates our impressions today, as we would a full picture of the experiences of Black people in Britain by investigating the circumstances of Lord Taylor and Lenny Henry as reported on the BBC, or of Black people in the United States by examining Bill Cosby and Oprah Winfrey as reported in *Newsweek*. Clearing up these historical issues will not lead to immediate change in action, but, as educators, we have a responsibility to provide a full appreciation of all the facts.

The factors that shape the identity of people of African origin, especially those of mixed African and non-African ancestry, today are complex. There is far more fluidity than ever before and the circumstances are not promising. In both Britain and the United States, the partners to sexual relationships across racialised identities has increased dramatically, as have the numbers of people of mixed origins. Whereas in the past, the partners and children of such relationships tended to find less hostility in Black communities (because of a virulent racism against them in white communities), this is no longer the case. More and more whites are less hostile. Also, more and more people of mixed origins are growing up in areas with few Black people. Even if one outcome was desirable it is hardly possible, or likely. No, we have to make choices, and I would prefer that the choices be linked to politics, community, etc, and not to the simple issue of identity or who you are, but what do you stand for. What we think about their identity is directly tied to what we think we might gain from their identity.

Images and discourses about 'race' mixture, and Black people of mixed origins, are far more pervasive than ever before, and continue to both reflect and shape attitudes, expectations and patterns. Unlike the past decades, where the dominant discourse was motivated by a largely hostile and similarly inclined racist response by white people, discourses today reflect far more divergent political, economic and social groups. And for the first time, people of mixed origins and their parents and families, are central players in these discourses. All these discourses, by their very nature, are predicated on ignoring contradictions, selective evidence, judicious highlighting of examples and, ultimately, subordination of the discourse to the goals and priorities of those that prevail in that particular institutional domain. This is another pattern that contributes to the increasing array of options for Black people of mixed origins.

We have always had to live with the disappointment that all Black people (presumed unmixed) do not embrace a Black identity, do not act and behave in ways we expect them to. Why else would we hear terms like 'Uncle Tom', 'Coconut' and 'Oreo'? The same is true for Black people of mixed origins. Neither ever have, nor ever will. Skin colour, as evidence of African ancestry, remains a decisive factor in identity formation and even where it is not the most decisive factor, it is still usually the first factor that comes into play in people's minds. One of the reasons I have consistently used the expression "Black people (presumed unmixed)" in this chapter is not to challenge their genetic integrity, but to remind us of the folly of making racialised identities the be-all and end-all, of our quest. We are all, from time immemorial, mixed, genetically. Some of us more than we would like to admit. And, more importantly, our identities, our Black identities, however we express them, are mixed with so many factors other than racialised group membership. These other identities, other needs, will remain inextricable from one another. Why should we keep beating our heads against the wall, expending our energies in bitterness, recriminations and contempt? We spend so much of our energies on indiscriminate recriminations that the efforts we devote to improving common goals are negligible. Is it not better to build than to destroy? Instead of chasing the fleeting illusion of getting everyone to embrace a common Black identity, and as we strengthen and embrace Black identities, let us focus on linking racism and racialised identities to other processes of exclusion, obstruction and denial; and on maximising the chances that we can share common political, cultural values that benefit us all. Acknowledgement of our African ancestry will be an essential component of this process. An indispensable part of this is recognising the role played by Black people of mixed origins, coming to terms with the variety of Black people of mixed origins, and with their particular needs, and working to build on what we share, rather than what divides us.

NOTES AND REFERENCES

1. Banton notes that "The expression 'mixed race' implies, unjustifiably, that there are pure races. To say that someone is of 'mixed-race' is to imply that his or her parents were of very different appearance, but in South Africa, that person's parents, grandparents, and great-grandparents may have been of similar appearance to him or her. What counts as 'mixed' depends upon popular ideas and is often in conflict with any scientific assessment." See Banton, M. *Racial Consciousness* (London and New York: Longman, 1988) p. 95. We still search in vain for a conceptually useful and unobjectionable language to differentiate people of African origins by phenotypical appearance. Too much of what we have, now, owes its origins to the colonising process of European conquest, and its premises to the untenable assumptions of racists. Stay with me for the moment, I will take up some of these issues in the text below, and outline my own position.

2. For example, see Whitten, N. E., Jr. and Torres, A. (eds.) *Blackness in Latin America and the Caribbean: Social Dynamics and Cultural Transformations, Volume II Eastern South America and the Caribbean*, (Bloomington and Indianapolis: Indiana University Press, 1993).

3. This point is explained by Christian, M. 'Black Struggle for Historical Recognition in Liverpool', *North West Labour History*, 20, (1995/6) pp. 58-66.

4. For an early challenge to these ideas, see. Sio, A., 'Marginality and Free Coloured Identity in Caribbean Slave Society' in *Slavery & Abolition*, 8, (2) (September 1987). A more sustained recent challenge is provided by Hodes, M. *Sex, Love, Race: Crossing Boundaries in North American History* (New York: New York University Press, 1999).

5. Higman, B. *Slave Population and Economy in Jamaica, 1807-1834* (Kingston: The University Press of the West Indies, 1995); Horowitz, D. J. 'Colour Differentiation in the American Systems of Slavery' in *Journal of Interdisciplinary History*, 3(3) (Winter, 1973) pp. 509-541.

6. Harris, M. *Patterns of Race in the Americas* (New York: Walker, 1964).

7. For an example of the economic and cultural legacy of transatlantic slavery today, see Small, S. 'The General Legacy of the Atlantic Slave Trade' in Tibbles A. (ed.) *Transatlantic Slavery: Against Human Dignity* (London: HMSO: 1994) pp. 122-126.

8. The notion of 'slave master' suggests an uncritical acceptance of the status of the enslaved person, and of the person who had enslaved him or her. I prefer to call them 'master-enslaver', which suggests a more active relationship between the person doing the enslaving and the person enslaved.

9. Higman, Slave Population... 1995.

10. Ibid. p. 141.

11. Long, E. *The History of Jamaica*, 1774.

12. See Small, S. *The Matrix of Miscegenation: Blacks of Mixed Origins Under Slavery in the Caribbean and the United States* (New York: New York University Press, 2000); Bardaglio, P. W. 'Shameful Matches: The Regulation of Interracial Sex and Marriage in the South before 1900' in Hodes M. (ed.), *Sex, Love, Race: Crossing Boundaries in North American History* (New York: New York University Press, 1999) pp. 112-138.

13. Johnson, W. B. *Black Savannah, 1788-1864* (Fayetteville: The University of Arkansas Press, 1996).

14. Alexander, A. L. *Ambiguous Lives: Free Women of Colour in Rural Georgia, 1789-1879* (Fayetteville: The University of Arkansas Press, 1991) p. 9.

15. Rich, P. 'Philanthropic Racism in Britain: The Liverpool University Settlement, the Anti-Slavery Society and the Issue of 'half-caste' Children, 1919-1951' in *Immigrants and Minorities* 3(1) (March 1984); Sherwood, M. *Pastor Daniels Ekarte and the African Churches Mission* (London: The Savannah Press, 1994).

16. Gabriel, J. *Whitewash: Racialized Politics and the Media* (London and New York: Routledge, 1998).

17. Brah, A. *Cartographies of Diaspora: Contesting Identities* (London and New York: Routledge, 1996).

18. In the context of the United States, I have described these social terrains in far more detail, and with regard to people of various racialised and ethnic origins, rather than just Black. See Small,

S. 'Institutional Domains and Discursive Terrains: Engaging the Mixed Race Movement in the United States' in Parker, D. and Song, M. *Rethinking 'Mixed Race'* (London: Pluto Press, 2000).

19. Quoted in Goodwin, Jo-Ann. 'The New Apartheid' in *The Guardian Weekend*, Saturday, 2 July 1994, pp. 6-11.

20. Phoenix, A and Own, C. 'From Miscegenation to Hybridity: Mixed Relationships and Mixed-Parentage in Profile' in Bemstein B. and Brannen, J. *Children, Research and Policy* (London: Taylor & Francis, 1996); Tucker, M. B. and Mitchell-Kiernan, C. *The Decline of Marriage Among African Americans* (New York: Russell Sage Foundation, 1995).

21. Modood, T, Beishon S. and Virdee. S, *Changing Ethnic Identities* (London: Policy Studies Institute, 1994); Christian, M. 'Black Identity in Liverpool: An Appraisal' in Ackah, W. and Christian, M. (eds.) *Black Organisation and Identity in Liverpool: A Local, National and Global Perspective* (Liverpool, UK: Charles Wotton College Press, 1997) pp. 62-79.

22. Sudbury, J. *Other Kinds of Dreams: Black Women's Organisations and the Politics of Transformation* (London: Routledge, 1998).

23. Ibid.

24. Small, S. *Racialised Barriers: The Black Experience in the United States and England in the 1980s* (London and New York: Routledge, 1994); Miles, R. and Small, S. 'Racism and Ethnicity' in Taylor, S. (ed.) *Sociology: Issues and Debates* (UK: Macmillan, 1999) pp. 136-157.

25. Christian, M. 'An African-Centred Approach to the Black British Experience. With Special Reference to Liverpool' in *Journal of Black Studies* 28 (3) (January 1998) pp. 291-308.

26. Small, S. *Racialised Barriers*, 1994; Small, S. 'The Contours of Racialization: Structures, Representations and Resistance in the United States' in Torres, R. D., Miron, L. F. and Inda, J. X. *Race, Identity and Citizenship, A Reader* (Malden: Blackwell, 1999).

27. Small, S. *Police and People in London. II A Group of Young Black People* (London: Policy Studies Institute, 1983); Small, S. 'Black Youth in England: Ethnic Identity in a White Society' in *Policy Studies* 4 (1) (July, 1983); Alexander, C. *The Art of Being Black* (London: Clarendon Press, 1996); Ackah, W. and

Christian, M. (eds.) *Black Organisation and Identity in Liverpool: A Local, National and Global Perspective* (Liverpool, UK: Charles Wootton College Press, 1997); Mirza., H. S. (ed.) *Black British Feminism*, A Reader (London and New York: Routledge, 1997).

28. As Barnor Hesse explains in Hesse, B. 'Black to front and black again: Racialization through contested times and spaces' in Keith M. and Pile S. (eds.) *Place and the Politics of Identity* (London: Routledge, 1993).

29. Christian, M. 'Black Identity in Liverpool' (1997) p. 72.

30. Small, S. 'Serious T'ing: The Black Comedy Circuit in Britain' in Wagg, S. (ed.) *Because I Tell A Joke or Two* (London and New York: Routledge, 1998) pp. 221-243.

31. Christian, M. 'Black Identity in Liverpool' (1997).

32. Alibhai-Brown, Y and Montague, A. *The Colour of Love* (London: Virago, 1992).

33. Some examples are provided by Weekes, D. 'Shades of Blackness: Young Black Female Constructions of Beauty' in Mirza, H. S. (ed.) *Black British Feminism, A Reader* (London and New York: Routledge, 1997) pp. 113-126.

34. Little, K. *Negroes in Britain* (London: Routledge & Kegan Paul, 1948); Banton, M. P., *The Coloured Quarter* (London: Cape, 1955).

35. A short video by Ngozi Onwurah in which her brother tries to wash himself white with a Brillo Pad and Vim. It came out in 1988.

36. Small, S. *Racialised Barriers*; (1994); Ifekwunigwe, J. 0. *Scattered Belongings: Cultural Paradoxes of 'Race, Nation and Gender'* (London and New York: Routledge, 1999).

37. Garber, I. and Aldridge, J. (eds.) *In the Best Interest of the Child*, (London: Free Association Books, 1994) pp. 89-102.

38. Small, S. 'Racialised Relations in Liverpool: A Contemporary Anomaly' in *New Community* 11 (4) (1991) pp. 511-537.

39. This point is made by Walter Rodney, cited in M. Christian, (1998), note 25, p. 298.

40. Phoenix, A. and Own, C. 'From Miscegenation to Hybridity' (1996).

41. Brown, J. N. 'Black Liverpool, Black America, and the

Gendering of Diasporic Space' in *Cultural Anthropology* 13 (3)(1998) pp. 291-325.

42.   Christian, M. 'Black Identity in Liverpool' (1997); Ifekwunigwe, J.O. Scattered Belongings... (1999).

43.   Solomos, J. and Back, L. *Racism and Society* (Basingstoke and London: Macmillan Press, 1996); Gabriel, J. Whitewash... (1998).

44.   James, C.L.R. *The Black Jacobins: Toussaint L'Ouverture and the San Domingo Revolution* (London: Allison & Busby, 1980; first published in 1938).

45.   Carmichael, S. and Hamilton, C. V. *Black Power: The Politics of Liberation in America*, (New York: Vintage Books, 1967).

46.   Some of the problems involved in relying on the evidence left by whites, or by men, are elaborated in Hull, G.T. Scott P. B. and Smith, B. *All the Women are White, All the Blacks are men, But Some of Us are Brave* (New York: The Feminist Press, 1982).

Chapter Nine

'COLOUR MATTERS, "RACE" MATTERS': AFRICAN CARIBBEAN IDENTITY IN THE 20th CENTURY

Shirley Tate

"African Caribbean? You know I've always been against that because to me . . . I always say to the kids yeah? Listen, you're living in England, in Britain and you're African Caribbean. That twice removes you from where you are. They can't go back to the Caribbean yeah? They don't want to. Why should they?" States Lionel.[1]

FOR SOME of us at the close of the 1990s in Britain, the term African Caribbean, as with other identity categories, is itself contested within a context in which naming is highly political. The citation above, from Lionel, reveals one aspect of this in terms of the political inappropriateness of the name for Black young people in Britain because it removes them, symbolically, twice from the British space to a space of otherness. That is the space of Africa and the Caribbean, which later he also constructs as a "space of no return". Perhaps the question now is how do African Caribbean identities prevail at the end of a millennium in which 'race' still matters? Alongside the continuing salience of 'race' at the level of lived experience, in the academy we have seen the emergence of the notion of 'translated hybrid subjects' that would seek to question the necessity for 'race' in Black identities. Through using extracts from speakers' life stories, I will argue that constructed essences of Blackness still remain central to African Caribbean identities. This places hybridity in a difficult situation, theoretically, and leads, then, to the consideration of an alternative. This alternative viewpoint, that Black identities are texts of social practice, seeks to account for the salience of 'race' as well as the change in senses of belonging that Lionel speaks about, produced by the context of Britain. Black identities, as texts of social practice themselves, emerge in talk as individuals selectively draw on identity discourses to construct the identity category, 'Black'.

IDENTITY AND 'RACE'

Although Lola Young[2] rightly criticises Frantz Fanon for his exclusion of Black women, the construction of pathological models of the psycho-sexuality of women and "the evidence of a deep seam of fear and rage regarding Black women", it is clear that his work has contributed to contemporary theorising of racial alterity and difference as well as Black politics.[3] Fanon examines the "violence of identification" in the colonial context.[4] Violence arises as it is about how white subjects accede to power and Black 'others' learn subjugation. In the colonial system of power/knowledge, the bodily schema is culturally and historically shaped.

There is a "racial epidermal schema"[5] in which "I am determined from without. I am the slave not of the 'idea' that others have of me but of my own appearance".[6] Moreover, for Fanon, 'race' as a discursive regime has the ultimate impact of the internalisation of oppression. Thus, in assuming the negation of Black selves, the colonised accept that any originality or multiplicity must be denied. So the colonised Black other occupies identities that imitate the coloniser's ideas of Black essential difference.

However, Fanon also reminds us that "Negro experience is not a whole for there is not merely one Negro, there are Negroes".[7] Therefore, producing a Blackness that is counter to racist images, facilitates the emergence of difference and the possibility for individuals to free themselves from the mental slavery of colonial stereotypes.

Individuals, then, have always required double or multiple consciousnesses in the colonial Caribbean situation. The question of Caribbean identity in fact has never been straightforward. This is especially the case if one supposes that identity involves a search for origins, as it is difficult to locate in the Caribbean an origin for its people.[8]

Africa, Europe, India, China, Lebanon and the Jewish Diaspora, are the historical sources for Caribbean people.[9] These are the cultural resources that allowed the construction of Caribbean identities in colonial spaces both during and after slavery. Within the colonial space of 1990s Britain, to be Black and British demands a double consciousness in order to negotiate the contention of racist discourses that Black and British are mutually exclusive. Occupying the space of Black British is, in itself, therefore, a subversive location.

However, "the fact is 'Black' has never been just there either. It has always been an unstable identity, psychically, socially and politically. It too is a narrative, a story, a history. Something constructed, told, spoken, not simply found".[10] Such constructions lead to the emergence of new political identities and a new conception of ethnicity as a counter to the discourses of nationalism or national identity within post-war Britain. A pan-Caribbeanisation has occurred as a response to these racialising discourses, coupled with the undermining of island chauvinism, the resistance to the undermining of cultural traditions and the valorisation of Blackness. So that in Britain, it is evident that Jamaican culture is hegemonic in the Gramscian sense of leadership and influence among Caribbean heritage communities as a whole.[11]

Stuart Hall claims that "we are constructing identities within which 'black' is essentially a politically and culturally constructed category which cannot be grounded in a set of fixed transcendental racial categories",[12] but must include difference in terms of what it means to be Black and British, simultaneously. I think that we should pause and take a look at this assertion. First, I agree with the idea that there is difference within Blackness, but I am not convinced by Hall's contention that Black is not grounded in understandings of fixed racial categories. This is so because the necessity of 'race' is very much a part of the social, of how we see and experience ourselves in interaction with others.

Perhaps an example would suffice at this point. Before we discuss the following respondent's extract, during the interview, Lorna spoke satirically about the general demise of Black culture and the fact that it now seems to be focused primarily on rice and peas on a Sunday, and Carnival once a year. She went on to talk about being asked to do a presentation about Black British culture. However, she does not want to follow the guidelines of what they want, but instead she intends to talk about Black experiences of inequality and racism and to trace the history of Black people's journey to the West through enslavement and colonialism. She explains why this will be what she speaks about:

> "I'm starting my presentation next week with a quote from Spike Lee which says that the biggest lie ever told is, it doesn't matter what creed, colour, or nationality you are. It's the person that you are that matters and if you do a good job, you know? And then it goes on to say bullshit. Colour matters. Race matters. It's everything to do with everything. And that's how I'm going to start my presentation next week because it matters. It shapes our whole life. You know what I mean? And to me, at the end of the day, you can have all your variations. But at the end of the day, when you bring it to the base line, it's between Black and white."

She uses the words of Spike Lee to show that, for her, 'race' and colour continue to be salient in terms of Black experiences in that they shape our whole lives. Indeed, it comes down, invariably, to Black and white.

That is the fundamental dichotomy that governs who it is possible to be. Lorna, again, makes us aware of this as she claims Blackness for herself, irrespective of the fact that she has a white mother, in the next extract. Her argument, here, is an interesting one for Hall's claim as she uses the very fixed transcendental categories that he claims no longer exist, to make her claim to Blackness when she says that she is Black as are other 'mixed-race' people because of their genes. Lorna states:

> "I believe that most mixed-race people, if they are left on their own, and not influenced, they would gravitate more towards the Black side. Because, whether you want to get scientific about it or technical in genetics, the Black gene is dominant and the white gene is recessive, you know? And dominant means strong and recessive means weak. So it doesn't matter whether you have a Black woman and a white man, or a Black man and a white woman, you are going to have a child of colour. You know what I mean? You are going to have a Black child because the Black gene is dominant, whether it's in the male or the female."

The point here is that, in the academy, we can theoretically suggest that there is no such thing as 'race' when we want to make claims about identities as hybrid forms. However, as Lorna maintains, this does not make 'race' cease to exist, as within 'the social' we have individuals acting to reify 'race' and using it to establish social identities that reflect authentic experiences.

THE CONTINUING SIGNIFICANCE OF 'RACE' ESSENCE

Hybridity became a 1990s watch-word within Cultural Studies and the theorising of Black identities. Indeed, for Stuart Hall,[13] identity is "never fixed, it's always hybrid. But this is precisely because it comes out of specific histories and cultural repertoires of enunciation, that it can constitute a 'positionality', which we call provisionally identity [...] So each of these identity-stories is inscribed in the positions we take up and identify with".

This is an interesting point of view and one that needs to be considered, as it seems to contain a contradiction. What could Hall mean by identity being hybrid, then? He seems, at one level, to be using it in opposition to fixity. So 'hybrid' takes on the meaning of fluidity and a temporariness in terms of his notion of identities as positionality. On the one hand, identity is not fixed, but on the other, there are provisional identities that come out of specific histories and cultures. Such fluidity, then, is questioned by his viewpoint that identity stories are inscribed in the positions we take up. This is so as if hybrid identities were fluid and free-floating they would refuse the boundaries of identity stories. Hall thus gives hybridity some boundaries of its own.

In other words, hybridity, too, is subject to the flow of discursive meanings, and without this, identifications could not proceed. Further questions arise, here. That is, would not these histories and cultures serve to fix such a positionality within discourses of identity, given the necessity for meaning? Therefore, would not such histories and cultures themselves produce and reproduce fixed notions of what it is to be Black?

If we again consider Lorna's words above, she is speaking within a British context but using international understandings of the impact of racialisation on Black women and men in order to make her own identity positioning known. For her, only two positions count – Black and white. Lorna later refers to, and produces, a discourse of 'race' with a very long history indeed and which emanates from 'the one drop of Black blood' test for Blackness in slave societies, such as in pre-1865 United States. As Black individuals, then, what Lorna shows us here, is that we are not hermetically sealed off from white supremacist discourses, but also use them to show distance from whiteness as we claim a Black identity for ourselves.

There are two other viewpoints on hybridity that can be considered. The first is that of Robert Young[14] and the second is that of Homi Bhabha.[15] For Young, there are two models of hybridisation in terms of culture. That which involves creolisation is about fusion, the creation of new forms, which can then be compared with the old form of which they are partly made up. Another model of hybridity, 'hybridisation as raceless chaos', is not productive of stable new forms but something closer to Homi Bhabha's restless, interstitial hybridity. Whatever model is chosen, for Young:

"Hybridity thus makes difference into sameness, and sameness into difference, but in a way that makes the same no longer

> simply different. In that sense it operates according to the form of logic that Derrida isolates in the term 'brisure' a breaking and a joining at the same time, in the same place: difference and sameness in an impossible simultaneity."[16]

Looking at Young's idea of difference and sameness in an impossible simultaneity as being central to hybridity, makes us wonder about the possibility of 'raceless chaos'. This is so as if the same continues to exist in terms of hybrid identities, then this means that within societies, which continue to be structured in terms of a racial epidermal schema, there is really no prospect for the de-racination which 'raceless chaos' implies. Indeed, the issue for Lorna, above, still is that 'race' and colour matter. They have an impact on our lives as Black people. Whatever difference emerges, because of context and experience, the sameness of skin remains. This sameness of skin, in itself, holds a contradiction, however, based on the policing of the boundaries of authentic Blackness by both Black and white people.

Some examples from Lorna and Dawn seem appropriate at this point. Before Dawn's extract she has been talking with her friend about her friend's experience of being asked by a white feminist are you Black or a woman? Dawn goes on to place this question within the context of a difference in imagining the self which she sees as existing between Black and white people. For us, in Dawn's view, being Black is an integral part of who we are within a society in which we are racially defined by both Black and white people. Dawn states:

> "It's like they . . . white people are all in compartments but we're not, you see. Because our Blackness is an integral part of our wholeness. Or when we're allowed to be Black. Because the amount of people I've had since I've come to London who've said to me do you consider yourself to be Black? And to me it's a joke because I think well all this time right . . . In a way, my Blackness is defined by white people. Because as long as white people call me a Black bastard, then I know I must be Black, then."

As well as white people putting us within the boundary of the Black other, through reading our bodies for signs of 'race', the Black community can be as equally ruthless in its policing of the borders of Blackness as Dawn makes obvious to us. Lorna continues this theme of her Blackness being questioned because of shade. Before this extract, she has been talking about herself as feeling totally Black, irrespective of having a white mother and not allowing anyone's ignorance to deny her a place in Black community:

> "Because I will choose where I want to fit into society and if a Black woman is hostile to me. You know I've been called a 'mixed-race bitch' or a 'half-breed' and other nasty stuff. I've been called it all in the past but it never hurt me enough to say that I don't want to be part of the Black community."

What both women show us is that shade, the actual colour of skin, is significant in their lives. They are two women whose bodies declare their mestisaje.[17] Their 'mix', if you like, is already there to be read off from their skin. Rather than, however, choosing this as a site of identification, what we see both women being involved in is a construction of themselves as Black. They choose a social space of negation as a site of identification. This implies to me that rather than being made to be different from Blackness, these women are choosing to be part of the Black same.

This, then, is perhaps how difference and sameness interact in the lives of individuals and, by extrapolation, how hybridity comes into being. This has taken me though to a location which is one step removed from Young's formulation because what we see here are individuals 'talking' their hybridity in terms of their lived experiences of being the same and different. They are occupying a space, then, of the intersection of discourses on the 'self', which, in turn, they have to negotiate in order to maintain Black identities. This idea of negotiation brings us to Homi Bhabha's work on the 'third space of hybridity'.

For Homi Bhabha, all cultures are in a continual process of hybridity, so the importance of hybridity does not lie in being able to detect two originals from which the third emerges but:

> ". . . rather hybridity [...] is the 'third space' which enables other positions to emerge [...] [it is] not so much identity as identification [...] a process of identifying with and through

another object, an object of otherness, at which point the agency of identification – the subject – is itself always ambivalent because of the intervention of that otherness."[18]

This appears to be an iteration of the notion of sameness and difference as central to hybrid identities, yet something else also emerges. It is that hybridity is not a neutral process. There are politics involved. This is to suggest the possibility that identities, of who it is possible to claim to be, can be crosscut by issues of 'otherness'. Black individuals, therefore, in recognising, giving meaning to and disavowing the otherness that they themselves embody, construct hybrid identifications for themselves, as we see happening in terms of Lorna's and Dawn's talk above. Such identifications are based firmly, though, on the continuation of essence through a constructed Black sameness.

This is made obvious, also, in the example that follows in which Lola speaks about her identity as not African but Black British. She presents this identity in opposition to what she sees as negativity and a lack of Black political knowledge on the part of the state and her white colleague at work. She situates her identity as a point of certainty within the state's confusion in terms of what is a politically correct term for Black people, and demonstrates her awareness of how colour signifies difference by placing, for example, Norwegian as an identity category which does not count. Indeed, being Norwegian does not count because, after all, 'whiteness' is the colourless, neutral but all pervasive norm in a racialised context. She, thereby, criticises the implied homogeneity of the white 'nation' and speaks back to the discourse of white supremacy that would deny the salience of her Caribbean heritage, her nationality as British and, her right to assert the colour-signified political identification 'Black' in conjunction with her identity claim. This example, then, makes me wonder where is the ambivalence of which Bhabha speaks as this woman makes her identification with otherness but proclaims a space of affirmation[19] of Black and British simultaneously? Let us now consider Lola's words:

"This lot at work, they just make me laugh. They try and discuss things like they say to me 'what would you call yourself, Lola,' you know? We were talking about this . . . it was something in Parliament you know, what [is the] politically correct way to call a Black person you know? Like African or whatever. I said, well I'm not African, as in being born on the continent. Why can't I call myself Black? I'm British you know? Because if they can say whatever they say in America. But she says, no you can't say that. I said well why can't I? Do you know what I mean? Then she says but then I could say my ancestors came from Norway and stuff like that. I said oh give me a break."

Lola also shows us something else. That is that she has to negotiate several worlds at the same time in terms of identity discourses. In her claim for Black Britishness, she has to position herself as not African in contradiction to how she would be identified by the state. This, in itself, is a bold and controversial identification denial within Black community politics. However, while there is this denial, there is also a simultaneous affirmation of connectedness to the African Diaspora through the use of the word 'Black', itself, and her use of Black America as an example. Africa, as signified, continues, then, to be connected to its signifier, Black. She places herself very much within the space of the necessity for the assertion of a right to be Black and therefore Diasporic, but also British in terms of nationality and location. Her assertion of not being African can now be seen within an overall claim that she is making to the right to construct Black British as an identity within this space of 'the British same' but 'the British different'. In this interplay, the same and different is signified by 'race'.

What Lola makes us notice is that, as Black women and men, we are continuing to live within a consciousness affected by Diaspora awareness. Paul Gilroy in *The Black Atlantic: Modernity and Double Consciousness* also looks at this phenomenon. For him, double consciousness is a double vision which ensures that Diasporic people are in two places at once and maintain a double perspective on reality. Diaspora opens up an historical and experiential rift between the place of residence and the place of belonging. As such, Diaspora-consciousness, for Gilroy, is opposed to the power of nation states.

Lola's talk, above, on being not African but Black British, shows that doubleness. What it also shows is the possibility that there is more than double vision at play here. I say this because we have in Lola's argument the interaction of three identity discourses. That is, African, Black and British simultaneously. This indicates a multiplicity of vision.

This is so as, while being firmly placed within Blackness as 'race', she then has to negotiate a space of identification for herself using the discourses of African, Black and British. A recognition that we constantly negotiate identity discourses in establishing Black identities, leads us to look at Black identities within Gilroy's conception of 'the changing same' as he sees this as a valuable extension to the idea of Diaspora. For Gilroy, this 'changing same' is not some invariant essence that gets enclosed subsequently in a shape-shifting exterior with which it is casually associated. It is not the sign of an unbroken, integral inside protected by a camouflaged husk. The phrase 'the changing same' names the problem of Diaspora politics and Diaspora poetics. The same is present but how can we imagine it as something other than essence generating the merely accidental? The same is retained without needing to be reified. It is ceaselessly re-processed.[20]

What are we to make of this when individuals talk about themselves as though Black is the sign of an unbroken integral inside, an invariant essence because of the intervention of 'race' in their lived experiences? Further, how can the same be re-processed without there being any reifications of it? Also, how will we recognise that something has been re-processed without recourse to such reifications? Let us look at an example in which Tracy speaks about changes in the younger generation of Black women in terms of what is considered to be attractive to illustrate that we work with reifications in terms of Black identities:

And another thing that really gets me is that they, especially ragga girls, will tell you how much in touch with themselves they are and they know absolutely nothing. The first thing they go off and do is put extensions in their hair. And I'm thinking, well why are you doing that you know? Is it to look good? And if you hear them, a lot of them turn around and say they want really long, long hair. You know? The old image of right running around the playground with a jumper tied to your head because you wanted to have long, blonde hair? Or they'd straighten their hair and I'm thinking you know aren't you going the other way? Can't you just be happy with what you've got? There's plenty of Black women out there for them to look on who are positive natural Black women. And they've got short Black hair. You know the way they let their hair grow now and it's short with tight little curls and they look so good. And they've portrayed such a positive image and it's like these girls don't want to know about it – they just want the long relaxed hair.

In this extract, Tracy constructs herself as authentically Black because of consciousness as opposed to young Black women involved in the ragga sub-culture. These latter are presented as choosing a style which is, to some extent, anti-Blackness while they proclaim that they are in touch with themselves. To be in touch with oneself is to acknowledge one's Blackness as a necessity for natural beauty, as a political choice, as Tracy makes obvious through critiquing ragga girls' practice of wearing long extensions. She translates this practice as being to do with a yearning for whiteness when she relates it to "the old image of running around the playground with a jumper tied to your head because you wanted to have long, blonde hair". Through this critique, she makes her position on the politics of Black beauty as naturalness known, before she continues critiquing the straightening of hair as being to do with "going the other way" through unhappiness with Black hair. The 'other way', here, is towards whiteness. She then shifts to talking about "the natural Black woman" as presenting a positive image because of their short, tightly curled Black hair. This, then, is the Blackness that underlies her objection to ragga style. Through using the discourse of the natural Black woman she constructs herself as more 'conscious' than the ragga girls she was describing.

Although 'the changing same', then, could be useful as a phrase to describe what emerges in the interplay between same and different in Black identities as individuals talk about their lived experiences, it needs to acknowledge that discourses of Blackness serve to reify Blackness. Further, it needs to acknowledge that these discourses are what individuals negotiate as they construct their identities. Acknowledging the centrality of discourses in identities leads us to looking at Black identities as texts of social practice.

BLACK IDENTITIES AS TEXTS OF SOCIAL PRACTICE

What can be drawn from the discussion, so far, is the centrality of the discourse of Blackness as a 'same' in Black identities. Whether or not theorists want to use the term 'hybrid' to refer to Black identities, cannot be allowed to negate the fact that 'race' continues to matter to us. There is no such space for us as that of 'raceless chaos'. Within a space in which 'race' matters, what can be said, then, about the nature of Black identities? What has been a constant above is that individuals negotiate identity discourses in talk and it is this that underlies my conception of Black identities as 'texts of social practice'.

The concept of 'text' implies both a specific piece of writing and much more broadly social reality itself. Therefore, a view that identities are constructed texts implies that they are written into and onto social reality by actors. They are constituted by 'social reality' but also come to constitute that reality as 'text implies that human reality is fundamentally discursive'[21] because of the interaction of discourses of difference and sameness in the struggle for meaning. Conceptualising Black British identities as texts of social practice, subject to the continuous play of meaning, entails that identity is dynamic but it is also 'raced', gendered, 'classed' and sexualised. Its dynamism arises from the fact that 'like a text, human action is an open work, the meaning of which is in suspense [...] waiting for fresh interpretations which decide their meaning'.[22] Being dependent on the interpretations of self and other to come into the world, the quest for meanings produces the capacity for the emergence of difference, and in so doing, secures the possibility of multiplicity in Black identities.

The struggle for meaning, in the making of texts of social practice, reminds us of the dialogic nature of Black identities as, in the constitutive interplay between identities and 'the social', individuals are inscribed by and through identity discourses. Texts represent socially constructed identities that are used as points of reference in order to cull the meanings of individually constructed identities in this interplay. Social practice operates in the dual sense of discursive construction and interpretation of that which is represented. It, therefore, removes the focus from the mind to that of interaction, or social groups or societal structures. Stuart Hall represents this as:

> . . . the articulation [...] between a social force which is making itself, and the ideology or conceptions of the world which makes intelligible the process they are going through, which brings onto the historical stage a new social position, a new set of social and political subjects.[23]

This appears to be a viewpoint that places hybridity within this notion of Black identity as texts of social practice and would help to ground it at the everyday level as a possible descriptor for such identities. Moreover, as texts, hybrid identifications would become the negotiation of positions produced by identity discourses of the 'self' and 'other' in order to arrive at new identifications. These new identifications, though, are still embedded in essence because of the performativity[24] of 'Black' itself within these identifications. Friedman reminds us, then, that:

> . . . hybridity is always, like all aspects of identity, a question of practice, the practice of attributing meaning. It can be understood only in terms of its social context and the way in which acts of identification are motivated.[25]

We have considered how the British context impacts on the meanings of Black as 'race', 'shade', consciousness and origins. Let us now focus on another example of what 'Black' entails. For Sonya:

> [Black identity] shifts for me. It shifts because of the experiences which I have with regard to Asian people. My ideal is where Black identity is a political one. And where you know because of the shared experience of racism, people whatever their ethnicity, are able to come together to be able to fight racism collectively but recognising ethnic differences.

Black, for Sonya, lies within the continuation of a pan-ethnic Black consciousness based on an anti-racist politics, alongside a recognition of the continuing significance of the differences produced by ethnicity. We construct ourselves as Black, then, in a multi-faceted way so that texts of social practice contain both 'the same' and difference, simultaneously. This same and difference is also present at the level of ethnicity which Sonya speaks about as being so fixed, above, in terms of establishing a distinction between the Caribbean and Asian categories. There is contestation at the level of African Caribbean ethnicity, itself, as a marker of identity, though, as is made obvious by Dawn and Sharon in the next extract. They speak about two reifications of Blackness. The cultural practice of food as a signifier of identity which they both critique and that which relates to a darker shade as somehow making us more aware of our Black identity. Dawn ends by saying that she has to prove herself all the time as a Black woman because of her light shade and that she does not confine herself to food which is seen to be African Caribbean. The Black 'same' then is open to the contestation of difference:

> D: People feel like if you have a Black identity it's got to be like you know, rice and peas on a Sunday and Nutriment.
> S: Oh tell me. I know. Every Sunday as well. You can't have a break. And peas soup on a Saturday.
> D: Yeah. Yeah and you know if you don't do that you know [you are not Black] and it's like awareness of identity to them is based on how dark you are.
> S: Mmh, I know.
> D: So like me I have to prove myself all the time.

In speaking of awareness, Dawn and Sharon make us remember another 'fact' of Blackness within the British context. That is that we also construct Blackness as being about consciousness and this has been at the core of the examples above. Next, Dawn talks about herself as a Black woman who, because she wasn't the fashionable shade of Black (that is dark-skinned), was never regarded as Black even though she had worked for years at a national and local level within Black politics. In recounting this aspect of her lived experience she explains that even though we know that Blackness is about consciousness, we are also policed by those who believe in the doctrine of 'dark skin equals authenticity'. Dawn states:

> I mean that was the thing that got me towards the end of like the stuff I did in national Black workers. It was like my politics and my contribution and my history didn't count for nothing. It was like you know because I wasn't the fashionable shade of Black what I had to say wasn't worthy to be listened to you know? And the fact that I'd been there and struggling all those times and I'd never given up the faith and all that, it never counted for anything amongst those people. And I was very disappointed […] But it's like I was never as a Black woman recognised within that organisation.

Crucially, this primary research demonstrates that the discourses of Blackness as 'race', colour, consciousness, politics, ethnicity and heritage are negotiated at the level of the everyday social world. What we also see, through looking at discourses, is that at the everyday level, Blackness is reified in terms of being a 'same' whilst individuals simultaneously show their difference from this same when expressing their identities.

CONCLUSION

For African Caribbean heritage communities in Britain, the issue of identity has never been easy nor will the advent of the new millennium make it more so. We are in a situation in which we recognise that anything more than a symbolic return to African Caribbean origins is problematic. This return, therefore, consists of continuing the construction and reconstruction of markers of authentic African Caribbean ethnicities such as food, language, music and other cultural expressions. The challenge with which we are faced is how to claim Blackness and Britishness simultaneously without asserting assimilation to whiteness as a necessary part of our future. That is, how to remain within Africa while being Diasporic. Individuals are already doing this, as is obvious in the examples above, as they deconstruct and reconstruct the meaningfulness of Black identity within this context. We are involved in the complexities of negotiating identity discourses to produce texts of social practice where 'race' matters, which, as individuals at that moment, we give the meaning of 'me'. Or rather, the meaning of 'my identity'. Perhaps it is this continuing significance of 'race' in our lived and social experiences that hybridity theorists need to consider more thoughtfully in order to understand the simultaneity of sameness and 'otherness' in our identities.

NOTES AND REFERENCES

1. The data that is used throughout, is drawn from primary research (in-depth interviews) conducted during the period 1996-1998 in London, Birmingham and West Yorkshire. The respondents were Black British women and men of Caribbean heritage aged between 16-38 who were asked to have conversations about their lives here in Britain with someone with whom they felt comfortable.

2. Young, L. 'Missing Persons: Fantasising Black Women in Black Skin, White Masks' in Read, A. (ed.) *The Fact of Blackness: Frantz Fanon and Visual Representation* (London: I.C.A., 1996) p. 88.

3. Hall, S. 'The After-life of Frantz Fanon: Why Fanon? Why Now? Why Black Skin, White Masks?' in Read, A. (ed.) *The Fact of Blackness: Frantz Fanon and Visual Representation* (London: I.C.A., 1996a) pp. 12-37.

4. Fuss, D. *Identification Papers* (London: Routledge, 1995).

5. Fanon, F. *Black Skin, White Masks* (London: Pluto Press, 1986; first published in 1952) p. 112.

6. Ibid. p. 116.

7. Ibid. p. 136.

8. Hall, S. 'Negotiating Caribbean Identities' in *New Left Review* No. 209 (January 1995) pp. 3-14.

9. Gilroy, P. *The Black Atlantic: Modernity and Double Consciousness* (London: Verso, 1993).

10. Hall, S. 'Minimal Selves' in Baker, Jr. H., Diawara, M. and Lindeborg, R. (eds.) *Black British Cultural Studies: A Reader* (London: The University of Chicago Press, 1996a) p. 116.

11. James, W. 'Migration, Racism and Identity Formation' in James, W. and Harris, C. *Inside Babylon: The Caribbean Diaspora in Britain*. (London: Verso, 1993) pp. 232-288.

12. Hall, S. 'New Ethnicities' in Donald J. and Rattansi A. (eds.) *'Race', Culture and Difference* (London: Sage Publications/ The Open University, 1993) p. 254.

13. Hall, S. 'The formation of a diasporic intellectual: an interview with Stuart Hall by Kuan-Hsing Chen' in Morley, M. and Chen, K. (eds.) *Stuart Hall: Critical Dialogues in Cultural Studies* (London: Routledge, 1996) p. 502.

14. Young, R.J.C. *Colonial Desire: Hybridity in Theory, Culture and Race* (London: Routledge, 1995) p. 25.

15.   Bhabha, H. 'The Third Space: Interview with Homi Bhabha' in Rutherford J. (ed.) *Identity, Community, Culture & Difference* (London: Lawrence and Wishart, 1990) p. 211.
16.   Young R.J.C. *Colonial Desire...* p. 26.
17.   Mestisaje is a Spanish colonial word which denotes mixture in terms of 'race'. I have come to use this word because of the contestation around the use of 'mixed race' or 'mixed heritage' within Black communities in Britain.
18.   Bhabha, H. (see note 15).
19.   hooks, b. 'Choosing the Margin as a Space of Radical Openness' in hooks b. *Yearning: race, gender and cultural politics* (London: Turnaround, 1991); hooks talks about this as a space of 'radical openness' (p. 153).
20.   Gilroy, P. 'Diaspora and the Detours of Identity' in Woodward K. (ed.) *Identity and Difference* (Milton Keynes: The Open University/Sage publications, 1997) pp. 335-336.
21.   Pinar, W. 'Notes on Understanding Curriculum as a Racial Text' in McCarthy, C. and Crichlow, W. (eds.) *Race, Identity and Representation in Education* (London: Routledge, 1993) p. 60.
22.   Ricoeur, P. 'The Model of the Text: Meaningful Action Considered as a Text' in Rabinow, P. and Sullivan, W. (eds.) *Interpretive Social Science: A Reader* (Berkeley. University of California Press, 1979) p. 86.
23.   Hall, S. 'On Post-modernism and Articulation: an Interview with Stuart Hall' in Morley, M. and Chen, K. (eds.) *Stuart Hall: Critical Dialogues in Cultural Studies* (London: Routledge, 1996c) p. 141.
24.   Butler, J. *Bodies That Matter: On The Discursive Limits Of 'Sex'* (London: Routledge, 1993). On p. 2 she cites two understandings of performativity, "the act by which a subject brings into being what she/he names [...] [and the] reiterative power of discourse to produce the phenomena that it regulates and constrains".
25.   Friedman, J. 'Global Crises, the struggle for Cultural Identity and Intellectual Porkbarrelling: Cosmopolitans versus Locals, Ethnics and Nationals in an Era of De-hegemonisation' in Werbner, P. and Modood, T. (eds.) *Debating Cultural Hybridity, Multicultural Identities and the Politics of Anti-Racism* (London: Zed Books, 1997) p. 85.

Chapter Ten

WOMENFOLKS: RACE, CLASS AND GENDER IN WORKS BY ZORA NEALE HURSTON AND TONI MORRISON

Diedre L. Badejo

THIS CHAPTER explores the work of two renowned African American female writers: Zora Neale Hurston and Toni Morrison. Although there is approximately four decades separating Hurston's *Their Eyes Were Watching God* and Morrison's *Sula*, there is continuity in their themes of race, class and gender. Both writers relate to the twentieth century and their works, it is safe to assume, will continue to influence African American literature in the twenty-first century. In particular, women writers of African descent in the present and future will benefit from the rich legacy and foundation provided by Hurston and Morrison's historical and cultural perceptions through their narratives and folktales of African American life.

Zora Neale Hurston's publication of *Their Eyes Were Watching God* in 1937, is a fitting close to the literary era of the twenties and thirties known as the Harlem Renaissance. W.E.B. Du Bois had set the tone for this literary era with the publication of *The Souls of Black Folk* in 1903. During this golden epoch of creativity, Langston Hughes shone as its brightest literary star giving life and meaning to the voices of Harlem's thousands of Black souls. Together, Du Bois, Hughes and Hurston exposed the beauty and humanity of African American folks to a world that was often amazed by their resilience and defiant love of living. All three writers became the instruments through which these souls of Black folk would speak; and together both the folk and their clarions have left us a brilliant legacy.

Hurston's *Their Eyes Were Watching God* reflects the abiding interest in the voice and the vision of Black folk. It gives testimony to her talent as a folklorist and a writer, while sharing the texture and clarity of African American women's voices and visions. *Their Eyes Were Watching God* is an odyssey both for Janie, the main character and narrator, and for Black women. The historical root of the novel takes us to the pre-Civil War era of enslavement, sexual violence, and dehumanisation. Its social vision questions the relationship between class aspirations and personal fulfilment. This book explores race, class and gender issues with which the Black community must struggle. But most importantly, *Their Eyes Were Watching God* examines gender and class as these issues impact upon Black male and female relationships. Finally, the novel speaks with the unmistakable power of a Black women's voice. Because of this, the novel is about Black women and class as much as it is about the quest for self-fulfilment and love.

In her essay, 'God's Divas', Andrea Benton Rushing notes:

> . . . the single most prevalent image of women in African American verse is the image of woman as mother. That makes this body of literature quite different from British or Anglo-American poetry, where most verse to women characterizes them as the beloved.[1]

This image of woman as mother has persisted despite enslavement, rape, empoverishment and racism. Unfortunately, it was the Black woman's ability to reproduce the slave labour needed to develop this country which distinguished her oppression from that of her male counterpart and white women. Despite this, the Black woman nurtured and protected that which she bore. Irrespective of the paternal source, the African American woman has continued to mother her offspring, oftentimes, at a cost.

Nanny exemplifies this image of the Black woman as mother, and her story sets the tone for Black women's struggles as illustrated by her granddaughter, Janie. Nanny's story recounts how race, class and gender oppression of Black women distorted their lives and the great wellspring of human emotion that is usually associated with the mother and child image. Nanny's brutal treatment under enslavement and her heroic escape with her newborn daughter, Leafy, instead, conjures up images of Black folks' humanity under siege. The permanent scars of this experience, and the later rape of Leafy, forces Nanny to presume that "de high chair" where the white woman sat was a seat of protection for her offspring. Therefore, once her daughter is destroyed by a violent rape, Nanny attempts to protect and isolate Janie from the cruelties of their world. In a passage that summarises such impositions, Nanny tells Janie's withering innocence:

> . . . Yo' Nanny wouldn't harm a hair uh yo' head. She doesn't want nobody else to do it neither if she kin help it. Honey, de white man is de ruler of everything as fur as Ah been able tuh find out. Maybe it's some place way off in de ocean where de black man is in power, but we don't know nothin' but what we see. So de white man throw down de load and tell de nigger man tuh pick it up. He pick it up because he have to, but he

don't tote it. He hand it to his womenfolks. De nigger woman is
de mule uh de world so fur as Ah can see. Ah been prayin' fuh it
tuh be different wid you. Lawd, Lawd, Lawd![2]

Despite the cruel ring of truth, for Janie, however, her grandmother
represents the restrictions of race, class and gender. She tells her
friend, Pheoby:

> She (Nanny) was born in slavery time when folks, dat is black
> folks, didn't sit down anytime dey felt lak it. So sittin' on porches
> lak de white madam looked lak uh mighty fine thing tuh her.
> Dat's what she wanted for me – don't keer whut it cost. Git up on
> high chair and sit dere. She didn't have time tuh think whut tuh
> do after you got up on de stool uh do nothin'. De object wuz to git
> dere. So Ah got up on de high stool lak she told me, but Pheoby,
> Ah done nearly languished tuh death up dere. Ah felt like de world
> wuz cryin' extry and Ah ain't read de common news yet.[3]

Because of the class oppression of Black people as a group during
enslavement, and the gender oppression and sexual abuse of Black
women during and after enslavement, Nanny attempts to secure for
Janie a new class position which the former feels will protect the latter.
Nanny is trapped by both her own victimisation and that of her daughter.
As a result, she arranges a marriage for Janie that secures the property
and title that will elevate her above these oppressive forces. For Nanny
believes that the world is run by white folks and that is enough to
know. For her, to know the world is to know destruction.

This dislocation of her sensibilities makes Nanny oblivious to the
wonderment life that Janie dreams about. For Janie, life is a singing bee
buzzing in and out of a pear tree. Life is sensual, fertile, and ever-growing,
a horizon that a traveller moves forever towards but never reaches. Living
is a path of experience and human contact; living is a way of knowing
and touching one's self and the world. For Nanny, the kiss of the honey
bee is a 'laceration',[4] but for Janie, its kiss stimulates the nectar of life.

Thus, the pursuit of life's sweetness and nectar is Janie's odyssey.
At the opening of the novel, Janie lacks an identity, and she is therefore
as curious about herself as she is about the name she is called,
'Alphabet', an enigmatic identity because different people gave her

different names. Her failure to recognise herself in a photograph also suggests Janie's lack of self-knowledge. In short, she remains undistinguished from those around her. Later, her role as a 'wife' in her first and second marriages further suppresses her soul, although neither entirely destroy her spirit.

Unlike her mother or grandmother, Janie enters her womanhood without the scars of rape, but not without the scars of a loveless marriage of convenience. Logan Killicks provides Janie with the property and title, Mrs, which elevates her class status within the Black community. But he cannot, and does not, fill her with the love necessary to enliven her spirit or her sense of fulfilment. Janie's marriage to Logan represents a new form of oppression, that of 'wife'. Even with this new status, Janie still lacks an identity and knows nothing of living. Wife becomes a 'black hole' in which she is swallowed up by his 'often-mentioned sixty acres' and her attendant spousal duties. Her marriage to Logan is her first experience with gender oppression.

Nevertheless, Janie continues to peer down life's highway, looking for something, desiring to know. Jody Starks's appearance on that highway gives her another chance to follow the buzzing honey bee. Before their marriage, Jody talks to her in rhymes and paints pictures of a challenging life. Hurston tells us:

> . . . they managed to meet in the scrub oaks across the road and talk about when he would be a big ruler of things with her reaping the benefits. Janie pulled back a long time because he did not represent sun-up and pollen and blooming trees, but he spoke for far horizon.[5]

In spite of the disappoint which follows their marriage, Janie's courtship with Jody is significant because this represents the first time that she makes an independent decision, and the first time she speaks her own names.

Moreover, the decision to run off with Jody signals the first real break with the gender oppression imposed on her. She refuses to be bridled and brutalised by Logan, a man whom she married involuntarily.

> . . . Logan was accusing her of her mama, her grandmama, and her feelings, and she couldn't do a thing about any of it . . . What was she losing so much time for? A feeling of sudden newness

and change came over her. Janie hurried out of the front gate and turned south. Even if Joe was not there waiting for her, the change was bound to do her good.[6]

Indeed, the action is definitely 'for her' survival. Her second marriage to Jody Starks provides Janie with middle class status and a venue for knowing herself and her world. However, Jody's possessiveness and egoism prevents Janie from fully entering the arena. Although Jody knows himself, he refuses to allow Janie to fully know herself. In this instance, his oppression of her becomes a classic example of the kind of oppression which spearheaded the feminist movement and against which middle class white women have fought. Indeed, Janie's gender and class oppression is ironic because instead of freeing her, as Nanny thought, she is bound all the more tightly. Her second marriage carries status but lacks reciprocity and the cross-pollenation that she seeks. Moreover, Jody's physical abuse of Janie destroys her illusion of his grandeur and eloquence.

> Janie stood where he left her for unmeasured time and thought. She stood there until something fell off the shelf inside her. Then she went inside there to see what it was. It was her image of Jody tumbled down and shattered. But looking at it she saw that it never was the flesh and blood figure of her dreams. Just something she had grabbed up to drape her dream over. In a way she turned her back upon the image where it lay and looked further. She had no more blossomy openings dusting pollen over her man, neither any glistening young fruit where the petals used to be. She found that she had a host of thoughts she had expressed to him, and numerous emotions she had never let Jody know about. Things packed up and put away in parts of her heart where he could never find them. She was saving up her feelings for some man she had never seen. She had an inside and an outside now and suddenly she knew how not to mix them.[7]

Because Jody feels like a big man when he humiliates her in public, Janie closes him out of her life. He wants to think for her like men, so he says, must do for womenfolks and chickens. But he falls, and when she confronts him on his deathbed, he learns this all too well.

> . . . Listen, Jody, you ain't de Jody Ah run off down de road wid.
> You'se whut's left after he died, Ah run off tuh keep house wid
> you in uh wonderful way. But you wasn't satisfied wid me de
> way Ah was. Naw! Mah own mind had tuh be squeezed and
> crowded out tuh make room for yours in me.[8]

Indeed, Jody's favourite phrase is "I God" which suggests how he
feels about himself both in relationship to the town of Eatonville and
to his wife. Janie's life as the mayor's wife symbolises Hurston's most
poignant criticism of wholesale middle class aspiration.

Janie's third marriage to Vergible Woods, or 'Tea Cake', defies both
gender and class constraints. In this case, gender restrictions appear
under the guise of age discrimination since Janie is older than Tea Cake.
For him, however, age is not a factor in his love for her. He says:

> . . . You'se ah lil girl baby all de time. God made it so you spent
> yo' ole age wid somebody else, and saved up yo' young girl
> days to spend wid me.[9]

With Tea Cake, Janie has status 'within' their marriage. He teaches
her checkers, takes her fishing, and takes her into the marsh where she
learns to talk with the other "big picture talkers". Janie jumps down
off the 'high chair', to learn about life, to feel it passionately, and to
become a blossom in a pear tree. Tea Cake is her bee buzzing and
pollinating man. Unlike her former marriages, their relationship is
based on love of self and love of the other. Each expresses herself or
himself without fear of recrimination. Now, Janie can feel the bee
sting and taste its honey:

> He drifted off into sleep and Janie looked down on him and felt a
> self-crushing love. So her soul crawled out from its hiding place.[10]

Her love for Tea Cake liberates her, and she is free to roam the earth
moving forever toward the horizon and, for a time, she does:

> Now, dat's how everything wuz, Pheoby, jus' lak Ah told yuh.
> So Ah'm back home again and Ah'm satisfied tuh be heah. Ah
> doen been tuh de horizon and back and now Ah can live by

comparisons. Dis house ain't so absent of things lak it used tuh be befo' Tea Cake come along. It's full uh thoughts, specially dat bedroom.[11]

While Jody Starks's death is final, Tea Cake's death is not. His spirit has filled Janie's own spirit, and so he must live:

Tea Cake, with the sun for a shawl. Of course he wasn't dead until she herself had finished feeling and thinking. The kiss of his memory made pictures of love and light against the wall. Here was peace. She pulled in her horizon like a great fish-net. Pulled it from around the waist of the world and draped it over her shoulder. So much of life in its meshes! She called in her soul to come and see.[12]

Hurston's *Their Eyes Were Watching God* belongs to the folk because it is from the folk. In language and expression, the novel speaks with the voices of Black storytellers who have maintained our collective thoughts and experiences. Like Ma Rainey, Bessie Smith, and Billie Holiday, these verbal artists chronicle the struggles and achievements of their people. Thus, Janie as narrator becomes a storyteller also. She weaves her tale during the evening time, and passes its power on to her friend, Pheoby. Because Janie dares to travel the highway of life toward the horizon, her story empowers Pheoby whom, we are told, grows ten feet tall just for listening.[13] Subsequently, Pheoby, now as Janie's griot, will sing the epic of her friend's odyssey. The woman's voice speaks the truth of their particular lives.

How can we assess Hurston's view of race, class and gender as they impact upon people of African descent? From Janie's odyssey, we can pinpoint three major perspectives. First, the attainment of wealth, that is, the absence of poverty is desirable. Second, women as well as men have an unequivocal right to engage in life's many essences. And third, African American people must work out their own definitions and objectives. These three perspectives correspond to issues with race, class and gender.

Logan Killicks, Jody Starks and Vergible Woods are working African American men: a farmer, a politician, and a labourer. Each of these Black men make the money that is needed to support themselves and

Janie. The class question here differs from what we usually expect, but the absence of poverty in a Black environment raises the status of these men. Logan owns his land and wants Janie to submit to him in the same way that the earth submits to his plowing. His crudeness and Janie's lack of emotional attachment to either him or his land render his status impotent. Jody is a dreamer and politician who sees himself as "I God". He wants to be the one who does all the doing and thinking while Janie passively accepts his dictates. His power and position and his image before the folks of Eatonville are paramount, but in the process, they grow apart and lose touch with how each feels inside.

Tea Cake makes money as a labourer and occasional gambler, and provides for Janie within his meagre means. She accepts him and his lifestyle because he includes her in it. They do as they please, in part, because their money gives them the freedom of choice. Janie and Tea Cake have neither property nor position, but they do have prestige within their community on the muck and they know that they have one another. By their story, Hurston seems to suggest that class privilege without personal fulfilment and genuine human interaction is barren and lifeless.

Their Eyes Were Watching God unmistakably echoes women's voices. Written by a woman in the 1930s, narrated by a woman protagonist to a woman audience, this novel distinguishes itself in style and form as a song of Black womanhood. This female voice speaks about the inner desires and need for fulfilment of Black women from a folk perspective. The setting is the Black community and the problems of living are not entirely focused on the question of race, yet it is an ever-present feature.

Human beings do human things irrespective of the political and social climate. Yet, the novel is neither apolitical nor insensitive to the generational affects of enslavement, rape and poverty. Leafy and Nanny are the women who bare the evident scars of these social evils. It is their victimisation that ripples through Janie's life forcing her into one marriage and isolating her within another. Neither one of them had time to sit down and deeply discuss anything, they only had time to survive.

Hurston also suggests that gender liberation and equality must be mutual in order to be rewarding for both women and men. Tea Cake is an example of a form of gender liberation that evolves naturally because he is secure within himself and he loves Janie as a flesh and blood human being, not a possession or as a status symbol. As such, love is as fulfilling to men as it is to women, and Tea Cake enjoys loving Janie as much as she enjoys loving him.

Finally, Hurston implies that Black folks must seek their own definitions and objectives if they are to succeed. Nanny's desire to elevate Janie to the high seat like a white woman fails to acknowledge or fulfil her real needs. Historical experiences and cultural world views differ too radically to assume that social mobility will resolve the problems faced by Black women or Black people generally.

Jody Starks attempts to isolate Janie from the common folk and this eventually destroys their marriage. Even though he completes the grandmother's dream by placing Janie on the high chair, such placement isolates rather than elevates her. Janie's desire is to live with the community folk, engage in their life because it is part of her life. She cannot know herself mimicking an isolated white woman, for she is neither white nor does she aspire to be. Her desire to know herself cannot obscure the first fact that she is Black.

Janie's defiance of race, class and gender restriction proves successful. However, she works that defiance out within the context of her own communal environment, and in full appreciation of its liveliness and humanity. Janie passes this on to Pheoby and to us. That our values, community, loves, individual expression, gender liberation, work and play lay the foundation for our identity and fulfilment as members of the Black community.

SULA: THE THORNY SIDE OF RACE, CLASS AND GENDER

Toni Morrison published *Sula* in 1973 just two years before the United Nations declared the opening of the International Decade of Women. The novel's historical vision takes us back to the post-Emancipation era of the nineteenth century when racism firmly entrenched class and gender limitations upon men and women of African descent. The work's social vision explores the way that race, class and gender oppression often ensnares Black women, forcing them to rediscover and redefine their identities.

Additionally, the social vision of the work humanises the women and men who are trapped in such intricate oppression by exploring female friendship and bonding. Finally, Morrison's novel and her characters re-place women of African descent in the centre of the feminist debate by offering what could be deemed an African womanist view of the social and historical roles of women.

The International Decade of Women came to a close in 1985 in a celebration that was held in Nairobi, Kenya. Women from around the world joined together to discuss their common differences and common problems. The African hosting of the Decade of Women Congress signals this global perspective. It indicates a full circle for African women who are now 'returned' to the centre of the debate, and to the question of humanism and human endeavour.

In a related example of the centrality of women of African descent in the global dimensions of the women's liberation movement, a January 1988 article in *Newsweek* referred to the African DNA ancestry of humanity, a concept long held by scholars in African-Centred Studies. If the origins of humanity are in the Olduvai Gorge in Uganda, next door to the site of the 1985 Celebration of the Decade of Women, then the mother of humanity was certainly a woman of African descent. We have come full circle. Why is this important, and what has it to do with African American women? In relation to Zora Neale Hurston's *Their Eyes Were Watching God* and Toni Morrison's *Sula*, it offers a great deal of relevance and food for thought.

Indeed, these issues cite the origin and historical perspectives of African American womanhood, many of which shape the way Black women and Black women writers, such as Hurston and Morrison, perceive their world and the world around them. The combined forces of race, class and gender oppression in America impact directly as well as indirectly upon these Black women and their works. Such social forces have evolved from the history of enslavement that undermined the stability of an African contingent and its people, while simultaneously solidifying the position of European oppressors in new lands. These forces displaced women of African descent from their central positions of economic, social and political power, and for a time disrobed and dethroned them both on the continent and throughout the African Diaspora.

A return to the source of African descent womanhood, alluded to above, reminds us that our main character, Sula, blossoms within an historical perspective. The character, as well as her town, is placed in that context. Morrison explains the present in relation to the past, Sula, Shadrack and the Bottom in terms of their intertwining sources. And when we take that one step further back, before the 'nigger joke', we get a view of Black women in former diverse states of power and authority within their respective pre-slavery, African societies. Such a vision forces us to refocus our view of women of African descent in America. That is, from the despised position as slaves, and breeders of slaves, to women of culture and courage. It represents a legacy of human resistance and a collective will to survive the horrors of enslavement, rape and the disruption of the Black family. Toni Morrison's *Sula* is testimony to the historical forces that have helped shape African American women's identity from the seventeenth century up to the twentieth century.

Moreover, viewing Sula from the West African coastline juxtaposes the question of race, class and gender in North America against the question of power, fertility and culture in Africa. Morrison's use of nature as omens and Eva's readings of signs and dreams, refers to the remnants of a former status in another context from which her characters are severed, but remain, nonetheless, mysteriously tied. Viewed from the shores of the slaving forts of Elmina in Ghana or Goree in Senegal, the rape of the African continent, the selling of African women and their offspring, the rape and breeding of women of African descent, represent the rape of their humanity as well as all humanity. Such multiple 'rapes' mark the international breeding of a global underclass of labourers whose humanity and human worth are measured from that time to this in economic terms.

In other words, their human worth has been reduced to cost-effectiveness, that is, as assets or liabilities. As assets, women of African descent and their offspring are a commodity of identifiable market value, priced according to age, physique, breeding capabilities and physical strength. Their commodity status became entrenched as racism and economic exploitation maintained African peoples in Africa and the African Diaspora as a cheap source of labour. Such economic violence against people of African descent, as a racial group, ensured the growth of mercantile, industrial and technological based systems of Europe and Euro-America.

Sula's refusal to reproduce herself is as much a rebellion against racist class oppression as it is against gender oppression. For, as liabilities, women of African descent and their offspring are viewed as an excess supply of cheap labour. Further, they are made obsolete by emancipation and by those very same technological advances their unpaid and underpaid labour produced. In the United States, racism barred African Americans from the economic fruits of their own labour, and locked them into an economic class that was easily maintained by it. The few Black escapees from this economic prison were either co-opted, destroyed or further restricted by a system that released them on their own recognisance! The combined forces of race, class and gender oppression was the crux that recurs in post-emancipation North America. Reconstruction betrayed the African American. In *Sula*, this betrayal manifests itself as 'the joke, the nigger joke' of the Bottom:

> A joke. A nigger joke. That was the way it got started. Not the town, of course, but that part of town where the Negroes lived, the part they called the Bottom in spite of the fact that it was up in the hills. Just a nigger joke. The kind white folks tell when the mill closes down and they're looking for a little comfort somewhere. The kind colored folks tell on themselves when the rain doesn't come, or comes for weeks, and they're looking for a little comfort somehow.

Morrison continues:

> A good white farmer promised freedom and a piece of bottom land to his slave if he would perform some very difficult chores. When the slave completed the work, he asked the farmer to keep his end of the bargain. Freedom was easy – the farmer had no objection to that. But he didn't want to give up any land. So he told the slave that he was very sorry that he had to give him valley land. He had hoped to give him a piece of the Bottom. The slave blinked and as said he thought valley land was bottom land. The master said, "Oh, no! See those hills? That's bottom land, rich and fertile". " But it's high up in the hills," said the slave.
>
> "High up from us," said the master, " but when God looks down, it's the bottom. That's why we call it so. It's the bottom of heaven – best land there is."

And finally:

> So the slave pressed his master to try to get him some. He
> preferred it to the valley. And it was done. The nigger got the
> hilly land, where planting was backbreaking, where the soil slid
> down and washed away the seeds, and where the wind lingered
> all through the winter.[14]

Such an inversion of truth and values entraps the people of the
Bottom between heaven and hell. The women who would do
otherwise to escape are equally ensnared within the clutches of
economic blight, racial cruelty, and sexual exploitation. Sula then
exemplifies the local variety of global entrapment for women of
African descent and their offspring.

In structural terms, Black women and Black men under conditions
of domination, economic exploitation and racial oppression, share a
similar position of subordination in relation to the dominant group.
Therefore, what we have is not a simple issue of sex or class differences
but a situation that, because of the racial factor, is based primarily on
racialised characteristics on both a national and global scale.

Toni Morrison carefully sketches for us the position of
subordination in relationship to the dominant group when she uses
the metaphor of the 'nigger joke'. But more importantly, she
sketches them in their distorted and obscured humanity in the
characters who occupy her works. For example, the relationship
between Nel and Sula asks how female friendship can survive amid
the deadly claws of race, class and gender oppression. How can
two female children grow up, amid unemployment, poverty and
violence, unscathed? But, more importantly, their relationship also
asks how does a community so constrained by these forces absorb
the meaning of lives such as Nel's and Sula's? Morrison herself
best explains this last question:

> Black people have a way of allowing things to go on the way
> they're going. We're not too terrified of death, not too terrified
> of being different, not too upset about divisions among things,
> people. Our interests have always been, it seems to me, on how
> unlike things are rather than how alike things are. Black people

always see differences before they see similarities, which means they probably cannot lump people into groups as quickly as other kinds of people can.[15]

Nel and Sula exist within the Bottom because they reflect its metes and bounds as well as the vastness of its humanity. They represent polarities, good and evil, conventional and non-conformist behaviour, stability and fluidity. Nel and Sula are mirror images of the contradictions and inversions of truth which freely flow throughout the Bottom. These contradictions and inversions of truths are what bind Sula and Nel, like the Deweys, into one whole personality. Such contradictions represent balance within human and natural forces, and this is interwoven throughout the novel. Sula's first visit to Nel's home is a key example:

> Nel, who regarded the oppressive neatness of her home with dread, felt comfortable in it with Sula, who loved it and would sit on the red-velvet sofa for ten to twenty minutes at a time – still as dawn. As for Nel, she preferred Sula's woolly house, where a pot of something was always cooking on the stove; where the mother, Hannah, never scolded or gave directions; where all sorts of people dropped in; where newspapers were stacked in the hallway, and dirty dishes left for hours at a time in the sink, and where a one-legged grandmother named Eva handed you goobers from deep inside her pockets or read you a dream.[16]

Similarly, when Sula returns to the Bottom with the plague of robins, the counter-forces gather to rectify the imbalance:

> What was taken by outsiders to be slackness, or even generosity was in fact a full recognition of the legitimacy of forces other than good ones. They did not believe doctors could heal – for them, none ever had done so. They did not believe death was accidental – life might be, but death was deliberate. They did not believe Nature was ever asked – only inconvenient. Plague and drought were as "natural" as springtime. If milk could curdle, God knows robins could fall. The purpose of evil was to survive

it and they determined (without ever knowing they had made up their minds to do it) to survive floods, white people, tuberculosis, famine and ignorance. They knew anger well but not despair, and they didn't stone sinners for the same reason they didn't commit suicide – it was beneath them.[17]

Like the Deweys, Shadrack and Hannah, Sula is an aberration; but unlike them, she became a yardstick by which the people of the Bottom ironically measure their own 'goodness'. For a people caught in the middle of heaven and hell, who had fallen through the bottom, as if into a deep black hole, Sula becomes a sanctuary from their fears and failures because she absorbs and challenges these for them. She is their scapegoat, a receptacle of the collective evil that would otherwise remain like an acid gradually eating away their hearts. That evil is both internal and external; a factor of race/class oppression and their own human frailty. So her movement beyond the confines of the Bottom signals her challenge of the traditional gender roles imposed upon women, especially poor Black women, who view their offspring as the only human relationship of which they can be sure. Nel provides an example:

> It didn't take long, after Jude left, for her to see what the future would be. She had looked at her children and knew in her heart that would be all. That they were all she would know of love.[18]

Sula rejects the role of wife and mother, something Nel readily accepts, and in so doing, commits a form of social suicide. Her 'suicide', then, is juxtaposed against Shadrack's National Suicide Day, and suggests that she is both the communal sacrifice and the sacrifice carrier. In a confrontation with Nel from her deathbed, Sula debates the meaning of goodness and love, and in so doing acknowledges her own role as a communal sacrifice:

> Oh, they'll love me alright. It will take time, but they'll love me. (...) After all the old women have lain with teenagers, when all the young girls have slept with their old drunken uncles; after all the Black men fuck all the white ones; when all the white women kiss all the Black ones; when the guards have

raped all the jailbirds and after all the whores make love to their grannies; after all the faggots get their mothers' trim; when Lindbergh sleeps with Bessie Smith and Norma Shearer makes it with Stepin Fetchit; after all the gods have fucked all the cats and every weathervane on every barn flies off the roof to mount the hogs . . . then there'll be a little love left over for me. And I know just what it will feel like.[19]

Morrison continues:

> As an angry and frustrated Nel rises to leave, Sula engages her again in the question of goodness. How do you know it was you who was good? I mean it wasn't you. Maybe it was me.[20]

Throughout the work, Morrison openly explores the meaning of female friendship through Sula and Nel:

> Friendship between women is special, different, and had never been depicted as the major focus of a novel before Sula. Nobody ever talked about friendship between women unless it was homosexual, and there is no homosexuality in Sula. Relationships between women were always written about as though they were subordinate to some other roles they're playing. This is not true of men. It seemed to me that Black women have friends in the old-fashioned sense of Black people, but it seemed so to me.[21]

Perhaps this form of sisterhood has its antecedent on the West African coast where binding between women or between men, for that matter, is a more common social practice than binding between men and women as friends. Women hold hands with other women friends, men hold hands with other men friends, but men and women rarely hold hands in public. Intimacy and sexuality are separate concepts in most instances, and intimacy in the true sense of the word is reserved for friends, while sexuality is reserved for heterosexual relationships. This explains why women in polygamous marriages frequently form sisterhoods with their mates often to the detriment of the singular husband!

For Sula and Nel, being Black and female in North America makes their relationship unique because it thrives in a situation where Black females, more so than Black males, are almost non-entities:

> So when they met, first in those chocolate halls and next through the ropes of the swing, they felt the ease and comfort of old friends. Because each had discovered years before that they were neither white nor male, and that all freedom and triumph was forbidden to them, they had set about creating something else to be. Their meeting was fortunate, for it let them use each other to grow on. Daughters of distant mothers and incomprehensible fathers (Sula's because he was dead; Nel's because he wasn't), they found in each other's eyes the intimacy they were looking for.[22]

In North America, they are not just friends because it is the natural thing for them to be, but because race, class and gender oppression force them to bind as a measure of mutual security as well. Like the Deweys, their differences are welded together to forge one personality grand enough to withstand the terror of their existence. Through the deaths of Plum and Chicken Little, the cruelty of their mothers, and the thrill of their growing sexuality, Nel and Sula share each other's intimacy. It is Nel's marriage to Jude that alters that intimacy, and I believe that Sula leaves the Bottom to allow her friend and alter ego to fully explore this newfound intimacy and sexuality. Yet in their separate lives, neither finds the fulfilment that they enjoyed when they were together.

In *Sula*, Morrison also dares to suggest that the husband – in this case, Jude – plays a peripheral role in a woman's life. Jude marries Nel because she, as wife, will confirm his manhood. Although this concept, too, is found in West Africa, in America, Black men's sense of maleness as synonymous with familial responsibility is skewed by race and class oppression that turns Black women into the "mules of the world", to paraphrase Zora Neale Hurston's perspective.[23] Where procreation in Africa ensures the maintenance of prosperity and lineage, in America and the rest of the Diaspora, procreation for Black men is an explicit demonstration of their maleness and their otherwise racially obscured humanity. Jude exemplifies this because he believes that his marriage to Nel will secure his place as a man in this world. The impact upon Black women, and in this novel upon Nel, is frequently to leave them lonely because the race and class burdens imposed upon the men allow them little space for intimacy. Or as with Nel and Jude, the bonding remains incomplete because it lacks the reciprocity that exists between Nel and Sula. This lack of reciprocity, it seems to me, results from the imposition of gender roles, against which Sula revolts, and which force Jude to leave Nel.

Equally, Sula's relationship with Jude is peripheral to the intimacy shared by Nel and Sula. Although Sula sleeps with her friend's husband, she does not see the act as a violation of their friendship, after all, like the Deweys, they shared everything! As do the co-wives in West Africa, Jude was just something else to share. Besides, where Jude's view of Nel as wife and mother restricts her, Sula's perspective of Nel as friend and sister liberates them both. This is what Nel realises after Sula's death:

> Suddenly Nel stopped. Her eye twitched and burned a little.
> "Sula?" she whispered, gazing at the tops of trees. "Sula?"
> Leaves stirred; mud shifted; there was the smell of overripe green things. A soft ball of fur broke and scattered like dandelion spores in the breeze.
> "All that time, all that time, I thought I was missing Jude." And the loss pressed down on her chest and came up into her throat.
> "We was girls together," she said as though explaining something. "O Lord, Sula," she cried, "girl, girl, girlgirlgirl."
> It was fine cry – loud and long – but it had no bottom and it had no top, just circles and circles of sorrow.[24]

In *Sula*, Morrison suggests that female bonding offers security and liberation that differs from, and is unknowable through, traditional gender-defined roles of male/female relationships. The author submits that racial oppression imposes caste-like restrictions on the possibilities of Black females to racially oppressive gender roles. The use of an historical construct to contextualise the novel and of African American and African cultural metaphors to explore the content of these characters' lives, places an examination of *Sula* within the larger Black world context. As such, the global dimensions of class oppression force us to rethink Black women's liberation in terms of its combined racial and sexual objectives. Indeed, the explicit humanity of Morrison's characters, with respect to race, class and gender oppression, makes their liberation an even greater imperative. The real beauty of *Sula*, then, is in its humanness. Its love and hatreds, its sensuality and brutality, its passion and its coldness. The real significance of Morrison as a writer is that she gives life to those who live with the most extreme forms of race, class and gender oppression. And their womanness and humanity shines through it all, refusing to give in, always pushing to re-enter the centre stage.

Overall, both Hurston's *There Eyes Were Watching God* and Morrison's *Sula* provide us with a deep insight into African American womanhood. Interwoven within their respective works is the issue of race, class and gender. Both works emanate from the pens of twentieth century African American writers. Yet each novel is historically grounded in the profound folklore of the African American experience. In this sense, Hurston and Morrison each inform their readers about time and space and the relevance of the past, present and future.

NOTES AND REFERENCES

1. Rushing, A. B. et al (ed.) *Women in Africa and the African Diaspora* (Washington D.C.: Howard University Press, 1988) p. 187.
2. Hurston, Z. N. *Their Eyes Were Watching God* (London: Virago, 1986; first published 1937) p. 29.
3. Ibid. p. 172.
4. Ibid. p. 26.
5. Ibid. pp. 49-50.
6. Ibid. p. 54.
7. Ibid. pp. 112-113.
8. Ibid. p. 133.
9. Ibid. p. 286.
10. Ibid. p. 192.
11. Ibid. p. 284.
12. Ibid. p. 286.
13. Ibid. p. 284.
14. Morrison, T. *Sula* (England: Picador, 1991; first published 1973) pp. 4-5.
15. Toni Morrison cited in Claudia Tate (ed.) *Black Women Writers at Work* (New York: Continuum, 1985) pp. 123-124.
16. Morrison, T. *Sula*... p. 29.
17. Ibid. p. 90.
18. Ibid. p. 165.
19. Ibid. pp. 145-146.
20. Ibid. p. 146.
21. Toni Morrison cited in Claudia Tate (see note 15) p. 118.
22. Morrison, T. Sula... p. 52.
23. See Hurston, Z. N. (note 2) p. 29.
24. Morrison, T. Sula... p. 174.

INDEX

A

Africa 8, 11, 12, 17, 20-21, 34, 204
> African thought 155
> African unity 6
> 'Arab Africa' 25
> Axum 145
> benefactors, donors and NGOs, reliance on 26
> 'Black Africa' 25
> and the Caribbean 197
> children and elders 154
> classic civilisations of 145
> colonialism in 7
> conquest and partition of, late nineteenth century 36-7
> 'cradle of civilisation' 38
> cultures of
>> questioned in nineteenth century 9-10
>> and Western values 11
> its Diaspora 5, 8, 11, 12, 17, 20-21, 34, 47, 55, 127, 128, 132
>> Africa, new connections with needed 22, 23
>> and Black-led organisations 21-2
>> Black cultures in 144
>> in Britain 34, 204
>> double consciousness 204
>> enslavement era, illiteracy during 129
>> global associations of 6
>> intellectuals of 6, 7, 121
>> men, and procreation 230-31
>> and mixed origins, people of 169, 177
>> and Pan-Africanism 5, 126
>> politics and poetics 205
>> and WANS 51
> economic base, need to develop 26
> economic freedom of 8
> economical and technological progress, need for 11
> education opportunities for, nineteenth century 9
> ethnic tensions and violence 13-4
> family structure, twinlineal 150
> French colonies in 15
>> and Monrovia group 15
> humanity, DNA ancestry of 223
> independent nations of, post-World War Two 69
> inferiority, notion of, refuted 10
> Kemet 145

R

Y